# THE GETTY AND UCLA: THE LIFE OF A MUSEUM SCIENTIST.

## Or a Working-Class Academic: From UCL to UCLA.

## DAVID ARTHUR SCOTT

# The Life of a Museum Scientist

ISBN:978-0-9829338-6-2

CSP Press: Los Angeles and Hastings.

Printed by Lulu.Com. 2019.

# ACKNOWLEDGMENTS

As usual, all errors of grammar and omissions or incorrect stated facts are entirely the fault of the author. For those who have read parts or all of these scribbles and offered their corrections of fact or grammar, the author is very grateful. These are: Tony Garrett, John McGowan, Nick Evangeli, Professor Emeritus Clifford Price, Professor John Papadopoulos, Jerry Podany, Dr. Claire Lyons, Dr. Brian Gilmour, Professor Emeritus Elizabeth Pye, Lesley Moorcroft, Professor Charles Stanish, and Professor Ellen Pearlstein.

# DEDICATION

Dedicated to Lesley Ann Moorcroft, without whom much of what has been written here would not have occurred at all. To my children and grandchildren who may like to read this when the mood takes them or when they are old enough not to get too bored with rants and memoirs like these.

# BOOK CHAPTERS

# Chapter One: Inauspicious Beginnings.

The viridian of the horse-tails and the celadon of the cemetery gravel, which I wanted to touch and play with, but realised I could not, filled the trough of the graves themselves and entranced me, as my grandmother and I walked through Highgate Old Cemetery in the autumn of 1953. The New Cemetery seemed very new by comparison back in the 1950's. We were two of the living amongst the celebrated dead. There was no one else there: the cemetery was irrelevant to anyone but us, from our council estate flat on St. Alban's road it was just a short stroll to the impressive wrought iron gates which stood as sentinels over the departed within their guarded, tranquil territory. I was four or five years old. The decayed beauty of that Cemetery, with its rusty iron railings, ivy encrusted, the red berries of the holly in your face, and their polished green leaves holding them like a chalice, has never left me: the fallen angels of stone, as if they themselves had died. The ceremonial Greek urns, small Egyptian obelisks, maidens sorrowfully embracing a stone cross, carved delicately to appear as if made in wood, portico columns, sunken tombstones, the beautiful polished granite vaults, the flowers and ivy carved in stone. The horse-tails rose up around our feet, and the damp sandstone gravel of the pathways was the perfect complement to each other.

Death and the dead had been given the repose and space that is due to them. I never felt that such a walk with my grandmother was morbid or wasted time, scattering the russet dead leaves in autumn, fallen like a blanket over the graves and ploughing through them on the paths leaving a small damp furrow behind.

At five or six you are aware of death as a thing-in-itself, rather like Heidegger would put it I think, but it was not depressing at that young age because one was aware that death comes to us all, and besides the dead in the Old Cemetery had passed on many decades before and were happily at rest in a beautiful tapestry of stone, earth and leaves.

Some had simply fallen asleep, apparently, but even then that seemed a dishonest sentiment. There must be a real difference between falling asleep and actually being dead, but Christians often preferred the inscription that their loved ones had just fallen into a slumber rather than actually died, perhaps longing for them to reawaken. Odd that some people such as the philosopher Bryan McGee could never come to terms with death, since he thought that it made life meaningless, perhaps even absurd in the existentialist sense. He wrestled and fought with the problem throughout his life without escaping from the thought that all was in vain, as death came to take us away.

I suppose that if everyone thought like him, that is how religion took hold on the human psyche, but it never made me think that an afterlife existed, and I had no innate sympathy for the church at all, despite my love of the cemetery. Neither did McGee, which was part of his philosophical problem that spurred his embrace of the noumenal world of Kant. But that too still failed to solve the mental anguish, although it meant something to him, unlike the linguistic games so seriously pursued by the Oxford philosophers who tried to instruct McGee in the error of his ways. That is the only trouble with atheism: you are on your own. There is nothing external to the self that can be called upon to provide succor apart from an appeal to other human beings or sympathetic animals on which one might project the agonized thoughts normally given as prayers to a God or Gods.

The gravestones that made one pause were those for children who had died aged eight or nine, or the soldiers from the First World War, aged nineteen or twenty-one. I sort of understood how children could die aged eight or nine, but at the same time could not grasp how that could really happen to them, that, in a way, it was absurd. To go to all the trouble and joy to be born and to live, and then to die nine years later: that seemed tough and a bit pointless. The young soldiers I imagined as happy or brave souls, who might not mind being under the earth aged twenty, although I thought that a rather abrupt departure from life. It seemed that you went to war to die at a young age, and then to be given a lovely stone tablet with your name on it for evermore. Death had its capricious side which gave it a sinister edge, an edge for young heroes, happy in death, but who had been taken away from life at such a young age.

The cemetery owed its existence to the Victorian love of death and its celebratory joys, the longing for the Gothic revived or the eternity of the ancient Egyptian, the latter still with us after thousands of years. There can be no more suitable architectural styles for a cemetery than those, and the wonderful counterpoint of Waterlow Park just up the hill completed a scene of arboreal elegance and Ruskinian decay as one can walk from the gates of the cemetery directly into Waterlow Park above, from the land of the dead to the land of the living.

From Waterlow Park, similarly practically bereft of people on a sunny Wednesday afternoon in September 1953, we would walk back home content: my grandmother to her cooking and me to play with toy bricks and soldiers. My grandmother was Edinburgh born and bred and like most Scottish people, never really lost her accent. She had the Scottish snobbery of the displaced Edinburgh middle-class and, thanks to being disinherited by marrying an artist of little standing, became sociologically a member of the working-class, living in a council flat with my mother, father and me, and earning her money as a cleaner for the rich folk up at Holly Lodge Estate, except that my grandmother never conformed to that social designation: she remained in a genteel world of her own making, surrounded by Victorian plates and bits of old furniture that they had managed to salvage from the detritus of their former lives.

In this introduction, I will talk a bit about part of the family background, so this discourse may be more boring to most readers, but it is the sole remnant of its history. My grandmother, Anne Cooper Dickson, had fallen in love with her first cousin, Eddy Dickson, but the imperious grandmother (my great-grandmother) would have none of it: a terrible mistake for first cousins to marry she pronounced and Eddy was declared off-limits. My mum's grandfather had both his own mother and father dead from TB, as the stepson, he is listed as being three years old at the time of these deaths. He married Elizabeth Cooper. The Cooper family was very affluent and owned a substantial amount of property in Edinburgh. When Elisabeth Cooper died, she left a lot of money in the form of shares to the three sisters: my Grandmother, who was the Anne Cooper Dickson referred to above, Nellie Cooper Dickson and Bessie Cooper Dickson. Poor Nellie died of TB at the age of 16. My Grandmother sold her shares very soon afterwards rather than keeping them as an investment.

In the cabinet of curiosities in the ex-council house in Edgware, where my mother and one of my sisters had ended up, long after my grandmothers death, there sits a finely crafted pair of Serbian leather sandals, which has an Islamic air, brought back to Scotland by my grandmother's aunt Bessie, my great aunt, who volunteered to serve as a nurse in the First World War with the famous Dr Elsie Inglis. They even have some kind of memorial in Serbia somewhere to their work said my mum. And this is true: it is in Mladenovac, Serbia, where great aunt Bessie worked tending the sick, injured and the dying, funded, strangely enough, by the French. Patricia Fara, in her book, *A Lab of One's Own: Science and Suffrage in the First World War*, also mentions Serbia, where Florence Stoney, a pioneer in radiology, took her mobile x-ray unit to, when the British Army told her that she was not wanted or needed in England. Of course not: why would one ever need radiology?

The British Army had also refused to support Dr Elsie Inglis and those brave nurses in their work to help the dying troops in Serbia, and it was only possible because France had agreed to take on the financial burden: another example of the stupidity of the higher echelons of the British Army, and the realisation of the French that perhaps nurses might be a good thing to tend to the wounded.

This great aunt Bessie was both a nurse and a midwife. After the First World War, Bessie, like many during that era, immigrated to South Africa. Being rather religious, she had gone with a group of missionaries. My mum knew that at one time Bessie had gone to Bechuanaland, and had married late in life, a Jewish chap, quite a lot older than her called Julius Schulman. The marriage was a happy one, but in Johannesburg, due to the high altitude and the thin air, quite a lot of people died of heart trouble, according to my mum, and Bessie died in her seventies and the husband not long after.

My grandmother had married the disreputable artist mentioned above; a Mr. Anderson, and they had three children. Eric had been the oldest, then my Uncle Morris and then my mum, Diana Vera Anderson. Now my grandmother was born to the second wife of Mr. Dickson, as the first had died. Aunt Bessie was only nine when her maternal mother died and grandmother was only three. There were two other children, resulting from this second marriage, Ella and Norman. According to my mum, who had a memory for detail with an exactitude befitting a QC, my grandmother did everything for Norman and there was also an uncle, Uncle James. At the end of the Great War, he was in business in Australia with Thompson's famous oatmeal, and used to supply farmers in Australia and New Zealand. James had gone out to New Zealand and worked in the North Island. He had joined up in the Second World War and served with the New Zealand forces and had stayed with Ella in Scotland for a while whilst on leave. He was killed at El Alamein and died there of his wounds. In Edinburgh Castle, if you look in the books of remembrance, you will find his name; James Dickson listed there in the New Zealand books of the war dead.

That seemed to be the trouble with my relatives: they seemed to be very few in number, some seemed to have been dead for a considerable time, others might as well be dead, since we never saw them, and some of these scattered few had forsaken the British Isles and moved to California, South Africa, Australia, New York or New Zealand, never to be seen again, the only contact with them was through a Christmas card, dispatched with a religious devotion by my mother, to these far-flung relatives or, if dead, their children.

The cabinet of curiosities housed cast brass animals which grandmother had brought back from India in 1914. A small tarnished silver trophy cup and stand won by her dog, Tim, in Mysore, so inscribed with the date: 10.10.1913. Next, a rare-looking collection of Victorian plate, part of a set of six cups and saucers, from the wedding present of my grandmother's grandfather and his second wife. Grandmother had a very expensive set of Chinese porcelain, and one day for a children's tea party, she was persuaded to take the large tea-pot down from its shelf, dropped it, and promptly burst into tears as it shattered: presumably a loss in today's money of several hundreds of pounds. There were no sums of this magnitude in our household by then in those days.

My mother remembered that grandmother had worked as a volunteer during the Great War, at an hotel for the soldiers. She had made friends with some of the soldiers and still kept in touch with the family that grew up in New Zealand, with the soldier's son and his family, and that was in 2017, practically one hundred years after the Great

War! Auntie Ella had been very good to my Grandmother, once she had been disinherited, and always remembered Grandmother at Christmas time. She had had four daughters, now all dead. Margot and Cousin Valerie: Margot died of a tumour, Bunny and her husband immigrated to Australia in 1981, keeping up the family tradition of moving on and moving away.

My grandmother, shockingly, had left my mother when my mum was six, for reasons never explained (destitute on being deserted by her unreliable husband? Nervous breakdown? Both?). My mum was sent to Dean Bank Institution, which was less of an institution and more of a home, founded in 1832. 1932 was their 100 years anniversary. The girls all got bibles in red covers. All of this bible thumping must have had a negative reaction on my mother, as I never once saw her even hold a bible and she had utter disdain for organized religion. My mum *Type equation here.*was there until she was seventeen. My mother's brother, Uncle Morris had been sent to another Institution in 1928, but the family was so horrified at the conditions that Uncle Morris was kept in, that they arranged for him to live with a schoolfriend called Hugh. They were keen scouts.

My mum was allowed to go out of the institution to see relatives at 11 am in the morning until 7pm at night. My mum's grandmother used to get her servants from Dean Bank, so she knew Mrs. Gary, the chief Matron. I thought that was odd then, that my poor mum had ended up in Dean Bank, the place the family had got its own servants from many years earlier, especially after reading the content of Appendix II, at the end of this book, which I found on a Scottish list-serve, which makes for grim reading.

Miss Lovas was the new matron who came in after Mrs. Gary and the least said about her the better, according to my mum. My mum had left school at 15 and one of the ladies on the management committee introduced her to Margaret Aitchison, a member of the great lawyer family of prominent Aitchisons (born Innerleithen, 1889, died Rhode Island 1949). Margaret Aitchison paid for my mum to go to Skerry's College, because she seemed to have academic promise. Even after the First World War, the college was helping out with skilled recruitment for the Civil Service, probably due to the shortage of young men at that time, they were prepared to take on women, as there was no alternative.

Mum passed the Civil Service exams held over three days, further details about this are given in Appendix II. Dean Bank had four colleges: one was in Liverpool and two more, one in Glasgow and one in Edinburgh. My mum had a temporary job in the Ministry of Health and then she was made permanent, which is now the Cabinet Office, opposite Big Ben, where she had a marvellous view from her window.

Ella married Arthur Sandeman, of Sandeman sherry fame and fortune, the youngest of 10 children and when they decided to marry, the parents of Arthur were delighted because there was so much intermarriage between the Sandeman's and the Quakers as they were all Quakers, so Ella brought in fresh blood. Ella used to supply my Grandmother with beautiful coats and silks, and later, bottles of Sandeman sherry. In 1926, my Grandmother had gone to work for the family of Norman Wilkinson, presumably she was a servant who lived-in. Maybe that helps to explain why her children had to be sent off: no means of support.

In 1926 Grandmother had gone to Edinburgh, and when Uncle Morris left school at fourteen he came to London. Morris went to work for Harraps until the Second World War, when he had volunteered as a dispatch rider. His military interviewers had wanted to place him in the army as an officer as they insisted that he was much too intelligent to be a simple dispatch rider, but he told them that that was what he had wanted to do, and he felt safer as a rider than as an officer. A wise move, as our relatives just seemed to die off in battle, Uncle James at El Alamein for example, and goodness knows who exactly in the Great War. Uncle Morris got on well with my mother, and in 1937 they used to go out cycling, much to the disgust of Uncle Morris's wife, Florrie, who worked in Harrod's who was indeed an old-fashioned snob, which was amusingly incongruous to me, since my mother was essentially rather snobbish herself, and rather brighter than Florrie.

I remember Uncle Morris and Florrie saying to me, when I stayed there once on an uncomfortable single bed, aged about nine, that they expected that my dad went down to the pub a lot. This disparaging comment was totally wide of the mark: in fact it was my Uncle Morris who used to like a gin and tonic, while my poor dad never went to the pub at all. He could not have afforded to.

Uncle Morris worked for Odhams Press then, and had many good years in middle management and did well. He later became ill with a duodenal ulcer and they nicked a nerve during the operation which made him really ill. I reckon his ulcer was caused or aggravated by too much drinking of strong spirits. He worked part-time for the Gas Board when they made him redundant from Odhams. Like the golden age of publishing, a time long-gone.

His accident during the war may not have helped: in the pitch dark he met a dispatch rider in Camden Town who was riding on the wrong side of the road, he was unconscious for three days, and then he was shipped off to North Africa as a driver as well when he had recovered. I remember him telling me about the useful back streets around Parkway in Camden Town, where Lesley and I once rented, that he knew from the war days. As a dispatch rider here in London, my mum used to go on the back of the motor bike sometimes and Eric, the other brother had died a while back of MS, only it was called disseminated sclerosis then. He was aged twenty-six when he died and in the end he could only move one hand. He had married just before he became ill and they had a little girl called Sandra. After the wife remarried she did not want anything to do with our family and the misery of the MS remembered, and they now live in Crouch End.

The Ministry of Health was where my mum worked as a shorthand typist. When the war broke out they had asked for volunteers to go to the Admiralty, so that is how mum ended up on the teleprinters for the Admiralty, and while at the Admiralty she was promoted, first to Clerical Officer and then as overall Supervisor of the entire typing pool. Then it was on to the Air Ministry and working on the code and cypher machines, which must have been getting messages from the breaking of the Enigma Code or sending out heavily coded messages to those who ordered the pilots. They worked a fortnight of nights and a week of days, that was how their shift was set up, and when the blitz was on, they used to start their watch at 5pm in the afternoon, so that others could get home before the raids started, and used to get three or four hours of sleep in the batch of time from 3pm to 9am the next day. She was moved to a more secret area underground with six others, who were all Irish girls apart from mum, from the Air Ministry, and my mum was happy there.

The Air Ministry was located in Bush House and mum was working there when a flying bomb fell on the women coming on watch for 9 o'clock. The bomb dropped right in the middle of Kingsway and a lot of people lost their lives. Firefighters kept great big tanks of water in the street to fight fires and some of the men who were killed came from the Ministry of Health. It fell about lunchtime and the damage it caused was immense.

The special typewriters had drums with insets and the insets were changed when the code changed and mum used to put the insets in a different position each day and it had a switch on it, when you were decoding the message and when you were coding the message and out it came: in gibberish. Forms were issued of where the code was going to and passed through a hatch to the Air Ministry officials and it was all WAAFS on the other side of the hatch who regarded themselves as way above the typists. One day they had fun with the WAAFS and made up a code as a joke and send it through the hatch. The WAAFS said they couldn't find where this place was....some nonexistent Pier they had made up, and the WAAFS could not find it, but it was a joke as the place never existed. Nine at night to nine in the morning they worked then, and each person took a potato with her and used to bake them in the oven in the kitchen and have that as the supper at night. The girls used to have fun together, and in the morning, they used to go to a milk bar where they gave the girls a gammon slice with dressing on.

After the war they all agreed to continue meeting up and they did every year throughout the 1950's, the 1960's, the 1970's. the 1980's, the 1990's, the 2000's, the 2010's, until my mum was the only one left alive of them all in 2017, and all of them were more alive in her mind than some of the living, before my mother herself died at the age of 97 in the late summer of 2017, The last of them to join the departed.

The unknown and mysterious man, my grandfather Anderson took a job with somebody called Kennedy and he was teaching Indian students in Bangalore, and stationed somewhere in Mysore. When my Grandmother had married this mystery man, it was 1912. They went by boat through the Suez Canal. Grandmother was expecting Morris and he was born in December on Boxing Day in 1914 and she came back to stay with her own mother until the baby was born and the mystery grandfather, who I never knew, came back from India and then worked as a copy editor for the Scotsman Newspaper, getting good money.

On retirement from the civil service mum worked for a firm of solicitors at Oxford Circus, part-time. A new partner was taken on after a couple of years and she said she hated part-timers and they were all laid off. So my mum, now in her seventies, worked for Mr. Horne, doing the paperwork for his shower curtain business, down the Tottenham Court Road. Mr. Horne managed a shower curtain business for hotels across Europe and the UK. There was a firm that made them and Mr. Horne had all the patterns for the curtains that would be made up and sent across the world. That was back in the early 1990's I think, when showers needed those hideous polyester curtains to contain water and keep the body hidden. Now, clear glass is the new normal, with bodies on view. My mother continued to work well into her eighties.

My dad was a kindly man, whose own mother was confined to a wheelchair and seemed rather mad, and goodness knows what this side of the family had worked as in the past. My father's father had been a cobbler and also made children's toys, which rather appealed to me, in a sort of downtrodden way. I imagined him as a character from one of Dickens's novels. Perhaps Our Mutual Friend, or Martin Chuzzlewit. My father's brother, uncle Fred, a heavy-set man, worked in the goods yard of British Railways, had a handshake that could easily have crushed the fingers, appeared to have the DT's, chain-smoked Players or Rothman's cigarettes, and seemed decidedly less educated than my dad, who having had no schooling past the age of fourteen himself, must have been the brighter of the two.

Uncle Fred lived over a shop in Worcester Park with my aunt, Grace Maud Batchelor and the seemingly dotty grandmother, confined to a Victorian wheelchair of a lugubrious black design, with assorted black levers and pulleys, oddly forbidding, which helped to separate the normal living from those who could not escape from abnormal living, and as no-one ever bothered to explain what was wrong with her, the unknown being a whole lot more disturbing than the known, this grandmother seemed a frightening presence. Knowing that she had once tried to set fire to the apartment, only confirmed that this grandmother was a dangerous person, one who seldom spoke, whose life was limited to brooding in a Victorian wheelchair of various forms of revenge on a world which had spurned her.

Aunt Grace Maud Batchelor had once worked as an assistant, around the period from 1890-1900, I would think, for the cinematographer, William Friese-Green, mixing up cyanide solutions, then much in vogue for clearing silver residues from film or negatives. Silver cyanide is remarkably soluble, as well as being a deadly poison: its latter attribute is all anyone cares about today. Judging from an early photograph, she must have once been something of a looker. She had been married, apparently, but there was never any mention of this former husband who must have left the scene decades ago. My aunt had left the photographer's unscathed and was herself a heavy smoker for fifty years or so. What she did after working for Friese-Green, who died around 1920, I never knew. It seemed that Fred earned the money for the three of them, such as that was, in the British Rail refitting yard somewhere in Worcester Park, with the other two on state pensions.

After being born in 1948, the earliest period of consciousness for me was the 1950's.

## Chapter Two: The Council Estate and Beyond

At that time, around 1956, in my household, credit cards were unknown, no-one had any stocks or shares, my father putting aside the money for the gas, heating, insurance, and electric bills in old tobacco tins in his tallboy, a piece of furniture dating from the austerity period after the war, around 1948, when everything was still rationed.

Somehow it seemed that life was still rationed, not for everyone, but for those in our immediate environment on the Council Estate and beyond, the circumscribed psychology of existence had not yet been pushed aside by the societal rebellions of the 1960's or the liberation of the motor car for some, or the more subtle liberation from the Britain of the 1950's, even if this liberation did not come for us. During this time, the River Thames was officially declared a dead river, plutonium was much in demand for Britain's independent nuclear weapons, then being tested above ground, women were trained as short-hand typists, coal-fired steam engines pulled pre-war railway carriages through winters dense smog, and social class-consciousness was still very prevalent. Now, sixty years later, much of the Thames has been declared clean, coal is practically a dirty word, nuclear weapons are no longer tested in Australian deserts, we keep very quiet about plutonium, women are no longer trained as short-hand typists, and boys from rough inner London council estates can become distinguished professors even if they have not yet made it to a supreme court judge.

Once I reached school in 1956, I remember days at Netley Street Primary School, but not much of Hargrave Park Primary, apart from the fact that the boys toilet stank dreadfully and that all of the invitees to my 6th birthday party were girls. I don't remember having a birthday party after that, perhaps because of the impecunious family budget, or because it was thought a repeat performance with another solely female contingent might begin to look a little strange. I did have one schoolboy friend who collected bottle-tops, something that I think stopped being a hobby among school-kids sometime around 1958. I remember staring at them quizzically, perhaps wondering exactly what the attraction of them could possibly be compared with a new Tri-ang Rail Coach, a new set of points or more toy soldiers. I could see a certain curiosity in them, but not one lasting for more than about five minutes. I think my friend came from a very poor family in which none of the things that I desired could even be contemplated, not that we were rich in any sense of the word, in our Council Estate flat, but rich enough to rise above bottle-tops.

I remember seeing boys and girls in the age group of five or six, being hit with rulers or with the hand of the teacher on the legs, and thought how terrible and disgusting this was. It seemed rather primitive behavior to me. Being the era of shorts for boys and dresses for girls, legs were available for chastisement at primary school in those days, as for some reason, the authorities had deemed corporal punishment to be a good thing to apply to children of all ages. Personally, as more of a passive and introverted observer than a boy of action, I found it all rather disturbing, unwholesome, and too invasive. It probably did not do untold psychological damage to the recipient, but in an existential sense to this observer it did leave a memory of an event which recoiled from any association with the concepts of empathic interaction on a human level, or natural justice on an abstract one, or respect for the authorities in any sense of that word. There seemed, in the case I am recalling in my mind, no especial reason why the girl in question was smacked across the back of her legs by the female teacher that particular day. The lack of any obvious rationale that one could determine added to the perverse psychological lack of understanding as to the motivation of the teacher herself, which led even at that young age, to an enhanced distrust and antipathy to the dictates of authority. There was, nonetheless, a realization that not all teachers were tarred with the same brush as this young woman, but that her actions, in virtue of her status, were inimical to it. Was she a sadist? Did she simply have a short fuse? Did the Headmaster even know? Did she engage in this kind of punishment often? Even at the age of six it is possible to feel contempt for adults. There was one overweight boy at the school, and that was the extent of the overweight. Just one, who unfortunately was very "slow" and had to be placed in remedial English lessons. This only encouraged the idea that there must be a link between obese boys and dense brains, which one can see is simply not true but Billy Bunter and his creamcakes just seemed to be a natural fit to overweight dimwits.

One of the most irritating aspects of the first year at school was the requirement to take an afternoon nap around 2pm-3pm, presumably because such young kids were thought to need rest during the day to be able to carry on, or the teachers needed a rest from them. Either way it was staring blankly at the ceiling for an hour, wondering when I could get back to my toy bricks and soldiers or playing with Christine Triggs, the girl who lived in one of the flats below us. I liked Christine Triggs and we used to play on our tricycles with stuffed animals, ferrying them around the small path around the council block, or playing doctors and nurses.

There were no immigrants, or at least no non-white boys or girls at the school: a remarkable memory to recall, given the racial heterogeneity of the north London population today, in 2019.

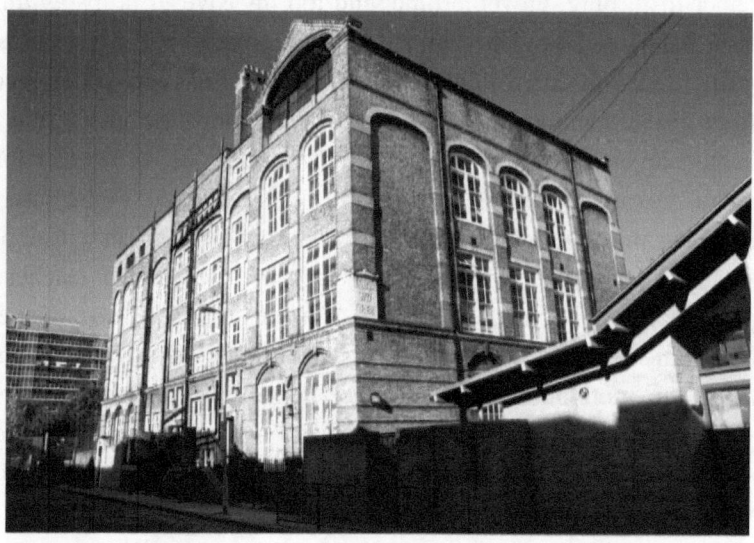

Netley Street Primary School. A recent photograph taken by John McGowan. The old Victorian structure now surrounded by 1960's tower blocks, otherwise nothing seems to have changed from the exterior of this typical school building, many of which were erected in 1883.

In fact, the last time Netley Street Primary School was featured on television, sometime in the 1990's, there seemed to be not a single WASP child there, I think they were all BAME, which I found a quite stunning reversal, except that if the population concerned was minority ethnic as BAME suggests, something had gone wrong with the idea of a minority: us old WASP's were now the minority here.

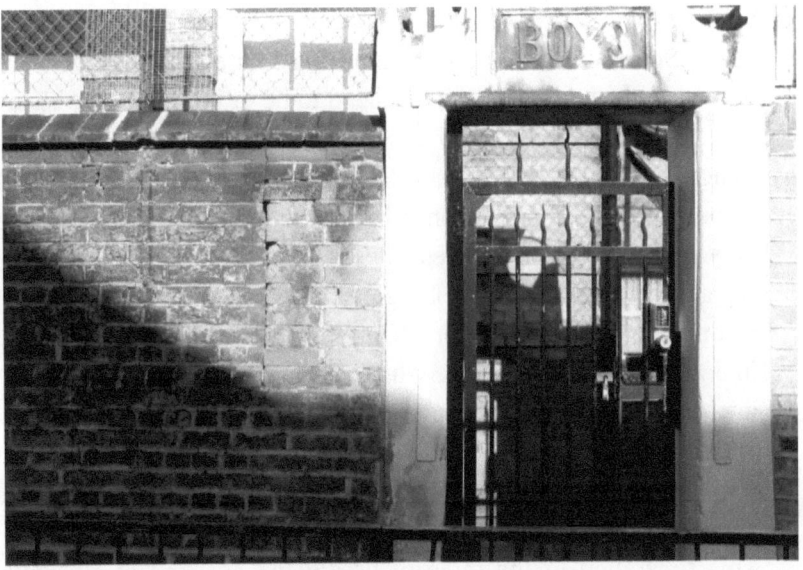

The street entrance to Netley Street Primary School, with the protective spiked railings and original Victorian brick wall. A nicely composed photograph by John McGowan.

It is not politically correct to point out this anthropological fact and makes me sound like someone who wants to leave the EU, but leaving the EU in my view is a complete mistake. Far too late to make any difference, as the damage, (if being overwhelmed with immigrants constitutes damage), as leaving the EU now will simply take us further away from Europe, when we need to be closer in every sense of the word to the rest of Europe, and the world at large. The influence of Europe and the ideals of the EU have been an important cohesive bond, now fraying due to right-wing Nationalism. The lessons of history have been forgotten.

Where was I? Oh yes, Netley Street. I was fascinated by one book in particular at Netley Street Primary School, and that was a worn-out book on biology. It had a half-tone illustration of a gas jar over a water trough with some water-weeds in the jar. The weeds liberated oxygen that then accumulated in the gas jar, displacing the water. This was amazing to me: oxygen could be collected from plants by downward displacement in a scientific experiment that could be set up in the lab. Not that Netley Street Primary possessed a lab of any description, but the image of the experiment in that green, cloth-covered battered textbook has stayed with me now for over sixty years. Somehow it was doubly amazing to me as having very little to do with biology per se, as it managed to be of interest to the chemist in me. There were three of us boys that hung out together, Bobby Langley, myself, and a kid whose last name was King, I think his name could have been Stephen King. I don't remember his first name very well. When the eleven plus came around we were all sent our separate ways: Bobby Langley to Grammar School, me to a Comprehensive and poor King to a Secondary Modern: an intermediate form of failure which disappointed my parents and made me feel depressed, since even at that age, there was a realization within me that I was hardly cut out to become a bank clerk, seaman, hospital worker, building site worker, baker, candlestick maker or anything remotely useful.

This separation of the three of us did me no good at all, while the others probably simply got on with their lives quite happily and never looked back, I was too introverted and unsure. So it was that I ended up at Acland-Burghley Comprehensive School in 1959. By that date there were a variety of backgrounds of the children who went to the school. I remember Jill Teague in our class, who had chosen not to go to grammar school because her sister was already at Acland-Burghley and she wanted to be with her sister. I still beat her in Science and English exams, which I do remember with a certain satisfaction. In some of the lower, streamed forms of the school, there were some especially gentle teachers whose intellectual qualities were somewhat in doubt, but they were remarkably caring and seemed close to the children in their care, who also seemed to lack the ability to even get a CSE, although as they grew older and somewhat more acculturated they did gain some CSE's before they left school. Some of these children were from directly immigrant families and you had to feel sorry for them and their lack of understanding of British cultural life, or their mastery of the English language or mathematics. Now many of the offspring of these children are earning more than my annual salary of £14,000 as a university lecturer in London in 1987, or in some cases, much more than the $220,000 annual salary of my UCLA Professorship in 2017, the year in which I retired, which just shows how resilient the human psyche is and what British society has made possible for so many refugees and immigrants since the 1950's.

One or two bright ones ended up in our A stream, such as Augustine Igbegbuna, the son of a Nigerian consular official whose grasp of English was simply astounding, his vocabulary greater than mine, and Nikos Evangeli, who was an ardent student of physics and mathematics.

In the fourth form we were sent down to have an interview at the Career's Office to try to help us with our future path in life. The Career's Officer stared quizzically at me across the worn and scratched melamine-coated desk. In the mundane 1960's building to which we had traipsed, down in Camden Town, hearing that a 14 year-old schoolboy, from what was then a rough and tough Acland-Burghley Comprehensive School, had ambitions to become a research chemist, must have appeared to be the pathetic ravings of an idiot, or at least a member of the educationally sub-normal, as those with special educational needs were so designated in those days.

There probably were a few kids bordering on the ESN at our school back then. It was an evocative phrase, which had the effect of either making you feel superior, or quietly worrying exactly what happened to those kids deemed to be educationally sub-normal, which brought to mind cretinous oafs sitting on council brick walls gazing vacantly into the distance, and there were a few of those, who one tried hard to avoid. Previously, the unfortunates who ended up in ESN schools, had been designated as MSN, or mentally-sub normal, which made them sound as if they might be portrayed in a Hollywood B movie-classic, doing unspeakable things, because they were so mentally impaired, that pulling wings off of butterflies was what they did most of the time. It was decided by the authorities, whoever they were, that being mentally sub-normal was a step too far in terms of empirical knowledge of the 'other', and being able to so characterize them. At this time the work of Michel Foucault, Jacques Derrida, Gilles Deleuze or even the psychologist R. D. Laing, still lay in the future. On the other hand, being educationally sub-normal might still mean that mentally you might be a genius, but had just gone unrecognized, something that the late lamented Oliver Sacks might have written about, had he not left old Blighty for New York a long time ago.

Nowadays these kids are designated as SEN (special educational needs), a sort of anagram of ESN, which makes them sound rather more special than sub-normal, especially given the problems of trying to define what is normal in the post-modernist world these days.

Such was the Career Officer's incredulity at my declaration of intent that I thought of him, reciprocally, as an idiot, as he attempted to make me see reason: his reason, not mine. The semiotic analyses of these kinds of aberrant personal interactions had not yet begun in 1962, but are ripe for reevaluation. If only one could distance oneself from the actual events.

There was no doubt what he thought: that the foolish notion of educational advancement to the level of a PhD, that had entranced my mind, must have been born from a psychological dissonance from the real world and sensible aspirational levels of achievement for one who had failed to get to grammar school.

I am sure that he thought the stark reality of life would one day bring me to my senses. My arguments against this proposition just seemed to confirm, in his own mind, just how deluded this spotty and pitiful-looking adolescent specimen really was. I walked out of the office at the end of the careers interview, it was too infra-dig to continue with further explications, both from his point of view and mine. Shaken and upset at the presumption of the total unreasonableness of my thoughts of the future, and the impossible nature of the aspiration to which I was wedded, I have never forgiven or forgotten this sorry interaction with the Schools Career Office. Since no-one had asked me before what my future intentions were, there was another saliency to this interchange, as a public declaration of intent, which I had never told anyone else; as an exercise in futility, it has stood the test of time well: as an example of careers advice for young people, it was an abysmal experience.

The careers advice centre was based in a prefabricated office of outstanding architectural mediocrity. I assume this is why the building no longer exists. It was down Kentish Town Road, near Water Lane, which also never existed back then, nor Camden Lock, nor Camden Market, nor Sainsbury's, while on the other side of the road contiguous to what is now Camden Market, the dark emerald-green waters of the Regents Canal was of interest to nobody. I used to stare down at the Dickensian gloom in which the lock was shrouded in the morning mist, its access gate firmly padlocked and bolted to the street, as if enclosing a forgotten secret. At one time, Dickens had lived in a house in Bayham Street, a stone's throw from the old gloom.

On the upper deck of the 137 or 134 bus, in the morning with the heavy smokers, the forlorn canal was always visible, as the bus stopped just shy of the railway bridge. The bus route, from my parents Council Estate flat on the Regents Park Estate to Acland Burghley, took me past there five days a week, in term time, for eight years. There was plenty of time to wonder exactly why it was that this neglected stretch of water, snaking unknown to all through London, deserted by humanity, and so silently, was locked away, presumably for its own safety and ours. It seemed sad. Sad as if displaced in time, it was a remnant of an old life that this part of London had once possessed, and which was now redundant, spurned in the name of a progress the canal did not understand or partake of. It couldn't be built over, but it could be hidden away, although as I will mention later, many wanted the canal filled in with concrete in the 1930's, a ghastly idea which was opposed by one man in particular at that time. The fact that you couldn't get at it, added to its mysterious appeal: I never once saw a barge go down this stretch of water, while now there are scores every day.

Remarkably, the canal architect was John Nash, who designed them around 1820, much better known for his fancy houses facing Regents Park, than for canals. I knew those well, because one of the benefits of the Regents Park Estate, was its proximity to the 'Park. You had to walk past the houses on the Outer Circle to enter the 'Park, and when I used to cycle through Chester Gate and the back ally of the Nashes to reach Albany Street, I once saw Michael Caine and Sharika Bakesh walking along next to my bike: that must have been later, around 1975.

Well, the back of the grand Nash houses is where you might expect to see Michael Caine in those days rather than in the vicinity of the prefab made in Canada residing in the Elephant and Castle, where he had been brought up at one time, with an inside toilet, then a luxury compared with his previous dwelling. In one way he had escaped the New Brutalism of modern Council Estate dwellings, as the architecture is referred to today, or just Brutalism, as it is no longer New, although I can't remember anyone in the 1960's referring to the style as such. I suppose it was known as Modernism, or portrayed as Modernism, as informing a council tenant in a brutal environment with drunks sleeping on stairwells, rough concrete repairs sodden with water, and the smell of rubbish from the bin room wafting across the landing was already quite brutal enough, without espousing the architectural philosophy of the New Brutalism, nicely satirized by Evelyn Waugh in the character of Otto in Decline and Fall.

As the architectural photographer, Nicolas Grospierre writes in his book on Modern Forms in Architecture "For me, modernism and architectural modernism in particular, is the embodiment of one of the greatest ideas in the history of mankind - progress" Quite so, although I think Grospierre must be living on a different planet. As the old Brutalism enjoys a revival of interest in 2017, it evokes in me a kind of horror of place that I was glad to escape from, rather than any thought of pleasure at the remembrance of it as a historical period worthy of study. Noteworthy architects of the time, such as Alison and Peter Smithson, as well as James Sterling, lived in Georgian terrace houses, now worth something like 4.8 million quid, rather than council estate dwellings, some of which are now worth nothing, as they no longer exist, having been demolished to make way for something else. Now, if these architects were so driven by the philosophy of the New Brutalism, why did they choose to live in a style of housing so utterly at odds with the dictates of their own writings and beliefs? I leave the reader to form his or her own conclusions on the matter. You might be influenced by a note from a reader to the London Review of Books on 1st December 2016, who writes that Alison Smithson refused to allow the school she helped design in Suffolk to be photographed when actually occupied by teachers and other irrelevances: people are a distraction, you see, from the minimalist functionality of pure space which is in no need of adornment by humans to be admired. The Smithson's much admired Georgian architecture in the way that Sir Gilbert Scott admired the Gothic: the major difference being that Scott built pseudo- Gothic but the Smithson's did not build pseudo-Georgian, but offered pseudo-living through their ghastly Brutalist blocks.

Our own UCL professor of building, Duccio Turin, reminds us of the brutal treatment of workers in the new era of 1960-1970's construction, with levels of death and injury only beaten by the mining industry, and the jail sentences handed out to pickets on building sites, deskilled by all of the concrete and glass, as easily disposable assets. It is all too easy to accuse others of hypocrisy, but the least they could have done was to emulate Arno Goldfinger's example and maintain an office in one of the blocks he designed and built, as a sop to the conscience of the conscientious. Goldfinger himself lived next to Hampstead Heath at 2 Willow Road in a large modernist detached house he had designed himself in 1939. The towers that he built, Balfron Tower and Carradale House, were described by architecture expert Nigel Warburton as "incredibly muscular, masculine, abstract structures, with no concession to an architecture of domesticity" Indeed Balfron Tower acquired an unsavory reputation for violence and squalor. Ian Fleming had been one of the objectors when Goldfinger had proposed to demolish the lovely old cottages on Willow Road to make way for his modernist dream home. The loss of the cottages gave Fleming the impetus to immortalize Goldfinger in the James Bond series. Goldfinger thought of suing but Fleming retorted that he would simply change the name to "Goldprick". The architects of our own Council Estate were less elevated than Goldfinger, but still managed to create a hideous conglomeration of tower blocks and passageways with no cycling, no ball-games, no pets allowed, no grass to lie on.

The architecture of the Regents Park Estate used to trouble me greatly, as I wistfully gazed at it with such a deep distaste, more than most occupants I think, as we had moved from an old 1930's block in Highgate, which seemed rather more genteel, with front communal garden and a rear concrete playing area surrounded by grassy banks not far from Parliament Hill Fields, to this monstrous environment with no garden and no access to outside space. We had no garden, despite being on the ground floor and overlooking a large expanse of grass to which access was deliberately forbidden, much as Otto would have forbidden.

It was reputed that some of the architects employed by Camden Council at the time were card-carrying members of the communist party, who probably saw human beings through an abstracted haze of socialist conformity to a newly disciplined life in which grass was only for looking at, as an integral design feature of an architectural landscape, not for touching or walking on. Communist grass rather than Georgian grass.

In 2016, a petition was signed by a number of prominent English architects and presented to Poplar Council, among them Richard Rogers and Peter Eisenman, to save Robin Hood Gardens council estate from demolition. The chances of Richard Rogers moving into the Robin Hood estate himself are remote, as he too lives, funnily enough, in a Georgian terrace house in Chelsea, probably worth 9.8 million, where glass, steel and space are the prime requirements, especially space and lots of it, according to Rogers, discreetly hidden behind a resplendent façade of London brick with finely finished stucco rendering.

Space has always been one of my personal bugbears, so I do sympathize with the desire of Rogers to have lots of it, as my wife and I raised three children in a two-bedroom house in Los Angeles, we have always had to compromise on space. Space has been a word with myriad meanings for those of us whose bedroom as a teenager was essentially a laboratory with a bed in it, and who have been battling with books, scientific equipment, microscopes, children, children's toys, wifely desires and (re)location ever since. Perhaps Richard Rogers and others like him should have been encouraged to build ersatz Georgian terraces, which they so admired, for the displaced rather than buildings which make a mockery of decent living, such as these inner London council estates. That would have been quite wonderful: perhaps some of them would still exist rather than being blown up forty years later, as so many tower blocks have been: a waste of millions of pounds.

On the return journey to the council estate from Acland-Burghley school, the bus skirted round Mornington Crescent, which seemed more of a triangular shape than a crescent. Mornington Crescent formed a kind of transitional function, as terrace houses gave way to oversized tower blocks, the inhospitable railway bridge, heavy and dour, and beyond them, the massive and grimy area of Euston station. Actually the triangle the buses traversed was Harrington Gardens- the Crescent itself was hidden behind the Carreras Factory. It was home in its time to Walter Sickert, some of the Camden Town Group, a school site for Dickens and still a place where Frank Auerbach lives.

In 1959 the small-enclosed Harrington Gardens was home to a destitute group of meth's drinkers. When these alcoholics took to drinking methylated spirits, it meant the end: one staggered against the railings, as if they formed a cage of his wasted life, his face flushed with an unhealthy reddish hue. It was a form of alcoholic suicide as the methanol and pyridine the authorities added to the ethanol took a heavy toll on the body: meth's drinkers did not survive for long. I knew methylated spirits well, because I needed alcohol for my home chemistry experiments and had to constantly battle against the azeotropic mixture that the authorities had concocted to prevent distillation and the production of pure alcohol. Dr. Nigel Seeley, my late lamented senior lecturer at the Institute of Archaeology, told me how the police had virtually eliminated every illegal still in England during the First World War, when coal and wood for heating were in short supply. They simply waited for the winter snow to fall and then raided every house where the snow had molten away in a patch on the roof. A large percentage of these were stills for alcohol, wiping out home production overnight. I thought this somewhat amusing, but there was poignancy to it, especially during the First World War, what with so many young men all dead or maimed, and the father in prison or out of work from his illegal still, they couldn't even drown their sorrows in an alcoholic lamentation.

Those fertile and febrile years of the 1960's, was full of the most naïve and misplaced enthusiasm for the new, the bold and the brash. The old London County Council (LCC) was just giving way to the enlarged 1965 superstructure of the Greater London Council (GLC), the former honoured in the memory of the rhyme recited by schoolboys and schoolgirls of the time: "London County Council LLC, You were born in the lavatree"

Whether the architect of London's new and much overdue change to the GLC, the imperious William Alexander Robson, ever heard of this rhyme is unrecorded, but his thoughts on the LCC Election, written around the time of the Labour Party's victory of 1935, under Clement Atlee, reveal a similar sentiment in more prosaic language. Robson wrote: "This, then, is the spectacle which confronts us in the London scene. There is the London County Council, which is supposed to be the principal governing body of the capital city. Its area was designed more than three-quarters of a century ago, and is about fifty years out of date."

Robson lived to see the LCC flushed down the lavatory, thirty-one years after he wrote those words, thanks to the Tory government of Sir Alec Douglas-Home (pronounced Hume). Since the LCC had existed since 1855, so many Tory voters had moved out (many have since moved back), that the entire area always returned Labour councilors and MPs. It was time to reorganize to give the Tories a chance of governing something in London, and Sir Edwin Herbert was charged with the task of its replacement, the metamorphosis to a transmogrified LCC, but now called the GLC, with the schools under the jurisdiction of the ILEA, the Inner London Educational Authority. The review board of the ILEA would prove to be exceptionally kind to me, several years later. Sir Edwin was rewarded for his work by becoming Baron Tangley of Blackheath, moving even further away from the workings and strivings of the comprehensive proletariat, well into the bosom of the establishment.

Knowing nothing of the political machinations of the power elites, the appellation London County Council, had a homely feel to it. There it was in the background providing beneficent support, such as free school milk, free castor oil capsules, blue-black ink, scratchy pens, exercise books, school meals, and school caretakers. There was an implicit thought that the London County Council was there for you, as a Londoner in St. Pancras (Camden had not yet been born) in a way that the GLC, with its greater ambit, which brought with it the transfiguration to the Borough of Camden, wasn't.

The change was not welcome for other reasons too, the Irish chess-player at St. Pancras Chess Club, where I was a regular member in the 1960's, and eventually club champion in 1974, strongly objected to the loss of the name of St. Pancras. Now, this could have been influenced by the fact that Pancras was a famous Catholic saint, who was fourteen when beheaded under Diocletian's persecution of the Christians in Rome sometime in 304 AD. So why did this boy become so famous in our benighted area? Oddly, because when Augustine of Canterbury dedicated his first church to St. Pancras, it was legitimated by the relics of the boy saint which he presented as a gift to the King of Northumberland, although Northumberland still seems a long way off from the Kings Cross area. Whether any relics made their way to St. Pancras Parish Church in our area of London seems doubtful. This however was not our Irish chess-player's motivation: his reason in opposing the adoption of the new name, Camden Chess Club, was because Lord Camden had been a much-reviled absentee landlord in Ireland. This was true: the second Earl Camden had served as Lord Lieutenant of Ireland, a colonial post much hated by Irish nationalists and republicans. Although the Camden family line still flourishes, they live in Hampshire, at Wherwell House, near Andover, oddly some miles from Camden Town.

Camden Town, for generations a run-down, shabby North London abode, home or hovel to railway workers, Irish navies, working-class families and assorted immigrants, would hardly have been suitable territory, even though it is named after Charles Pratt, the 1st Earl Camden, who had owned most of the freehold, the other major landowner being Oxford University.

The newly formed London Borough of Camden, inspired by the coat of arms of the Marquess of Camden, took the elephant from it for their own symbol, although an animal less suitable to be seen lumbering down the clogged streets of Camden Town or Kentish Town, often strewn with discarded litter or dog shit as was common in those days, would be hard to imagine.

The Irish chess players' protestations came to nothing, and Camden Chess Club it was to be. The vote was twenty-seven for the motion, with one abstention, and one vote against. The abstention was probably from the man who brought us round tea in the chess-club, a charmingly mentally-impaired chap who stayed on for years, quite happy to make and serve us tea and a biscuit, which made you feel rather privileged in turn, to be served by him every Wednesday: he played chess himself and usually lost, poor chap, although occasionally someone as lowly as he would be playing on the bottom board of an opposing team and our tea-maker might even win.

The Irish player decamped in protest to the Working Men's College Chess Club, across the road from our club. Ours met in Crowndale Road Junior Library, which I think no longer exists. It was a pity we lost him, as he played chess with an easy elegance which matched his Irish wit. Another interesting character was a rough lorry driver, who witnessed the murder of one of the regulars outside his local pub, The George IV, just near Holmes Road in the backyard of Kentish Town. He was practically illiterate, which made him rather special in my eyes, as a good natural player, not schooled in chess theory either, but with a good fighting instinct. Born in a different station in life, I am sure he would have been quite the thing. I remember getting a lift from him back from one of our away chess matches, probably with Metropolitan III, down at St. Brides, in a bone-shaker of an old lorry which hurtled and lurched in the darkness down Caledonian Road at 11pm as we made our way back to Euston after the match, which I think we won. In those days, around 1964, his lorry was practically the only thing on the road at 11 pm, apart from a couple of prowling buses, trying to avoid stopping at request stops on the last journey home to their depot in the evening.

Aged 14 or 15, I was a reasonable chess-player and good student at Acland-Burghley Comprehensive School; hardly outstanding in any respect. I was certainly one of the council estate kids so despised as a complete waste of time by Nicholl's character, the teacher Bri in the *Death of Joe Egg*, currently enjoying a west-end revival. Nicholl's play was from 1967, and the sentiments expressed are just so apposite for the time.

The newly formed comprehensive, circa 1962, had been created by the amalgamation of Acland Technical School and Burghley Secondary School, on two different sites in Kentish Town with a mixed catchment of English, Greek Cypriot, Irish, Turkish, Jewish, Caribbean, Nigerian and Others. Lord Burghley had been the political wheeler-dealer of the court of Queen Elizabeth I, a major land-owner in his own right, and Acland was named for Sir Arthur Dyke Acland, 13th Baronet, an old-fashioned Liberal MP, keen on educational reform, and a son of one of the wealthiest landowning families in England. The reality of life's spectrum is that many of the pupils at Acland-Burghley were some of the most pathetic and landless specimens of the English working-class, a few of whom had not taken, or been offered, a bath for several months. This was vaguely shocking somehow in the 1959-1964 period, since no-one ever seemed to mention it, or ever commented upon it. I was shocked.

Some stank terribly as one passed them on the stairwells. As they always seemed to be in one of the lower forms of the Comprehensive system at Acland-Burghley, this was as close as one came to them, and how their teachers withstood their offensive effluvia was a mystery to me: a tougher bunch I dare say with less Roderick Usher attributes than I possessed. I recall one of these kids bragging how his uncle was inside for murder. He lived down Tufnell Park Road in a shabby two-story house which today would set you back 1.7 million.

These smelly kids with their felonious relatives must have been the residue of the deprived working-class families of the area of Tufnell Park, Archway, and Kentish Town, which nowadays might seem like something almost exotic, as ripe for an ethnographic investigation; as ripe as the smell some of them emanated. It is strange the way the brain can store specific smells, for decades, and recall the memory of them in totally different contexts. In 1985 I stood in the rotunda of the British Library, then in the British Museum, the magnificent central dome above us, looking up the catalogue number of some obscure work in the green cloth-covered reference tomes which stretched around the central library desks in a wide circle of green baize cloths. The man standing next to me smelt exactly the same as those unfortunate schoolchildren all those years ago, and the smell took me straight back to that stairwell in Acland-Burghley. I furtively glanced at him in some alarm: an old scholar, somewhat disheveled, probably with no one to care for him, who had possibly not washed for weeks, but could still conduct his research at the British Library. That was the last time I recognised that particular smell, although when we lived in a flat in Archway, the ancient occupant below us had a similar smell of an unwashed body and home, perhaps not far from death. But there is a difference in the smell of stale urine from the furniture and clothes, as compared with the bodily smell of those who do use the toilet but just never wash themselves, and this latter smell is quite distinct. The ethnography of smell has yet to be written I think.

In the 1950's ethnographers and anthropologists took little interest in the social lives of the unwashed of Kentish Town, just as now these academics prefer to investigate the social interactions and lifestyles of upper middle-class Brits who have forsaken the British Isles altogether and moved in their tens of thousands to France, to enjoy the countryside, the air, the fresh produce, the absence of numerous assorted immigrants, except themselves, or the superior housing at reasonable prices that France has to offer in spades, rather than those living in Tower-Blocks in Peckham or Council Estates in Camberwell. Well, at least one imagines the number of Francophile escapees to be in the tens of thousands, but the actual figure in 2016 is just shy of 200,000.

There is a retrospective scholarly interest in the British families condemned to live in Council Estates in Peckham, in 2019, as native ethnographic specimens, but in the fifties and sixties, there was practically no sociological analysis or investigation of their lives. Camden is too mixed these days with some ex-council dwellings selling for over half a million quid to be an easy trawl for anthropological theories or an easy PhD, but parts of London still are.

Troubled or tormented individuals did extend to inhabiting our group of students in the 'A' stream. There was an extraordinarily handsome boy who arrived in the class, by the time we reached the fifth form, who was very knowledgeable about drugs and seemed to have a regular supply of cocaine. How he had come by this sophisticated understanding of marijuana and cocaine in 1965 was simply beyond me, although I was always socially somewhat backward. No-one I knew took drugs at all, and it was the same with the blokes I knew at University by 1970, none of them took cocaine, which made this Acland-Burghley druggy even more amazing, especially as he was tanned, tall and very healthy looking, the opposite of how drug-crazed teenagers were supposed to look.

One attractive girl, too advanced for her years at fifteen, wore lashes of make-up, short skirts, and volumes of hair. Tedious conversations could be overheard as this precocious creature was stopped by the lady Deputy Head in a corridor and cross-questioned over her appearance, her make-up, her skirts etc. etc, as she made her way to a class. It was a spectacle made even more poignant by the fact that this Deputy Head was rather lacking in height, walked with a limp, wore an old cape, had probably seen valiant service in the Second War World, and was nothing to look at. One could hardly imagine caning this pupil as a punishment, which is what the boys would have been threatened with, except to derive sexual satisfaction, as she was reputed to already be a prostitute and had seen more of life than I was to experience, quite possibly in a lifetime. When her honour was impugned, somehow our class was involved and it was decided that a burly and muscled boy in our 4th form class was to fight a mature fifth-former over the slight. The two classes made their way, one lunch-time, to the railway bridge, which separates the genteel area bordering onto Hampstead Heath from the back end of the school on the other side. The two boys sized each other up, and as both had glass beer bottles, each smashed them in half, and made as if to go at each other with the splintered glassy ends. Truly a frightening prospect to watch and I stayed, in typical fashion, somewhat to the back of the crowd, appalled at this level of violence. Thinking better of this, both of them dropped the broken bottles and went at each other with fists. The fifth-former seemed to land a hefty kick on the jaw of our class-mate and down he went. He was knocked out cold: the entire fight was over in less than three minutes. There was not a teacher to be seen, as he was carried back to the school grounds and revived, fortunately with no permanent damage.

The truth was that our well-built class-mate was fundamentally a gentle soul who had had the misfortune to have been born with the physique of a putative beach muscle-man. Later, I remember that he had developed an interest in art and was thinking of following an artistic career, rather than a career as a bouncer or boxer.

# Chapter Three: Museums and School Life

I recall running into this well-built schoolmate as I was off, playing truant, as I usually did on Wednesday afternoons from 1962-1965, while he was travelling between the two physically separated sites of Acland Technical School and Burghley Secondary School which made the early hybrid Comprehensive possible. My truancy was to facilitate study: the favoured locations were the British Museum and the Natural History Museum, the latter was easier as the 27 bus went all the way to South Kensington in those days, so one could hop off, and cross the road to the imposing edifice of the Natural History Museum, which on a Wednesday afternoon was nearly deserted, the entire building enveloped in a contemplative Victorian solidity and stolidity. Here I greatly enjoyed the rocks, minerals and fossils. The spectacular mineral hall was deserted, except for this one solitary schoolboy-truant.

The British Museum was the same: one could ruminate on the Aztec crystal skull, condemned as a forgery decades later, without interruption: tourists and other visitors were minimal. I was amazed and puzzled as to how the Aztec, without the benefit of power tools or iron bits could have created this masterpiece, as I had a smattering of self-taught geological knowledge, but masterpiece it must be, otherwise it could not have been displayed in the British Museum for decades, next to the rare book section on a tall plinth on a beautifully polished mahogany floor. Unfortunately, detailed scientific examination by Dr. Paul Craddock of the British Museum Research Laboratory, and others, in the 1990's were to prove that the Aztec skull might have been made by the Aztec's descendants sometime in the 1920's.

The Egyptian mummies in their polychromed coffins were always a source of fascination and awe, and I used to spend some time with them. The mummies were practically left alone in their glass vitrines to contemplate their dislocated fate: an incredible thought today, when they are so surrounded by legions of gawking tourists making it

34

practically impossible to stand next to one for any length of time in peace. In 2015 the British Museum received 6.7 million visitors a year, having started off in 1759 with about 75 a day. Well, 6.7 million is about 18,500 visitors a day, and at the time I was ruminating on the wonders of ancient Egypt in 1962, on a rainy Wednesday in February, I would have estimated the number of visitors at about 200 in total! Just as it should be for contemplation of the ancient world, although museums these days, such as the wonderful Museo Egizio in Turin have to rely for their income totally, on the paying visitors who now stream through their doors. Long live free museum entrance for all is what I say, another pleasure removed at one point by the Conservative Government, for many years, for which I have never forgiven them, as being especially penurious at that period of time any entrance fee at all was really very painful financially. A bit like you, dear reader, paying 250 quid per person as a fee to go in every time you went: that is about the ratio it would be to my personal GDP of the 1970's compared with an average wage in 2019. The Minister responsible for sport and culture in 1979 who had introduced these fees, under the ghastly Margaret Thatcher, was Hector Munro, Baron Munro of Langholm, whose interests were in Scottish land, country sports and vintage motor-cars. His direct interest in Museums or the poorer folk who visited them was never evident, and I have seen no reference to it in his writings. Some museums refused to toe the Conservative Party line and held out against entrance charges, the British Museum being one of them, thank God.

Over the next fifteen years, visitor numbers at many of the free national museums who rejected the Conservative philosophy grew spectacularly, while some of those who had introduced charges suffered from a marked decline in visitor numbers. The Victoria and Albert Museum introduced a five pound admission charge in 1979 and saw its visitor numbers halved as a result. The Conservatives could not care less: after all, those who did not pay did not vote Conservative, so it made no difference to them.

It was only due to the incoming Labour Government of Tony Blair in 2001 that free entry to my beloved museums was re-introduced again. I used to write letters to the Prime Minister, John Major and other MPs in protest, with no effect. When the Labour government got in again, under Tony Blair, nothing happened despite the promise of scrapping these charges. Back to writing to the Prime Minister again, and this time I did get a reply from the Prime Minister's office, to say that the matter was under review, but I was very displeased with Labour for the delay in repealing the horrible Conservative party policy of museum charges. The old retainer Labour MP for Camden, Frank Dobson, who I also used to write to on several matters, was quite useless, which added to my derision when Blair later tried to prevent Ken Livingston getting chosen as Mayoral candidate for London and suggested Frank Dobson as the preferred choice of the Labour Government: they must have been joking, surely. Frank Dobson, a loyal Labour lackey, of suspect intellectual merit or self-determination was hardly a suitable choice, so why did Blair suggest him? The party line would not have been put out of joint if Dobson had got the job, but the rest of us would hardly have been enthralled.

So why had it taken four years for the new Labour government to get the museum charges removed when they said they would go straightaway? The devil is always in the detail, and it was the VAT regulations that apparently prevented the change occurring in 1997 until the budget in 2001 got around to removing this hurdle. Those museums who had introduced entrance fees, such as the Museum of Mankind, got additional funding from Government to make up for the lost revenue from the entrance charges, which forced Scotland and Wales to do the same. In the case of several private collections that had been donated to major museums, such as the Natural History Museum, they had been so given on the stipulation that they were freely available for members of the public to view and study. Had I been an eccentric millionaire at the time, I would have sued the Conservative Government in the courts to reinstate free access to those collections, but no-one seemed to come forward, and it was left to the Labour Government to claim the kudos for the reversal, based on whatever remaining socialist principles New Labour actually possessed, which was not many.

I never saw myself as a member of the gawking tourist class on my truant visits to the museums: more as an independent observer and renegade school pupil, whose visits to the British Museum especially were an essential part of the fabric of my life. Fifty years after these truancies, I was to write a scholarly review of ancient Egyptian pigments, but at that stage of life, such a thought would never have occurred to me as even remotely possible. I greatly enjoyed my Wednesday afternoons, and found them wonderfully educational and psychologically restive, otherwise my fate would have been playing games, such as football, without any kit, at Cannon's Park Recreation Centre, which had to be reached by an assortment of hired coaches, with the Clitheroe Kid blaring out on the radio. Why the fuck did we have to go to Cannon's Park, when Hampstead Heath was just down the road? What was the point of it anyway, as I made an especial principle of never having any kit with me? This made playing practically impossible, and as one martinet sport-loving deputy headmaster, a Mr. Morgan, made us kitless specimens walk around the perimeter of the pitch one Wednesday afternoon in November, I resolved never to travel to Canon's Park ever again.

I should say that the meek working-class, of which my family was a member, even though they stood no chance of inheriting the earth, did not swear in the modern sense of this term. The expletives uttered were "damn" "blast" "bloody" and "hell". That was the extent of the swearing which went on in our household: rather dissimilar to Princess Anne apparently, whose language was described to me by a woodsman on a neighbouring estate as being "foul-mouthed". My family could never be so described, belonging to the genteel working-class, or dispossessed Edinburgh middle-class, as they read the Sunday Express, the Daily Mail, Woman's Weekly and The People's Friend, the latter a Scottish magazine that I used to kid my mother was actually a communist-inspired friend to the people of a subversive tendency. I suppose many working-class folk still read the Daily Mail: the newspaper which reckoned Nelson Mandela too dangerous to ever be released from prison, because he was too rabid to be trusted not to incite rebellion, and who ridiculed Bertrand Russell's Vietnam War crimes tribunal, because there were no war-crimes committed by American troops in Vietnam at all.

The Express and the Mail had a thing about the Rolling Stones and tried hard to bring shock and outrage to bear on them as far as possible, until there was a mysterious capitulation to the new super-rich pop stars, as stars they had clearly become and the subsequent tone in the Express and the Mail was something entirely different. They had seen circulation as the writing on the wall, not writing about drug raids on the new superstars or constantly trying to get evidence of new drug-taking by lesser pop stars of the time. As this time the public pronouncements of Prince Phillip were revered and accorded much press. Later we would learn of rumours of his gallivanting around town, and perhaps that is why he suddenly seemed to lose a great deal of height in his public profile and his public pronouncements in the Express and the Mail seemed to vanish: perhaps this was merely a coincidence and an example of the passing on of the old guard in favour of the new, for by the late sixties or early seventies, public interest in the Royal Family had waned to such an extent that you might think they were merely an anachronism, soon to be seen riding bicycles in broad daylight, like some members of the Scandinavian royalty do to this day. Then Diana happened in 1981 and the climb of the celebrities and their paparazzi began to bring a helpful trivialization to an increasingly shallow press, saving the Royal Family from Scandinavian oblivion.

The following exchange between two class-mates, around 1963, over a disagreement during a football match in the school playground, down Tufnell Park Road where we went for woodwork classes with a taciturn Polish teacher, named Mr. Svoboda, probably a Second World War émigré, whose command of English was somewhat limited, conveys something of the atmosphere of these playground interactions. First I have to attempt to capture Mr. Svoboda's irritating Polish accent. In describing how random pieces of wood were to be cut using a hand-saw, set-square and pencil markings or wood-scribe, he instructed us, repeatedly, that: "Everfing must be streight an squre" And as one of the principal functions of being able to cut wood with a handsaw, marked up with a set-square, it was true that everything was supposed to be rectilinear: straight and square. However, ensuring that the three-dimensional reality of the saw-cut was in accord with this Euclidean principal was something else altogether. It could all too easily wander off in curved space, proving the efficacy of Einstein's assertion of the curvature of the space-time continuum, and provoking Mr. Svoboda to utter his famous phrase yet again.

There was an afternoon break, much welcomed, as I enjoyed

woodwork and still do. I even have an O level in woodwork, but Mr. Svoboda's attempt to produce a squared world even managed to make woodwork appear tedious, because nothing actually seemed to be made during these sessions apart from short lengths of wood, cut in a straight and square fashion, which seemed to be of no practical utility. The entire class had a surreal ambience to it which made it both memorable, because of the total lack of interest of my classmates, the obscure location relative to Acland-Burghley itself, and because of the intangible nature of what was produced.

Here is the simulacrum of many such conversations of the time during these breaks:

"Tha wos a fucking gole!"

"No it never"

"Yes it was you ponce"

"You're a fuck'in ponce, it wos a fucking gole"

"Fuck off you cunt"

"Yu fuck off an'll u cunt"

And with that one of them would storm off, still riled up and swearing. I suppose that my past life has prevented me from laughing at all of those British plays and Television shows in which "fuck" and "fucking" are used in place of a more refined dialogue to elicit a comic effect, or which are supposed to provoke laughter just because the expletive is being uttered every third sentence. Having lived through the reality of it, I rarely find any humour attached to the use of swearing, simply to shock or titillate contemporary audiences. I think I must be a sort of working-class snob.

I arranged to take the 27 bus back home to my parent's council flat on the Regents Park Estate at the time expected for my arrival after my truancy episodes, although since my mother was out working as a shorthand typist for the Civil Service, she did not necessarily get home much before me, and had no idea that I had bunked off school the entire afternoon, although in my book, games at Cannon's Park did not count as school, but as a sodding waste of my time.

My family did not evince much interest in my educational life anyway, since having failed the 11plus, I think they had expectations of me becoming a lowly civil servant, like my father, who had left school at the age of 14, and had never garnished a single paper qualification of any kind in his entire life. My father had been sent to invade Sicily in the Second World War, but soon caught dysentery and was shipped off to Algeria from where he left at the end of the war to be demobbed back to civvy street with no qualifications whatever. I used to feel sorry for him and wonder why or how he had never thought of taking evening classes or tried to study in any way whatever. The one thing I remain grateful to him for, besides his generally benign presence, was teaching me how to play chess, although as I became far stronger a chess player than he, our games together became something of an embarrassment and I used to deliberately prolong the game by not making the strongest moves so as not to hurt his feelings too much, or even to contrive a draw, as his temperament was not one well-suited to losing at this kind of personal level. Even then, he once sent the pieces scattering across the board in frustration. I took a very dim view of that. In fact, one of the mental virtues of chess played at club level is the lesson of being able to stomach losing without letting it affect your subsequent play or approach to the game or indeed to life itself. Even the World Chess Champion has to occasionally suffer losing to other opponents, and this has to be accepted with Roman stoicism. You can reflect back on losses to blame yourself for a stupid move or being outplayed and sometimes this will not be easily forgotten, or in some cases ever forgiven, but it is a lesson that chess mirrors of our real lives, and it is a beneficial one to most of us, although there can be real pain associated with a particularly stupid loss. Grandmasters can go over losses from years ago at the board, from memory. You have to be able to distinguish between the abstract beauty of chess as a thing-in-itself and the psychological problems of coming to terms with winning or losing. The tension between these mental processes often results in very strong players effectively ceasing to play altogether, such as British champion W. R. Hartston, who ceased playing at age forty. Since he no longer studied, how would he feel playing ordinary club chess at a strong level? Even the World Champion, Garry Kasparov, a chess genius, effectively stopped playing, which seems a great pity for the rest of us. Aspects of these mental vicissitudes are well described in *Rookie* by Stephen Moss. It is the intellectual work of thought itself that makes chess both valuable and potentially dangerous to any establishment consensus, which is why it was never taught at the kind of schools I attended. The principal wider benefit of chess-playing is the development of abstract concentration in thinking how events or thoughts can be further elaborated as they progress or regress through time, and that, the close studying of chess can inculcate.

Now, one thing was certain in my mind at this time: I would never work as a tax officer, like my father, for the Inland Revenue, or enter the Civil Service, although somehow I did end up working for them in the school holidays when aged 16 or 17, to earn some extra summer money, most of which I gave to my mum, which only accentuated the boredom associated with Civil Service life and its tedious rituals.

In those days, PriceWaterHouseCooper's files groaned on pre-war pine wooden shelving in decaying manila envelopes, long saturated with the acidic emanations of the Euston Road, their folding endurance, as the paper conservator's would say, severely compromised. From the extent of their files, which consumed several feet of shelving, I surmised that they must be a big client of Her Majesty's Tax Inspectorate. I looked at a few of the carbon-copies of outgoing letters, written in the impersonal style of officialdom. From these I learnt to use "per pro", "without prejudice", the "15th Inst." etc., etc., in my own letters to officialdom in the years to come, in which I could give as good as I received, and sometimes better: even forcing Camden Council to completely revise their subsidies applied to student housing policy in the borough. This was a particularly satisfying triumph, as Lesley and I were both students, I was trying to claim two student rebates against rates rather than the one which the Council insisted was legitimate. The Council was not about to agree. I telephoned the Ministry of Housing in Whitehall, and by some serendipitous happening, I was put through to some high-ranking mandarin, who explained, that in his view, the Council were interpreting the legislation incorrectly. I took notes, looked up the appropriate documents, and wrote a long letter to Camden Council Housing Department. Complete silence. When I telephoned the Council offices, I was not allowed to speak to any junior staff, but my call had to be answered by someone in senior management only. Some weeks went by and eventually the Council replied to my letter to say that, as a consequence of my letter, the Council had been forced to revise its entire housing policy for students, and that, in future, cases such as ours, would receive two rebates.

On another occasion, I took the Ratings Agency to court and emerged, winning our case against them; I forced the Royal Bank of Scotland to pay up insurance for losses incurred in under-stair storage areas, and got the Gas Board to write-off our entire gas bill for several months due to the gross inaccuracies of their gas meter. All the more gleeful were these small victories against the massed ranks of the bureaucrats, as like Camden Council, the Gas Board would only allow senior management to talk with me on the telephone. Oh, the triumphs of an age now essentially lost to us as we struggle with call centres, automated response computers or send e-mails, or even letters, to which we never receive a reply. 2019 is not 1975.

All of these small triumphs helped form an education in bureaucratese, useful for the chameleon in my personality, who enjoyed the game of outmaneuvering officialdom, social colouration disguised or changed for the occasion to subvert, in my gentle fashion, the authorities.

My mundane job for the tax inspectorate was to ferry these files from the storage areas to the tax inspectors in their separate offices, on a wooden trolley, and to retrieve the files they had finished with and file these back in their correct location. It was not especially taxing work. The whole procedure was relatively fusty and subdued, like the offices themselves and their fustic-coloured files. When the frosted glass door in its oak frame was closed behind them, no sound seemed to emanate from the inspectors, totally absorbed in their arcane tasks of extracting those taxes due from business clients through perusal of mountains of paperwork, precise calculation, and a deep knowledge of the applicable tax code. It was work which never ended and which could have no end: taxes would continue to be assessed until the next Ice Age or Nuclear Devastation intervened. There were multiple locations of these Inland Revenue offices along the Euston Road, all equipped with brainy tax folk secreted in their solitary offices, the typists down the corridor somewhere, and the files mouldering away on their dusty wooden shelves, patiently waiting for attention. Those files unlucky enough to be unwanted or forgotten for years, leaned lethargically on their neighbours for support, some in danger of complete disintegration. Occasionally a new set of clothes would have to be provided for these decrepit residents in the form of a new manila folder, replete with the file number and case numbers transferred from the discarded folder in black felt-tip pen.

Back at school in the new term after the summer break, our class, although the supposedly brightest in the streamed comprehensive system, still had its fair share of potential criminals or nutters. As a consequence, there were several periods of detention for the entire class as a result of the antics of a few. This was very boring, resulted in school seeming mentally tedious, and made one wish that there was a reason to life in a school, beyond the superficial concept of what others might think were reasonable actions to follow or inflict on others, that there had to be, surely, a higher purpose even if it was implicit but never stated, of hermeneutics undeclared, waiting for you to discover what it was, not this banal existence which ordinary life decreed. It engendered a feeling of helplessness or ennui at too early an age, this semiotic analysis of one's fate beholden to forces over which one had no control. The unreason, both of teachers and some of the pupils, was truly stunning to behold and acted to make me more introverted than I already was, as a kind of retreat from all the nonsense, senseless detentions, inability to act independently, and some martinetically-inclined teachers. I recall one geography teacher who seemed superficially quite normal, but when one of the milder troublemakers was overheard making some kind of sexual innuendo, he flew into a rage, and the boy was made to stand at the front of the class, as we all looked on in fascinated apprehension as the master strolled grimly over to his desk. He took hold of a large heavy atlas and flew across the room, bringing the book down on the boy's behind with considerable force. The boy was propelled several feet forward, more or less coming to a stumbling halt just before the classroom door. The boy returned chastised to his desk, while the rest of us, or at least me, wondered what to make of this explosion from the geography teacher who had seemed ostensibly quite in control of himself. It was a matter for pondering in his future classes which I never solved, since he was generally amiable. Once, Christopher Dietrich, one of my school-chums got into a conversation with this teacher about swear-words and approached the front to whisper into his ear the secret words. The teacher told him that he should never use those words and

Dietrich returned to his desk, never revealing what they were: I have sometimes wondered over the past fifty years or so, what these words could possibly have been, without solving the riddle.

There was a physically large and unruly pupil in our class, who caused a fair amount of mayhem, who mysteriously disappeared one day, not long after he had stood up, literally, to one of the female teachers in class, refused to sit down, used language best described as disrespectful, and reduced her to tears. The long-suffering male Deputy Head, a noted martinet, a mirror-image (mentally if not physically), of the other Deputy referred to in games, was called in. After we had all ceased banging our desk lids or feet against the floor, following the fracas of the stand-up, we had to sit still for half-an-hour while he glared at us, as if he was proleptically aware that an argument could be made that we were all potential trouble-makers, just a few steps away from being sent to the headmaster's office for caning, which could almost be predicted as an inevitable event in our case.

The line between being caned and not being caned seemed a fragile one, potentially completely fungible, especially under these circumstances of guilt by association. The disappearance of this mature-looking oversized lout was explained by his removal to Borstal, later to be reconfigured by the 1982 Criminal Justice Act into Approved Schools. What went on in these Borstal establishments was unknown to ignorant types, such as myself, but it did not sound too good, as if it signaled the end of normal life as a schoolboy to become some kind of confined schoolboy prisoner devoid of personal volition to be able to leave. Indeed, the Borstals were run by Her Majesty's Prison Service, and those shut up in them were not free. If these Borstals were filled up with uncontrollable, unruly and potentially violent types such as our vanished class-mate, this did not sound too appetizing a prospect.

Later, it was decided by the Thatcher Government that treatment of inmates in these borstal establishments had been far too lenient, and Willie Whitelaw, one of Thatcher's loyal enforcers, announced the introduction of the "Short, Sharp, Shock" treatment for these unfortunates who had had it too easy. The speech he made, introducing the new treatment, in a phrase borrowed from Gilbert and Sullivan, met with rapturous enthusiasm from the Conservative Party

Conference in 1977. Subsequent events conspired against its effectiveness, as crime rates in the 1980-1989 period were certainly not going down: the short, sharp, shock treatment was obviously not sharp or shocking enough. According to the authorized biography of Whitelaw by Garnett (not Alf) and Aitken (not Jonathan), the Prison Officers Association remarked that this Conservative Party policy was merely producing very fit young burglars able to out-run the police at a cost of one thousand pounds per month, then twice the cost of attending Eton: it was, in fact, another failed Tory strategy whose financial implications had never been properly costed, and whose practical implementation resulted in increasingly agile youthful offenders. In former times, the Whitelaws of this world would undoubtedly have increased the range of offences for which transportation for life would have been prescribed, removing more of the criminal classes from London schools to a new life in Australia, which would presumably have been much more cost-effective as well as practically more efficient.

Whitelaw was less keen to investigate the rumours of high-class pedophiles which apparently floated about at the time, and which has resurfaced in recent years, to be buried again under official obfuscation as well as a badly flawed investigation by New Scotland Yard, based on the fantasies of a nutter. Coming from a very wealthy Scottish land-owning family, Whitelaw was alarmed to discover that he was responsible for the upkeep of a decrepit castle on his lands, which he tried to give away to the contiguous village inhabitants, so that the cost of upkeep became their problem, not his. His farming lands, according to my informants, included several ancient monuments or earthworks, for which tax relief could be claimed. Whitelaw made sure that the maximum tax benefit was always claimed from Her Majesty's Government, even if the land was not being farmed at all, salient cases where a short, sharp, shock should have been administered to Viscount Whitelaw, but then in those days tax avoidance by the upper classes was a standard feature of their lives, only now, in 2019 clamouring for attention due to the activities of drug lords, arms dealers eastern oligarchs, facilitating bankers, the ability to buy citizenship of soft option countries, such as Cyprus, and residents-in-exile, such as myself.

Back at Acland-Burghley School, later in the next term, yet another, more cunning working-class kid, a quieter member of our class also vanished, after breaking into the caretaker's flat and stealing whatever there was to be stolen, which can't have been monetarily very rewarding. He too ended up in Borstal: I used to wonder idly what had become of them. Of course, there are no live-in caretakers to be burgled in these schools or university premises anymore, their function redundant, the days of the concept of such care finished, their flotsam generously rehoused by Camden Council in the 1970's and now no-one can even imagine why they existed in the first place, despite the need to preserve well what they had once cared for over decades.

Some Council Estates in Camden, such as our own, clearly went downhill after the abolition of the caretakers, with more rubbish, graffiti, drunks, and general neglect apparent. I recall going up in a lift in one of the tower blocks in the 1980's, not far from where my mother's council estate stood, to buy a tatty second-hand bookcase from one of the inmates, with the lift floor swimming in urine. The huge rubbish-bins waiting to be loaded directly onto the council lorries on the ground level below, bubbling with overflowing trash, their offensive smell wafting on the wind, a multicoloured froth, some blowing away in an updraft, escaping collection to provide the depressing source of their own secondary litter, squashed underfoot.

After the various flammable disasters, which have afflicted council estate buildings in the first two decades of the twenty-first century, their desirability ratio compared with a large detached house in East Sussex (our current location), has gone into an even steeper decline.

While I am back in the 1970's, let me remark on a few of the dismissive statements made, even in the Guardian, concerning life in 1970's England. The only thing that younger commentators can recall is the three-day week, the UK having to be bailed out by the IMF, and the problems faced by Gay people. In any era, some things are lost and some things gained, and a hell of a lot has been lost since the 1970's. You only have to read Bill Bryson's book, *The Road to Little Dribbling*, to appreciate just how much. I will add a few sundry items to Bryson's litany: the dawn chorus; the extraordinary decline in wildlife in the British Isles; cheap Italian restaurants down Parkway in Camden Town, a single bare lightbulb casting its meagre illumination upon excellent Italian fare; the humble clothes-peg, successively redesigned to make a cheap and weaker product which bears little comparison to its sturdy 1970's equivalent. Your typical rent for a bed-sit in London was around 15 quid a week. Fish and chips in 1970 cost 25 new pence. Chicken and chips made with chicken so succulent, even from a takeaway joint down the Faringdon Road, that I can still recall it today as we munch through chicken breast in 2019, somehow rubbery and unsucculent even from Sainsbury's. Back then, I could afford to rent a bedsit in Swiss Cottage on the insubstantial part-time earnings from a temporary job cataloging cervical smears at a Hospital on the Holloway Road.

Cadburys chocolate bar: a wonderful confection in the 1970's has been replaced with a blandified product by the new owners of Cadburys which is of lesser quality than that made in the 1970's. Flying, even in economy class, was a real pleasure, with plenty of room for the legs and for taking with you five or six suitcases. Room under the seats on the unbeatable Boeing 747-600 series was so generous that some economy passengers simply slept, laid out on the floor under the five central isle seats. The seats on the Boeing 747-600 series was a reflection of the much smaller distance between economy class and first class: they were essentially the same, just with more leg room, as the seats with the ash-trays in the arm-rests were padded, generous, and not in much need of improvement. Contrast that today with the huge difference between first class and economy class seats, which reflects the now enormous distance between the rich and the rest of us in 2019. There was a good in-flight magazine. Travellers conversed with their neighbours or relatives, often standing in the isle and moving about. Food and drink came round with trays and real knives and forks, ending with an ice cream and scones, clotted cream, jam and tea. It took about a couple of hours or less to check in for the flight from LA to Heathrow, half an hour to check in for Paris, on a regular flight costing 45 quid.

In the film *Withnall and I,* the protagonists could travel in a beat-up Jag, and we could all park on Oxford Street for free. Free concerts in Hyde Park and cheap train travel for all with British rail canteen staff wheeling a trolley through the carriages with tea, sandwiches or fruitcake. Since the 1970's starlings have declined by 90%, the same with so much of our wildlife as front gardens get converted into car-parking spaces while hedgerows and trees go the way of the dodo in many areas of the country. Our cars and population have massively increased as the bird numbers have relentlessly gone down. What causes the decline in starlings is, of course, unknown, since it is not a government research priority. The dawn chorus of the multitude of birds has given way to a pitiful and muted muttering. Some say this is due to global warming, others to the fact that vast swathes of British front gardens have disappeared under brick or concrete and others that the 10 million quid that us Brits spend on slug pellets each year, combined with the pesticides used everywhere has killed off a huge percentage of British birds or their food source. Research into the disappearance of starlings and sparrows seems to be a low priority to the Brits. Whatever the causes, the 1970's is an era still of birdsong and morning choruses, of starlings, blackbirds and robins. According to the RSPB, writing in 2019, there are 44 million birds less now in the UK than there were in the late 1960's. That makes the number lost since my younger years in the 1950's about 78 million. Even the partridges in pear trees almost became extinct until the efforts of a few bird conservationists.

Easy MOT certificates were on offer. Good dole money, strong unions and no pressure to get a job. That was the experience of life and travel in the 1970's: sod the three-day week, life in the 1970's was a whole lot less stressful, the number of overweight people was miniscule, the gap between the rich and poor not too bad, air pollution in London was not yet a problem as serious as it has become in 2019, and the city was not overwhelmed with immigrants: there was a good balance to life in many ways.

Having said that, air pollution might not be such a good example, for the simple reason that in the 1970's the only person banging on about it was me, although today it has become much worse through the pervasive and much elevated levels of nitrogen oxides. I remember cycling past a primary school on my way to South Kensington about 1975, where the playground was adjacent to a very busy road with dense lorry traffic and heavy levels of toxic pollutants were being spewed into the air, to be breathed in by the unfortunate primary school kids in this rough area of Kensington. I told Lesley that this was a disgrace and that something must surely be done about it, but that no-one gave a fuck. I went on and on about this topic for years, one of my idee fixe, a mental hobby-horse, to the general boredom of anyone listening. But as a chemist, I knew that the official disinterest was another blind by the authorities to sideline any complaints, by pretending that there wasn't really a problem at all. Best just to ignore it really, since no-one in authority even gave a toss.

Well, of course, their own children were being brought up in fancy schools with grass verges or next to tree-lined roads, not tarmac playgrounds ringed with a six foot wire-fence two yards from a busy industrial London artery with lorries chugging out a gross assortment of pollutants, and cars roaring past all day or spewing out a whole range of nasties, waiting at the traffic lights nearby.

As a London cyclist, I regularly used to wipe the spots of smog from my face, resulting in residual brown streaks. It is hard to believe that in 2019, some forty years later, that this is still a major problem. The so-called modern measurements of air pollution that I used to moan about only apparently came into action in 2000 AD. 2000 AD?? What on earth were they thinking? It is so pathetic that it makes one want to jump up and down in total frustration with the authorities. So what is the problem, apart from government inaction over the decades? The problem is caused by sulphur dioxide, the nitrogen oxides, ozone, smog, brake-lining dust, petrol fumes, ammonia, hydrocarbons, sulphur hexafluoride (especially in the UK as opposed to Holland), and fine particulate matter from a variety of sources. Some of these pollutants have been in decline for years, such as sulphur dioxide, which tends to come from coal, coke and manufacturing and engineering activities, now rather thin on the ground in the UK, so that has diminished. Others, such as sulphur hexafluoride, nitrogen oxides and fine particulates, have been steadily rising especially due to the popularity of diesel automobiles, heavy traffic, and electrical sub-stations. If we go back far enough, in the days before the so-called "Clear-Air Act", Norman Brommelle, then working as a conservation scientist at the National Gallery of Art, London, told me that one day in 1956, you could see the smog rolling across Trafalgar Square and floating into his office window, like a wraith. He had to shut the window to keep the noxious fumes at bay, and very damaging to artwork and antiquities this kind of acrid pollution is too. The Clean-Air Act began to clamp down on the coke and coal burning chimneys, as the effects on human beings were obvious and in some cases dire, although the effects on artworks might be a long slow process of insidious acidification, they could be equally dire. Less obvious now are the effects of micro-particulates and nitrogen oxides on the human body and on works of art. It is the human body that has come in for some damage function studies here, a little after we did the same for pigments and organic colourants. In fact, recent research suggests that working-class school kids are at risk of higher concentrations of pollutants within the classroom itself, as compared with the levels found outdoors, for a whole variety of reasons. The World Health Organization (WHO) sets levels of airborne pollutants for ten micron-size nasties (PM10) and tiny micron-size nasties (PM 2.5) with WHO levels at $20\mu g/m^3$ and $10\mu g/m^3$ respectively. Air pollution limits set by the EU or WHO are regularly exceeded in London and elsewhere. The current major of London, Sadiq Khan, wrote of his own efforts of tackling air pollution, stating that he has one hand tied behind his back due to government policies and inaction. The UK government has been dragged through the courts three times (up to 2019) by ClientEarth, and has lost three times, at a cost of over 500,000 quid to the taxpayer. Things are slowly getting better, but at the usual glacial pace of government departments not too keen on upsetting things or making any changes that would mean immediate action or in some cases, any action at all. It now takes a month before London hits illegal limits rather than a week or so a few years back. UK law required that the hourly measurement of nitrogen oxides must not exceed 200 micrograms per cubic metre more than eighteen times in a year, but Brixton Road exceeded this level on far too many occasions in 2018 already. Putney High Street, more than 1200 times in 2016! . The government now plans to halve the number of people living in areas with particulate matter in breach of WHO levels by 2025!! How are they going to achieve that? Well, 2025 is sufficiently far into the future that it will be another politicians problem, not theirs. So what happens to the working-class school down Brixton by 2025? Basically nothing, as they will be one of the areas still in breach of these limits by 2025, for sure. Of course, 2025 is a safe bet, not only will more electric cars help to avoid taking any action at all, but seeming to take action is better than actually having to spend too much now to render that action effective. As a chemist, I have to wonder how they arrived at the figure of 200 micrograms per cubic metre of nitrogen oxides. It is a high level, and continuous exposure to such a level will probably exacerbate asthma in children or adults, even if it is exceeded only eight times in a year.

The cult status of the film *Withnall and I* in 2017, is redolent of a recent past which has now gone: the decrepit Jag Withnall drives, spewing forth numerous pollutants, would no longer be on the road, so they would have no car. In the 1970's one could easily park a car without any cost on the streets in London, there was plenty of room, and the MOT cost about 15 quid, so Withnall could afford to keep the Jag going. A typical insurance cost was 75 quid a year, and repair costs were minimal compared with new-fangled engines with computer driven drives and programmes. If the radiator leaked, one just got a new or reconditioned one for 40 quid and fitted it yourself, and then you were back on the road again, as I did myself with our old Fold Cortina. Not in the UK of 2019, when the combined costs of insurance, tax, MOT, and repairs makes driving an expensive pursuit. Withnall reflects a past when the cheap rents in Camden Town meant that students could live there within their budget, like us, while the wrecking balls were tearing the old houses down to make way for a future of high-rises, higher rents, and high Brutalism. Not in 2019: now you are lucky to be able to afford to live in the living-room while you sublet the actual bedroom to make ends meet, as my eldest son did for several years. Not necessary in 1970, even in Kentish Town and Camden Town, where, on page 45 of the A to Z, we had at one time or another, fourteen different addresses over the years, financed either by student grants, part-time work, unemployment benefit, the dole, and total reliance on the bicycle or bus as a means of transport. In the 1970's if you wanted four pints of milk delivered to your door every day of the week you could do that, and pay the milkman every couple of weeks. On his electric milk-float there was little carbon footprint, and lugging the milk home every day now is more reliant on having a car which is only now having its footprint reduced by going electric. The milk would be pasteurized with top-of-the-milk cream, wholesome and authentic milk. Milk-bottles would be collected and returned to the dairy, washed and reused: reducing the carbon footprint even further compared with today's plastic or cardboard cartons. I challenge you student of today, to live within your means with no credit card, on a student grant (or its loan equivalent) and consume food of quality while living in Goldhurst Terrace, a stone's throw from Regents Park.

Carbon footprints, and their size, used to be fashionable around 2008, and some Guardian readers even publicly announced that they had ceased flying anywhere, but as the economic doom, created by the US of A by getting dying hospital patients to take out a 30 year mortgage (I kid you not) began to bite, the recession in the UK was not a joke. Some Brits had to give up on Spain and returned to the UK because the economy was so badly affected, some UK residents had to go into hock to tide themselves over, some struggled on, and a few never noticed. Bankers continued to reap bonuses, some businesses flourished while others went under, and now, in 2019, the banker's bonus pots have recovered to pre-2008 levels. The pages of the newspapers are no longer obsessed with carbon, but we used a good deal less of it in many ways in the 1970's. Books tended to be much shorter, as producing 600 pages on a typewriter or in handwritten manuscript was quite a feat and most novels were less than 500 pages. The UK government still lags behind Scandinavia and Germany in all issues concerning child-care, and even in France the French government provides you with a free cot and a bit of dough! Enough already. And this is written just at the time the stupid Brits are set to leave the European Union.

# Chapter Four: From the Fifth Form to University

Well, for the moment that is enough of the olden times and the agony of the present. Back in the early 1960's now, desirability has other, more personal connotations, as it is always the strange occurrences that you remember from these distant events. One afternoon, our fifth-form class was deemed ready to undertake a certain amount of sex education, or rather a couple of hours of it. We went, expectantly, to an odd part of the old Acland School to be instructed by a sombre-looking priest attached to the St. Benet's church where we went to "sing" each Wednesday. He had not got very far into the lesson when there were titters from the back of the class concerning some relatively innocuous sexual matter he was expatiating on. The priest seemed about to explode with a pent-up fulminating rage. He summoned the principal titterer to the front of the class, bellowed at him, and immediately ordered him to report to the headmaster for caning. It was not even that this guy had been subjected to much barracking before this event. His extreme reaction, and the sense that the whole class had of the injustice of it, and the danger of uttering another sound, meant that we heard him out in a sullen silence. Clearly, sex for this priest was meant for the procreation of other Christians only; it was a solemn affair: very solemn. That there should ever be any joy in sex, heaven forefend. Sex was a really serious business not to be (under)taken lightly. There were real risks associated with sex which meant that most of it was obviously best avoided altogether, apart from sex in the full confines of marriage. This is long before the aids epidemic, but this priest would surely have seen it as the price of sin for those souls gone far astray. Good material for a Monty Python-like sketch. In fact, Saint Benet, a somewhat obscure Catholic worthy, of the 6th century AD, was sorely tempted himself sexually, by some Italian beauty, and despoiled his naked body, wallowing among nettles, so that his flesh was torn and pained, by which he managed to heal the wounds of his heart. After that, he felt no more temptations of the flesh and never thought of that Italian beauty again. Temptations of the flesh were what a number of us desired the most. Clearly the Church was not for the depraved among us, some, such as myself, already rather fascinated by the slender bodies of nubile school-girls and by the flash of a pair of black knickers on long bare legs. Sting, who had been a schoolteacher, might have felt the same with his early hit with the lines, *Don't stand so, don't stand so, don't' stand so close to me.*

Mr. Alan Breed was our talented music teacher, but he had a number of idee fixes when it came to popular music. It was the early days of The Beatles, and Mr. Breed made the pronouncement that The Beatles would not last long and would soon be forgotten. My classmate Paul Membrey had a perspicacious understanding of popular music, as it was then referred to, while I was somewhat indifferent, and he was almost apoplectic at Mr. Breed's definitive statement. Paul rose to his feet and told Mr. Breed just how wrong he was. Mr. Breed was not about to change his mind, but I think that we can conclude that history has consigned Mr. Breed's assessment to a tiny minority of musical critics: perhaps making him unique in being totally wrong, as The Beatles have not been completely forgotten, while Paul Membrey has been fully vindicated by the historical progression of musical taste and culture.

A temporary, and attractive young female science teacher, on secondment to our school, laboriously set up a classroom experiment in front of the class, to demonstrate how oxygen could be produced by the slow heating of potassium chlorate, the oxygen being collected in a gas jar by downward displacement of water. I am quite sure that such an experiment is now totally banned by the draconian health and safety regulations now prevailing. Being an amateur chemist, I watched her demonstration with interest, as I would not have risked heating up potassium chlorate in my own bedroom-cum-laboratory myself. Besides, you could never quite trust potassium chlorate not to have slowly decomposed by itself to potassium chloride, relieving the oxygen content in the process, and rendering the experiment quite futile, or alternatively, the chlorate salt might decide to explode by itself if sufficiently irritated by contact with sugar, dirt or rough glass. Well, this poor teacher tried and tried to get any oxygen to be generated in her experiment and after an hour of futile heating with the Bunsen burner, burst into tears, to the general amusement of the class. I surmised that she was probably a biology teacher seconded to general chemistry for the want of anyone else. The problems of this kind of inadvisable experiment were even felt on the Russian space station Mir, much later. When oxygen was needed in a hurry the Russians made it by reacting sodium chlorate with iron powder, the mixture exploding in the face of the Russian astronaut Aleksandr Lazutkin! Well, they should have known better, and not having more knowledge than a fourteen-year old comprehensive school kid, is a kind of laughable failure of Russian chemical acumen.

As far as oxygen generation was concerned, personally, I always loved the electrolysis of water with platinum electrodes and gentle applied direct electrical current which could magically decompose dihydrogen monoxide (water to you), into its constituents, the gases hydrogen and oxygen, which displaced the water in the two inverted glass tubes of the electrometer as the gases filled up, in the proportions of two volumes of hydrogen to one of oxygen. It was clean, mysterious, and definitive all at the same time, and it never failed to work. It was thermaturgical and stunning. You almost felt that one could take the whole thing a stage further, that hydrogen and oxygen could be decomposed to electrons, neutrons and protons, and then another stage of disaggregation could be forced on these poor particles until they became quarks, until eventually there was nothing resembling matter as we know it at all.

Our most famous teacher was one Jo Kusner, MBE, an artist and expatriate Lithuanian, who taught at the school for over three decades, although I think I never had a class with him. According to his obituary, Jo began working at Acland-Burghley in 1963 because a Professor Tim Bain (who I have googled without success), who knew Jo, had been teaching a bit of art at the school previously and found that he "couldn't cope dodging the stones the boys were always throwing at me".

Jo Kusner had suffered much more than stones in Lithuania during the war, having had his sister shot dead by a German soldier in front of him, so rose to the challenge without a second thought. One day at Kentish Town Public Library, where I took out books on Chemistry and Chess mostly, I spotted a small volume of paintings by Paul Klee, and borrowed that too. There was something about the delicacy of his touch, which intrigued me, and the whimsical colour spaces of his work that attracted my attention. There was an energetic art teacher, probably before Jo's time, another lost soul whose love was the artistic beauty to be found in natural forms, the wonder of the shapes inhered in rocks worn by the sea from Dorset and their fossils, the kind of inspiration that Moore sought from architectural forms of the human body set in a landscape. As this teacher had set us the task of doing something of our own, I took out the small book of the works by Paul Klee from my brief-case, and got a couple of the other students to copy it, and then present it to the art teacher. The work was similar to the well-known Klee painting of 1922, *Red Balloon*, oil on muslin, but a little easier to copy in a geometrical sense. On being asked what he thought of the work, the art teacher pronounced it to be very poor indeed and of no interest. The pupil then told the art teacher that it was a copy of a work by Paul Klee, which did not amuse the art teacher at all; he was angered and infuriated, especially when he came across another rendition by the pupil next to me. However, he quickly went on to other matters: I suppose Paul Klee was not someone he had any interest in emulating. I had set the whole thing up but did not produce a copy of a Paul Klee but something of my own interpretation, which was very sub-standard. The art teacher in question did indeed need pastures new, away from the tiresome bustle of London, and the plebs of Acland-Burghley. He took himself off to the Hebrides at one point, I recall from later information, when some teachers and former pupils attempted a re-union with Eddy Grant at Acland-Burghley some years later. I was in LA at the time, and I think that Eddy did not turn up at the School for this event, which must have been a disappointment.

The teacher I felt closest to was Mr. Bobby Brown, an articulate and energetic teacher of English. John McGowan, or it might have been Michael Lalley, and myself even visited him in his flat in later years as a friend, although as my general interests were rather limited and my knowledge of literature scanty, Mr. Brown and myself were never exactly on the same wavelength. I remember that Mr. Brown had the idea of making our class take part in a debate between ourselves, the topic to be chosen being suggested by the pupils themselves. These were then written down and passed to the front of the class for Mr. Brown to evaluate. Mine was 'Unilateral or Multilateral Nuclear Disarmament'. This was a class of 14 year olds and Mr. Brown made the sleight of hand remark that the title was not clear exactly what was intended, which was, of course rubbish. I think that Mr. Brown thought the topic too much for a group of 14 year olds, and I had a suspicion that such overtly political and scientifically orientated debating topics was not exactly what Mr. Brown was interested in anyway.

One of the 'establishment' teachers was a Mr. Montgomery, upright and rather proper, who one day announced to our fifth-form class that no-one here was going to get a first-class degree, because otherwise you would be at grammar school and would not have fared so badly in the eleven-plus, which meant being realistic about your educational prospects. It must have been some kind of careers talk, because we never had Mr. Montgomery as a regular teacher. Even at that time, in 1963, the deterministic logic applied by Mr. Montgomery which proved us incapable of reaching such academic heights made me quite angry: I had no such limitation in my own mind, even if the thought of it was some distant dream, an unattainable idea like a Platonic form whose essence would always evade the grasp of the merely tangible. Eventually, I did get a first from University College, London.

Our form teacher for quite a while was a Mr. Bradsell, a louche, handsome chap whose personality was somewhat mysterious with a kind of natural elegance which was oddly dissociative and detached. His allegiances were understated and undeclared, but he was no yes-man, you could just tell. He drove to the Acland School in an old Sports Car, slumped low down in the driving seat, wearing a trilby hat, and remaining very anonymous-looking as his hat whizzed by without any sign of a body. It might have been an old Triumph, from the 1950's, but certainly added to the stylish aura of Mr. Bradsell. Mr. Bradsell had a penchant for Sherlock Holmes and once asked the class to describe what they had read during the previous few weeks. Some, of course, had read nothing except the Beano, Bunty, or possibly the Eagle Comic, and when he got to me I blurted out "A Textbook of Semi-Micro, Semi-Quantitative Inorganic Analysis" which produced the not unanticipated reaction in Mr. Bradsell of uncomprehending dissatisfaction, as his interest and knowledge of the subject was something less than zero, but I followed this up with "The Complete Short Stories of Sherlock Holmes" which was clearly a relief to Mr. Bradsell and he complimented me on my reading. Some years later there was a report in the Daily Express that a certain teacher, a Mr. Bradsell, who by this time had left Acland-Burghley, had eloped with an attractive teacher at the school he had transferred to, and the pair of them were never seen again. Exciting stuff.

Some kids were already gainfully employed while still at school: the other end of the working spectrum from the layabouts. There was just the inconvenient necessity of turning up for school at all. One class-mate had begun to work as a milkman's assistant on the milk floats round Camden Town, arriving for school sometimes late and often tired out, or even knackered, by 9.30am. He was later to deliver milk to my mum's council estate, right through the 1990's until the abolition of milk deliveries occurred in that part of London, by which time he was already a grandfather and heading off into retirement in a few years' time. While I had only been working for fifteen years or so at that stage, he had already done over thirty, and was off. Thirty years later, after this event, I am still not a granddad, although just about to become one, in late 2019. And now I have made it: another grandson was born in Chicago to our daughter in August 2019, so I have a respectable number of two grandsons!

Our milkman school chum also used to deliver milk, on the same round, to a posh car showroom on the Euston Road, which had been a former transport café long before the Euston Road turned into the monster of a road it is now. The son of the transport café owner was another of our classmates, who made it big as a result of the location of the café and his working-class nous. After transforming the greasy café into an upmarket car showroom, he ended up, some years later, only needing to sell or renovate one Jaguar a week to make a tidy profit, never acknowledged his milkman school-chum, and eventually bought a fine spread at Kingston-upon-Thames in the 1980's, which by now must be worth several millions. I ran into this very smartly dressed old school-mate one day, sometime in the 1970's, in a sharp suit in the lower reaches of Tufnell Park Road, where it finally gets swallowed up by Kentish Town Road. Kentish Town Road is that kind of road, a road with a big appetite, with plenty of people, awash with cars, mostly stationary or moving at 3 mph, untold numbers of buses and shops to match, which move in and out of existence over the years in kaleidoscopic fashion. While I had a beard, long hair, a tatty pair of jeans, no money, rode a bicycle, and was possibly on the dole at the time, Mickey exuded wealth, success and social respectivity. Bicycle riding was totally unknown to this guy. I found this inversion strangely disturbing, since being something of a lazy sod, he had never exerted himself at school and had probably left with a couple of O levels, while I had strived to rise above the system and had eventually got eight O levels and three rather average A levels.

While getting a series of form prizes for achievement at O level, I walked to the St. Pancras Town Hall for the event from our council flat, down Euston Road. I walked through Somers Town, then a strangely dangerous area for youngsters: when I told a couple of my classmates that I had indeed walked to the Town Hall, and traversed Somers Town, the comment was "Cor....hee waulked daun Somers Tuwn"

This meant very little to me, but I got the message and have regarded the area with suspicion ever since. One year, around 1994, when we were back in London from LA and I was teaching my ancient metals summer school course at UCL, I was riding a borrowed bicycle that was too small for me. A group of local Pakistani kids were passing through Somers Town as I rode past, looking daft, and one of them called out "Look at that fucking git...fuckin tosser" And the accent of these immigrant occupiers of the area was exactly the same as the working-class brits I knew from back in 1965. Strange how cultural assimilation can so easily cross over from one sub-group to another. Also strange is that I have no memory if my parents bothered to attend the prize-giving ceremony or not: I think not, I think that they were working too hard at this juncture to take the time to be there and my two younger sisters were at home as well.

Euston Road is a supersized road, too large for the human psyche to cope with, or even to cross, with wide lanes and scores of buses, choked with taxis and delivery vans and sundry pollutants for the lungs. The Euston Road was also the making of D.E. and J. Levi, property developers, in a big way. The Levy's had an inkling that something was going to happen to the old, trundling, Euston Road that I knew so well, and they began to buy up some of the property on the periphery.

This went on unnoticed by Camden officialdom for a couple of years, until the time came for the dramatic redevelopment of the road and surrounding area to be announced by Camden Council. They were shocked to discover that practically all of the property affecting the development was owned by the savvy Levy's who had no intention of letting it go without a sweet deal for them. Hence certain buildings, planned in advance by the Levy's, received planning permission without opposition, or other favours were granted to them in turn from Camden Council, which they otherwise would not have been given under any circumstances. The Levy's went onto ever bigger things, even more profitable, and Camden Council got its new and rather hideous Euston Road redevelopment, which is like a scar across the landmass, dividing the area into boundaried zones, those belonging to London University, Friends House and the UCL Hospital, on one side, and those of Euston Station, Somers Town, Camden Council Buildings, The Shaw Theatre and Camden Reference Library, on the other, some of which is no more. The Camden Reference Library, once one of my regular haunts, was sold off and turned into a bank or something equally useless.

Our most famous classmate was undoubtedly Eddy Grant of The Equals fame, who ended up living in the former British governor's house in Jamaica, following the financial success of his group and his own musical talents. Eddy Grant tried hard, but was worried about his ability to pass any A levels without extra coaching. He was tutored in Physics by my mate Nikos Evangeli at his place, and used to come over to my mum and dad's council flat for a few chemistry lessons, since, as you know, I was a chemistry nut and my bedroom was, as you heard already, essentially a laboratory with a bed in it. We sat at the small Formica-topped table in the kitchen to go over a few equations, followed by a visit to my laboratory for a couple of lessons employing actual reactions. I demonstrated how chlorine gas could be produced, and despite the makeshift fume-hood which I had rigged up, we had to poke our heads through my bedroom window to take in gulps of fresh air to counteract the chlorine gas, which was issuing forth at high concentrations and threatening imminent asphyxiation.

Chlorine gas was used to kill or maim British troops by the German military in the First World War. I was quite interested in chemical warfare, employing mustard gas or chlorinated derivatives, and their synthesis, and how chemicals could be used to create small explosions was a particularly fascinating topic, as it was for many schoolboy chemists of the 1960's.

The still-familiar names of the chemical companies, BASF, Hoechst and Bayer, made the killer chlorine, much in the same way as I had just demonstrated to Eddy Grant, and the German army had employed Dr. Fritz Haber, a noted chemist, of the Kaiser Wilhelm Institute for Chemistry in Berlin, to devise a way to get the noxious gas into the British trenches, to kill or blind as many soldiers as possible. It wasn't easy but he managed to do a good job and many British soldiers were indeed blinded for life. Haber was convinced that the way forward in warfare was the use of poison gases, and he developed nitrogen mustard, used on British troops for the first time at Ypres, where thousands died and many endured a lingering and very painful death over several weeks. It made no philosophical difference to Haber, who said that if you were dead, you were dead, no matter how you had died, and if you were simply blinded, then that also made you useless, so it was a win-win situation. His wife, Clara was also a chemist, so she knew exactly what Fritz was doing, and begged him to stop, but Fritz never would. One night she took his service revolver from their bedroom, went outside their house and shot herself through the heart.

Oddly, it was the English chemist, Hans Thacher Clarke, born in Harrow and educated at my own college of UCL, who was partly responsible for coming up with the reaction to make mustard gas, when he was in Germany doing some research. Other countries soon followed suit and even after the Second World War, the British were dumping their stockpiles of Mustard Gas off the coast of Port Elizabeth, causing much environmental damage which was hushed up, and many skin sores to fishermen, which no-one did anything about. This is why the British sent the stuff to the deep off the coast of South Africa, rather than off the coast of Norfolk: everything to do with nuclear or chemical warfare has to be kept out of the public gaze in England, as far as possible, never commented upon, unless in a good light, and even then it might be better to never mention the subject at all.

The populace is too ignorant to constantly be reminded of the dangers of the new neutron bombs, so much more effective than the old atomic bombs used on Japan in the Second War World. Now the trouble with neutron bombs is that they only kill, for the most part, animal life forms and leave buildings standing, unlike the hydrogen bomb of today which would destroy an entire city. There is an interesting autobiography written by Samuel Cohen, the inventor of the neutron bomb, available on-line, which he called *Fuck you Mr. President*, where, with mixed emotions now, he still castigates the US Executive branch for their failures to engage in neutron bomb development. As a conservator, neutrons are of course preferable, as our function is to preserve the past, but for most other people it seemed as if the scientists had gone a step too far, and the great powers promised to not use neutron bombs at all, but instead to wipe out civilizations including the buildings, with hydrogen bombs instead which seemed to make everyone much happier.

The population is also kept away from extensive knowledge of VX nerve agent, a tiny drop capable of killing you, which Russia, China, The United States, North Korea, and possibly Britain, stockpile or possess, even though chemical warfare is officially totally banned these days, but not if you are mad, like North Korea, or a member of the elites, like the rest of the pack. So just a minute, if it is totally banned, how come Russia, China and America have huge piles of the stuff? Because what applies to countries under the international ban on chemical weapons does not apply to the big boys who can do what the fuck they want in the name of their own defense. As a back-up to the nuclear weapons under their control, chemical weapons would be the last resort used by these countries, because by then the international agreements would be meaningless. MACD: mutually assured chemical death follows MAD, an analysis never discussed in public for obvious reasons.

Yes, even the airmen who dropped the hydrogen bombs were blessed by the Christian Church in America. Death can come with a blessing even when you are vaporized while walking along a street doing the shopping in Hiroshima.

I had no time for religion, and none of my family ever went to church. There was a feeling that the Church of England was a remote institution which had very little to do with the teaching of Christ, and even less to do with my family members. My mother, in all other respects a veritable pillar of rectitude and conventional views, was very definitive about the Church: she would have absolutely nothing to do with it. It was as if, being financially penurious, that the Church of England was of little relevance: its genteel beneficence reserved for Anglican priests working on farming projects for poor Christians in Botswana rather than the uncouth working-class of Camberwell, who had had their chance of becoming upstanding Christian citizens, but had squandered their opportunities in the ungodly world of pubs, the races, the dogs, ignorance, and unbelief. For a brief time, when I was about seven or eight, my parents tried to send me to Sunday School up the hill at a very middle-class Church on Highgate West Hill, called St. Anne's Church of England, probably with the dual aim of getting rid of me on Sunday mornings and in a futile attempt to improve or create behavioral mores associated with the middle-classes. I remember gawking at one or two of the cars parked in the church car park, as I seemed to have a natural proclivity to admire polished wood rather than church catechisms. One version of the Morris Minor had varnished wooden decorative and structural elements as integral to its design, a style which lasted for years so it must have appealed to others, as it did to me. We had as much chance of driving around in this superior version of the Morris Minor as taking a holiday in the South of France. There was also a Porsche 911 parked nearby, which not having any wooden parts, was of less interest to me: it also lacked the two hinged doors on the back of the Morris Minor, which allowed contents to be stored directly from the back of the car, of much more practical utility I thought.

Clearly, something was wrong with my mind-set, as these cars were making a much stronger impression on me than anything to do with the Church of England and Sunday School lessons, although I liked the association between personal wealth and St. Anne's carpark, which perhaps Christian values might promote, but I had no idea how one might get to enjoy both. After three visits, I announced to my parents that I was not going back again: they took this with resigned good grace, as if it was an inevitable realization that the genteel Anglican mind-set was already passé for me, which is how I thought of it, as totally irrelevant. I do not think that my mother had thought that there was any real benefit to be gained from this anyway: her views were too Scottish rather than C of E, even if they had existed, which they did not.

Many churches around the world venerate the grandmother of Christ, some only established because of the relics stolen from Constantinople during the crusades, but although supposedly adhering to the Catholic tradition within the Church of England, I doubt that any relics made it to Highgate West Hill. If I defined anything about the Church of England it was entirely apophatically: by the absence of that which it sought to affirm, the presence of one singular God: the Gods of ancient Greece or Egypt seemed like a lot more fun to me, and despite having some reservations about Nietzsche, his analysis of the twilight of faith and his assertion that God was dead, struck chords with me. *Thus spake Zarathrustra*: what an amazing work, written with such intensity and power.

For thousands of years people had worshipped Osiris, Thoth, Isis, and a whole host of others, who had brought great wealth and influence to Ancient Egypt: I saw no reason for their inferiority to God Almighty which had already made two Christian nations kill millions of other Christians during the First and Second World Wars, and whose priests blessed each of their own soldiers on their way to kill the other, by whatever means possible, including being gassed to death.

I was an ardent admirer of Professor Bertrand Russell, who had been a conscientious objector in the First World War and who had been imprisoned as a result. Reading Bryan McGee's book, *Confessions of a Philosopher*, many years after this initial hero-worship of Russell, came as a salutary reminder of the difference between Russell's thought processes and the actual consequences of any action which they might entail. McGee writes that Russell had at one point advocated the bombing of the Soviet Union, in order to prevent Soviet possession of nuclear weapons. Russell denied to McGee that he had every said such a thing, but McGee found the text, and Russell was flustered for the only time that McGee ever noticed. Obviously the passion with which Russell regarded the problem of nuclear weapons was such that it had clouded his judgement in one of the statements he had been impelled by his inner intensity to utter, even if he had come to see that this statement was totally without the humanitarian justification we associate with the great man. But he was truly great: his work on logic, the demise of logical positivism, the hiring of Wittgenstein, his work on the limits of human knowledge, his opposition to nuclear weapons and his endless works for the general reader. While in Los Angeles, I was touched to learn that the favourite author of one of the automobile breakdown guys who come round to get my car started in the cold morning of rainy February was Bertrand Russell. Russell never spared himself or took much time for self-satisfaction from his many achievements.

If I had been the age for conscription in the 1950's, which by the Grace of God I was not, I would have refused to have gone and would have been dealt with severely by the authorities, but like Russell, there was no way I was going to be associated in any of my activities or life with the British army, without a major philosophical argument.

It was the Labour Government, shame on them, who had introduced conscription in 1948, why when the atomic bomb was the all-powerful influence of the time, is beyond me, and what good did it do? In 1958 this ghastly Labour law was still going: like sheep many of those who did partake of National Service without giving it a second thought were dead by 1964, some in remote Korea, fighting the mad North Koreans, and a fat lot of benefit that has done the world since. Bryan McGee, who described himself as a socialist in the 1950's, undertook his Military Service without any discussion of the issues at all, in his autobiography, referred to above. Strange, since McGee was mentally tormented by the constant questions which the inevitability of death threw at his logically empirical brain, to such an extent, that Kant and Schopenhauer were the muses he followed, convinced that, despite not being religious, that the followers of modern linguistic philosophy were missing out on the mysteries of life in the name of endless refinements and arguments concerning language. Now, I do find that a strange omission, as if being culturally more conditioned to a sensible view of life than myself, he undertook this service simply as a matter of course, without giving it a second thought, rather than viewing it as a social or moral problem, or a philosophical problem of the instances of death. Is it worth dying to defend South Korea against North Korea? What was left of North Korea when it had been carpet bombed by the USA? Is it a social duty to go to a foreign war at the behest of the establishment who has called you up which has nothing to do with you, unless you hate communists like they are vermin to be exterminated at all costs? Have your views regarding death been of any influence in your decision to serve or not to serve?

It was not the Second World War: that was a whole different kettle of fish, which Russell thought justified, and I am sure he is right. I had no intention of being dead in North Korea, although unlike Bertrand Russell, the underprivileged often died during their First World War incarceration, exactly what was done to them by the authorities is seldom spoken of, but it must have been exceptionally brutal. The Church of England, unlike the nonconformists and the Catholics, encouraged its clergy to undertake National Service. Anglicanism was intimately linked to the concept of "manly morality" which was promoted by the military authorities and the Anglican Church, the latter just part of the establishment order, so what would you expect? I preferred the Catholic approach as at least being in some sympathy with the dictates of Christ.

An English army guide of 1947 declared, "the sexual appetite was implanted in man for the lawful use in wedlock". I am sure the priest who provided our first excursion into sex education at Acland-Burghley would have agreed. However, hundreds of those conscripted never got the chance to test out this maxim in wedlock as they were already dead.

Before they decided it was not quite such a good idea, the United States had nuclear weapons posted on South Korean soil, to deter the North. The trouble is that Koreans are a tough-minded, very capable, hardworking and determined race, and the United States action just seemed to encourage the North to secure its own nuclear and chemical warfare arsenal, which it has now done. The USA withdrew its own nuclear weapons back to the US, without huge fanfare, but one could argue that by then the psychological damage had already been done, and the North determined to get nuclear weapons of its own.

Years later, in Los Angeles, I worked on a few Korean ceramics for one of the expatriate South Koreans. His grandfather had been the first Korean to be educated at Oxford, and he showed me a picture of a young man in pigtails, looking very exotic and foreign with an Oxford College in the background, not like Korean gentleman in the west today. Another Korean chap I had done work for on his bronzes, was the man responsible for the wire fence on the 38th parallel, which separates the North from the South: he was a businessman who had been awarded the contract. His coins were mostly genuine, but the market for ancient Korean coins hardly amounted to much in Los Angeles. For a time in the 1960's, I was a member of the boy scouts, although being sexually rather aware at an early age and at the same time very introverted and physically cautious, I was conscious that both the Scout Master and one or two of the scouts themselves, were not so much interested in the Brownies, as I certainly was, but their fellow scouts, possibly even me. This seemed to me to give the whole enterprise a rather sinister and salacious edge: homosexuality was not even legal in the Britain of 1962, and at that time 'poofs' were much scorned and subject to ridicule: the upper class homosexuals, such as Benjamin Brittan and Peter Pears, were known at the time to be homosexuals, to those in the know: in my ignorance, I thought they just worked well together. Some were rounded up, such as Sir John Gielgud, for cottaging in public toilets, by plainclothes policemen and carted away. What good that did was beyond me at the time, even though I had no interest in homosexuality at all, I thought it was simply farcical, and a total intrusion into the private life of citizens. As a youngster I felt that one should live and let live, that if one's activities did no harm to society, then that should be tolerated by society and not condemned by it as an offence which merited a term in prison or cruel treatment with drugs prescribed by Prison psychiatrists, as in the famous case of the Bletchley Park mathematical genius, Alan Turing. What business the State had in deciding on the morality of sexual conduct between consenting adults was clear to me: none whatever. In my view the State had no place in deciding on the morality of such interactions, but then I am a radical. Presumably those who thought otherwise were heavily influenced by the apparent pronouncements of Christ or the actual views of the Anglican Church, who regarded homosexuality as a terrible sin against God. Of course, in those countries of Africa where the Christian faith is bound to a traditional past, homosexuality is still a serious crime in 2019. In 2019 England, even those who illegally joined the armed forces twenty years ago, because of their sexual proclivities, have been forgiven, largely due to the efforts of radicals and outsiders such as Quentin Crisp and Peter Tatchell. The power of the church to shape public opinion regarding homosexuality in 2019 is not what it was in 1975, and homosexuality has ceased to be a sin against God. The scout troop used to meet in St. Mary Magdalen's Parish Church in Munster Square, near the perimeter of the council estate, where it gave way to a couple of magnolia-coloured pre-fabs, with green painted surrounds, buildings lost in time from the emergency housing set up after the end of the Second World War, an enterprising idea of Sir Winston Churchill's. These prefabricated structures were only supposed to last for ten years, although these two survivors seemed quite happy and contented after twenty years in the same spot, with their small and attractive front gardens, convenient location, and illustrious neighbours: so much more desirable than living in the hideous council estate. Remarkably, just across the road from the strangely-named Munster Square, in a juxtaposition which now seems impossible to imagine, rose the stately form of the White House Hotel, between Albany Street and the Euston Road. Today, the White House Hotel is still going, but the prefabs have long since been demolished. A room for one night at the White House Hotel now costs more than the annual salary of a typical Prefab occupant back in 1964. Munster Square is still an odd area, as someone was stabbed to death there in 2019, part of the young gang violence phenomenon which overtook many parts of London in those days. I write as if for the future, so I look back on these events as I look back to 1964 as in the past.

St Mary Magdalen's was an interesting church, with exciting catacombs, enclosed by iron railings in the basement of the entrance from the Street side of the church, which looked dark and foreboding. The catacombs could be accessed from the lower church hall where the scout meetings took place, from a large hole hacked through the wall, probably from its use as an air-raid shelter in the Second World War, which was a more reassuring entrance, full of mystery and far less scary. The vaults were filled with old church furniture, pictures, candles, and wood, permeated with the competing smells of incense and the mouldering ambience of decay and damp. One week, the Scout Master announced that a donor intended to give a large collection of chemical equipment to the Scout Group. I was ecstatic. We could put part of the disused catacombs into service as a laboratory. This euphoria was unfortunately short-lived; the vicar vetoing the idea without further discussion, which was a major disappointment to me.

One week, I had been making a variety of gunpowder in my home laboratory and had a glass vial of it in my coat pocket. It was an experimental powder with rather more potassium nitrate than usual. The Scout Master announced that we had to raise a Billy-can five feet in the air using poles and assorted string within three minutes; otherwise we had to imagine that a bomb was to go off. We were split up into five groups of four for the competition. I timed our group: after three minutes they had failed to secure the Billy-can at the specified height, so I emptied my vial of gunpowder into the Billy-can, at five seconds past the three minute mark, stood back and lit it with a match. This I would not have done had my little group succeeded in their task, but they did not. I knew that igniting this small amount of gunpowder in an open container was not that dangerous: there was no possibility of an explosion, although the whooshing sound followed by the lower church hall filling up with dense clouds of smoke from one end to the other was good enough for a dramatic effect...or far more than enough for the avuncular Scout master who bellowed "You Scott – Out!"

I was glad to go, especially as the spoilsport vicar had it coming, but increasing sophistication, such as listening to the Third Programme on the Radio at night (swearing no problem for the cognoscenti in those days on posh radio, long before the famous Kenneth Tynan incident, when he uttered the word 'fuck; on BBC television for the first time), reading the Listener Magazine, the Confessions of J. J. Rousseau, Crime and Punishment by Dostoyevsky, the Sherlock Holmes stories of Sir Arthur Conan Doyle, the Textbook of Inorganic Chemistry by Partington, The Handbook of Semi-Micro Semi-Quantitative Inorganic Analysis (already referred to above), A Textbook of Psychology by McDougall, and a host of other books on chemistry, psychology, philosophy, and astrophysics from the library at Regents Park, all played their own part in the demise of the scouts.

For some reason this library branch was especially well-stocked with rather advanced books on the space-time continuum, relativity and astronomical theories: perhaps to encourage the council tenants to make a move to a different universe or region of the astral planes. The bending of space and its relationship with time was an exotic pursuit in the rectilinear world of Council tower blocks. The library on the perimeter of the council estate, the Regents Park branch, is long gone now: the haven that I took for granted, three minutes' walk from our front door is no more, just as the BBC Third Programme is no more: it was replaced with the Music Programme, devoted to classical music, which I used to listen to instead, but never with the same intellectual curiosity that the Third Programme inspired.

I had elevated tastes, dismissive of the Home Service or the Light Programme, or whatever-it-was called, as just so much trivial rubbish lacking any serious purpose or intent. I would listen to the Third Programme, but had no time for popular music or popular culture, and was therefore leading a rather insular and insulated life, which I daresay I still do in a manner of speaking. Only with the advent of the Rolling Stones, which so shocked the readers of the *Daily Express* and the *Daily Mail*, obsessed with the evils of drug-taking, that even a few milligrams of cannabis was a crime meriting a jail sentence of some length, did I warm to popular music. We had no record player and the radio was an old valve monster with reception from Hilversum, Berlin, Triana, The Home Service, The World Service and the Third Programme.

I did not even smoke at that time, but dismissed the *Mail* and *Express* as publications intended for stupid people who could never know any better. Even *The Times* used to rail against the evils of cannabis smoking, which although I had never smoked myself, I had decided that condemnation was a load of rubbish based on the medical evidence. I did have the occasional cannabis cigarette, much later, and liked the hashish called at the time "Paki Black" which seemed aromatic and flavourful without making one feel sick. Of course, this was highly illegal in the Britain of the 1960-1970's. Even being found to have cannabis under the fingernail could lead to a prison sentence. In 1968, an innocent journalist, a Miss Finnigan, was writing an article on the misuse of drugs and went to a flat in London to buy some cannabis. Caught, she was arrested and pleaded guilty to possession and was sentenced to nine month's imprisonment. Being an educated person, she appealed against her sentence and the appeal judge dismissed the case against her, for the obvious reason that the judiciary would be held up to ridicule by that time. A year earlier in 1967, Keith Richards and Mick Jagger were arrested in their house, also for cannabis. The cops claimed that Marianne Faithful was dressed in nothing but a fur rug that she would let slip and that this lack of inhibition was an indication that she was under the influence of cannabis. The Chichester judge, Leslie Block, a conservative and naval veteran, sentenced Jagger to three months for possession of amphetamines and Richards to one year in jail for allowing cannabis to be smoked in his home. Thanks to an editorial by William Rees-Mogg, of all people, in *The Times*, the authorities began to wonder about the wisdom of judge Leslie Block and came to the conclusion that an appeal would be a good idea, and in which case the Rolling Stones would just be released. Sure enough, judge Block was overruled as once again, the judiciary was being shown up as fucking stupid. I had already come to the conclusion that it was the UK law that was so stupid by 1968, that its logic was totally flawed, and let me see, how long has it taken the authorities to come to a partial agreement with that conclusion? Yes, a full fifty years! Fifty years?? That is partially because of American influence and pressure on the UK government not to rock the boat over cannabis legalization, or to relax drug laws in general, as they might begin to look too much like Holland or even Portugal. They should have listened to *The Little Red Schoolbook* [*Den little røde bog for skoleelever*] originally published in 1969, which stated "since pot hasn't been proved to be more dangerous than alcohol or tobacco, it might be better to make it legal" There was no chance that the authorities would ever listen to this sane Danish advice!

With the Rolling Stones something happened to popular music that I could relate to. Bringing down the old order was very much a part of my psyche, even if the path it chose was only destined to be a small thorn in the flesh of the establishment. The idea that I could ever vote Conservative is still totally absurd. Like Jeremy Corbyn, I was in a political wilderness, but unlike Mr. Corbyn in 2016, after thirty years of voting against the government, I have never been plucked out of it, even though I reckon Corbyn is destined to be sent back to the backbenches again in the course of time, despite the lost dreams of a youth angry with life and their lot which has seen the honesty of Corbyn's statements over-ride the cant of conservative austerity. How dare they offer the nurses a 1% pay rise and then take a 10% pay rise themselves, recommended by IPSA in 2015 with another 1.3% pay rise recently on top of that. The job that nurses do should be honoured by society, and sympathetically rewarded, not subjected to mealy-mouthed mean rises of 1%. But that is what the elites do: take everything they can get as long as the lower orders are reasonably content. If discontent were to swell to unmanageable proportions, then the elites offer comfort by deciding that the 1% pay cap was a feature of a philosophy now in need of revision, so that the offer of an increased percentage point, or half-a-point might even be seen as quite generous. Public opposition to this mean-mouthed government rhetoric may yet see the Treasury being told what to do by the PM, but all of this is in constant flux: the only thing that remains the same is the ever-increasing gulf between the low-paid and the high-paid in the UK.

So, my role is to be an exception to whatever general rules apply to those brought up on inner London Council Estates who went to comprehensive schools in the days before the gentrification of Camden Town, Kentish Town and Archway. There were other exceptions of course: just along the balcony was a Jewish family, obviously displaced, whose children were very bright and who went off to good schools, one to Westminster I think. There was John McGowan, whose family lived in a block of flats close by our estate, who did end up going to Acland-Burghley School. McGowan tried to take me in hand, which was very gracious of him, and attempted to introduce me to jazz and modern art. McGowan was an elegantly dressed aesthete who decided it was worth trying to round-out my education as a scientific-obsessed nerd, although the word 'nerd' had not been invented by 1965. I can still recall the Giacometti exhibition at the Tate Gallery that he took me to around 1965, which made a strong impression. John McGowan remained true to his calling: art. He taught printmaking at Oundle College (fees 15,000 quid a year) and is an accomplished artist and printmaker in his own right with solo exhibitions to match.

Clearly he is more of a pragmatist than myself, who refused to have anything to do with fee-paying establishments. That however, is an unfair statement as John told me that he had turned down the offer of a job at a private Girl's school in Reading many years before, so his thoughts were rather similar to mine. John's fine print-making has resulted in several solo exhibitions, the latest one in Kettering, and when we visited in 2019, we liked three prints based on old scenes in Venice so much, a signed limited edition of twelve, that we bought a set for our own living room wall, the last of the set of twelve, and we often look up from our table to admire them: so much more restful and interesting than a Duchamp urinal.

After my first degree in Chemistry, I aimlessly wandered into doing a teaching qualification at London University, Institute of Education. For the teaching assignment, they were going to send me to some posh fee-paying private school. I had to notify them that I had no intention of teaching at such a place and could they find me a comprehensive school instead. Reluctantly, they did: I am never sure whether these principles are daft, self-justifying or delusional: whatever, if I was in Jeremy Corbyn's place, Prime Minister May, would not be able to accuse me of having gone to a grammar school when the Labour Party might have been seeking their elimination. I would still seek their abolition, just as Old Labour education policy thought of doing away with private education altogether back in the early 1980's. They would not dare to suggest that today, not when Diane Abbott's children go to private school, not when the increased need for a leg-up became ever more desirable as the 2000's rolled on, with the ever-increasing gulf between the rich and poor, why saddle yourself with the poor end of the spectrum when it is so much more beneficial to move with the rich?

Now, in the UK, the gulf between the rich and poor is many times greater than it was in the 1970's, my golden era, generally a period reviled by most commentators today, but we were much more equal then. The adult pay gap between those born into wealthier families and those from less well-off parents is widening, according to research by the Institute for Fiscal Studies. In 2012 a 42-year-old man whose parents were among the richest fifth of households earned an average of 88 per cent more than those from the poorest families. The equivalent gap in 2000 was just 47 per cent, and what on the earth the gap was in 1975 is probably so astounding that it can't be reported: it must have been of the order of 18 per cent. Britain is one of the most unequal societies in Western Europe in 2019, much to our collective shame. I think it is the size of the pay pyramid that is so disgusting in today's Britain, where private water board CEO's receive salaries in the millions with huge pension contributions and bonuses, where shareholders take up most of the rest of the pot and the public sector in terms of corporation tax, gets very little. When questioned about these obscene rates of pay, we are told that the director's salaries are still below those for FTSE top 100 companies CEO's rate of remuneration. And to think that this is a resource for us all, once in public ownership, or in shared ownership, as it is still in many countries of the world. In others, such as in Japan, Canada, Egypt, Pakistan or Scandinavia, there are no private water companies at all! Nicaragua, the Netherlands and Uruguay have even passed laws banning water privatization while in Italy a law favouring water privatization was repealed by an overwhelming majority of Italians through a referendum. In the case of Italy, the spectre of cartel and former mafia control of what should be a public good was too scary a prospect and convinced the public to outlaw private ownership, even if one lays aside the socialist nature of that wise decision.

Compared with Britain, some of the laws in the Netherlands make the latter seem almost like a communist state, except that the truth is it is Britain that seems like an enclave of the worst excesses of capitalism, thanks to Margaret Thatcher's government, and the Netherlands with reasonable policies that favour the population at large rather than lining the pockets of the few.

Where was I? Oh yes, the teaching: I gave up this teaching lark, although I was to become a Professor in time, secondary school teaching was certainly not for me: much too much like hard work. I was a wayward chemistry student who disliked the mathematics associated with chemistry, but who knew a lot about general chemistry, balancing equations, making varieties of gunpowder, inorganic chemical reactions, the name of compounds, their chemical constitution, what they were good for, the history of chemistry (a subject of interest to few even today), and a whole lot else beside. Not necessarily the kind of disciplined knowledge to get an A at A level, but enough to get by. Our council flat lacked any form of central heating, relying on a half-baked (pun intended) conception of heat provided from a central oil-fired boiler-room in the Combe, a massive tower-block nearby, which was supplied to the flat through a couple of movable vents downstairs. It was truly pitiful, had perhaps been inspired by Scandinavian versions of communal distribution of heating for a group of flats, and the whole estate had won design awards from the Royal Institute of British Architects (RIBA). As I stared mournfully out of my bedroom window which overlooked the asphalted roofs of the garages below, thoughtfully covered with loose grey chippings as an apparently desirable architectural finish, youths could be seen on the roofs pelting each other with the angular granite gravel, gradually resulting in bare patches of asphalt visible from above, while the helpful sign in the open space to the side, announced that no ball games or any other form of recreation was allowed, including the riding of bicycles. The sheds below us were open to the general area of the garages outside and various drunks would bed down there for the night or piss on the lower stairway on their way back from the pub. At some stage I wrote a letter of protest and complaint to Camden Council Architects Department in the 1970's, and received a sympathetically worded letter back, but the RIBA was not criticized in any way, which clearly they should have, from my standpoint as an inhabitant of this award-winning wonder, especially as I had specifically asked them to comment on that award.

I remember going bob-a-job with the Cubs before the estate was built and entering the small house whose ancient and contented occupant kept budgerigars in her modest dwelling. All bulldozed to make way for the Le Corbusier-inspired vision of the modern metropolis in the air, removed from the ground and the sights of trees or bushes. One year I taught a weeklong seminar on ancient metallurgy in Le Chaux-de-Fronds, and was amused to see where Charles-Édouard Jeanneret (Le Corbusier) had been raised: in a nicely apportioned detached house. Yes, exactly: I would love to see the elite of the RIBA living on my mum's council estate for five years in the 1960's and see how they liked living in award-winning accommodation for a while.

One night, in the 1960's, the temperature dropped so low in my bedroom, that the glass bottle of Industrial Methylated Spirits, which I had to use for my experiments instead of pure alcohol, shattered, spilling the IMS all over the old chest of drawers we had bought from one of the posh houses opposite Regents Park for five shillings. These were the Nash Estate Homes, one could say, rather than the Council Estate Homes. The finish was ruined, but there was no possibility of replacement, so I tried to repolish it as best I could: the thought of spending money on a replacement was out of the question, as there was none.

There was no Uncle Tungsten available for me, as there was for Oliver Sacks: Sacks came from a whole different social class as his father was a doctor, his mother a surgeon, a cousin owned a cine recorder, there was the influential chemist uncle, a very extensive extended family of physicians, scientists and other notables, and they even had a garden! As his mother was one of eighteen children, Lithuanian Jews, it does make one wonder about the contributions of nature or nurture to one's ability to get on in life. My own feeling is that in some cases there is a considerable influence from the inherited genetic stream and some Lithuanian or Iranian Jews are particularly blessed. I was just listening to an excellent lecture by Stephen Greenblatt on Lucretius and the survival of the *Nature of the Universe*, and, yes, this eminent scholar is also of Lithuanian Jewish descent! In the mediocre gene pool in which my own family nexus wallowed, we were never likely to mount to very much. At the same time, I was an ardent admirer of Jean-Paul Sartre, whose existentialist creed could result in any transcendence of limitation, because the individual existence of the self was the predominant feature of our lives, not a pre-determined bad faith or avoidance of freedom of choice. We were free: free to choose or make our own destiny. It just might help, however, to have those genes into the bargain.

Without an Uncle Tungsten, I had to make do with my own company and my own laboratory-bedroom, which gradually filled with chemicals, including such delicacies as sodium metal, magnesium ribbon, picric acid (which I synthesized myself), sodium hydroxide, concentrated sulphuric and hydrochloric acids and chromyl chloride, a wonderfully corrosive crimson liquid, synthesized too by distillation, to name a few friends from those days.

There was a very helpful dispensing chemists located on Stoke Newington High Street, that advertised as selling chemicals and equipment for the schoolboy chemists, like myself back then, who could buy things now totally banned for public use. Being a schoolboy chemist in 2019 must be incredibly frustrating, with sulphuric acid now heavily restricted even, thanks to those acid-throwing bastards, which began to happen to women somewhere in India decades ago, and has now spread as a fashion to the UK, to get revenge or destroy the looks.

The journey to Stoke Newington on the number 73 bus in the 1960's was like a major expedition for me, since Stoke Newington represented the back of beyond, its only appeal being this special chemists shop. Stoke Newington, I imagined, as being filled with disadvantaged and potentially violent types who were somewhat inferior to us Camden Town-Regents Park inhabitants, by virtue of their location. Trying to buy 0.88 SG ammonia or cobalt aluminium sulphate (cobalt alum for crystal growing), from a chemists anywhere near us in the Regents Park area was next to impossible, the stupid assistants would just shake their heads, and some did not even know what 0.88 SG even stood for, so down to Stoke Newington it had to be, even if it was a forsaken and unknown region of London compared with Camden Town.

I was especially entranced with atomic models and longed to be able to build a version of DNA or even the amazing structure of vitamin B12, long on display at the Science Museum, where I used to stare at it in wonderment, worked out by Dorothy Hodgkins at Kings College, London, whose chemistry department closed down a few years ago, in 2003, although they may have been forced to open it again since. I saved up some money and ordered a set from a chemical supply company. The lorry driver had difficulty getting into the Regents Park council estate area, and even more reversing to get ready to leave and was amazed to discover that he was delivering to a schoolboy living in a council flat, as the rest of his deliveries would all be to prestigious institutes and chemical laboratories at UCL with delivery ramps!

I once went for an interview at Kings College in 1964 with a very upper-crust chemist who looked askance at my interest in chemistry at home, and the fact that no-one at Kings College had ever heard of Acland-Burghley Comprehensive School. He wondered if it was such a good idea to turn one's hobby into a career. What a load of crap: no career in chemistry at Kings, that's for sure.

In some ways my approach to knowledge has never really changed that much. I moved at random between certain fields, the hedgerows of which are supposed to contain them, for good reason, but which I never really paid any attention to. This has been both an advantage and a disadvantage. The perpetual amateur can continue to find enjoyment in knowledge and study, while the focussed can become weary and disinterested, as they plough one field in a methodical manner, which I could never do. Those who wander are not necessarily lost, but making connections and receiving sustenance from different sources and motivations which can result in benefits of different sorts, even if these are long-term, inchoate, never realized, or slowly matured, rather than immediate.

After eventually getting three A levels of modest rank in Chemistry, Physics and Pure Math's, I left the confines of Camden Town and the Regents Park Estate, to head off to the University of Reading, fundamentally ill-prepared for University life. My sheltered and introverted working-class existence had not taught me to swim, to drink, to drive, to travel, to speak a foreign language, or any number of other normal activities. No-one in my family could drive or had a motorcar, no-one drank, went to the pub, or ate out, no-one had been abroad apart from my maternal grandmother, who had been in India before the Second World War for a while, and my dad during the war in Sicily and, after dysentery, in Algeria before being shipped back home. My mother never smoked or drank, and always went out to work. I never used to think of her as a teetotaler, as indeed she was, for teetotalers in the 1950-1960 era were seen as remarkably self-

78

disciplined and self-denying. Many of the upper classes at this time smoked like chimneys, drank like fish, and fucked like rabbits when they could, while the lower orders fretted away in their desire for social respectability and moral rectitude, eeking out the pennies.

I did have a student grant, provided by the Inner London Education Authority, an enlightened and liberal body who played an important role in my life, not only at this juncture, but in years to come. In theory, there was supposed to be a parental contribution to the student grant, as it was means tested after a fashion, but having two younger sisters at home, who my parents were still looking after, the idea that they had any spare money at all was simply laughable. The Government mathematicians who had made these calculations had clearly not based their economic model on our household, which could hardly have been accused of extravagant living, since they never went dancing, or to the cinema, the pub, or ate out, or had foreign holidays, or a decent home holiday, or a mortgage, or colour television. One of the tobacco tins would have to have been raided, perhaps resulting in the electricity bill going unpaid. I had to manage on the amount of grant money I did receive and be grateful.

I could play chess and study chemistry, do a little geology, mineralogy and math's, but very little else. While at Acland-Burghley Comprehensive, I had been sufficiently enthusiastic to form a chess-club, as there was one schoolmaster there who was interested in chess as well, although I could beat him fairly easily. The chess club was quite a success, and we purchased cheap plastic sets and roll-up plastic boards. We decided to enter the British Schools Chess Championship, just to see how far we could get. The first team that the Championship organizers fixed us up with was Dulwich College. Perhaps this was some kind of sick joke on their part, as Dulwich College had a chess team of considerable strength and experience, while our putative team had only just been put together. On board one, I was playing R. D. Keene, who by then was practically of master strength. Our team lost 6-0. Dulwich had to play away from home, and so these public schoolboys had set foot in an inner London poor comprehensive school for the first time in their lives. What an extraordinary event. Raymond D. Keene went on to become a grandmaster, one of the strongest players in the country, acted as a second to Victor Korchnoi in his world title match against Anatoly Karpov, and still writes the weekly chess column for the Spectator magazine. I was to play against him one more time, when he had recently been awarded the title, some years later. This was a 10-second a move tournament at Hastings. My strength as a player at 10-second a move chess was considerably greater than my actual board strength, which was strong club level, nothing more. I played black against Keene and we ended up in a Dutch Defense, stonewall variation, in which Keene became increasingly uncomfortable: he offered me a draw after about 35 moves, which I naturally accepted. Having played thousands of games between the events at Acland-Burghley and our meeting in 1978, Keene had no recollection that he was playing the same person he had met so briefly all those years ago. Another 10-second a move match saw Camden Chess Club pitched against Cambridge University First Team at the British Championship Speed event held in Bristol around 1974 I think it was. I was on board two, playing against Grandmaster Michael Stean, who had just been named co-winner of the British Championship. I was black in a Sicilian Defense, Kan variation, and was gradually getting outplayed. Stean however, made the mistake of over-reaching himself and at one point offered a queen sacrifice which I declined, as I had been plotting something else of danger to white involving a knight sacrifice of my own on the other side of the board, if I ever got the chance, this might be it! In those 10 seconds, Stean was temporarily at a loss, he made an inconsequential move, I sacrificed my knight, which Stean had to accept and then my Queen, supported by a fianchettoed Bishop moved in and mated him. Stean pulled a face, shook hands limply, and slowly rose from the table. Score: Cambridge University 3, Camden Chess Club 1. A point they could ill-afford to drop to stay on top.

I won the Camden Club Championship in 1973 and 1974 and at one annual prize giving, the Mayor of Camden, I think it was the time of Florence Evelyn Cayford, I am not sure if she was the one, but the Mayoress was the Chairperson at any rate, puffing away on her pipe. Yes, there was a time in the 1970's that meant the liberation of women had advanced to the stage that it seemed quite normal for her ladyship to light up a pipe of tobacco. Meanwhile in the Camden of 2019, one might even be thrown out of a meeting for smoking the same pipe. Or even vaping. Besides, Mayors probably have more prestigious ribbons to cut than wasting time on us chess-playing losers, even if I did win the Championship that year.

The adjustment to life at Reading University was superficially easy, but essentially flawed. Psychologically, I was younger than my physical age, more or less the reverse of children in 2019, who seem so mature and worldly-wise at the age of twelve. I was in Whiteknights Hall, with an interesting group of students, one from Winchester, whose love was the opera and the theatre. As he was doing no work at all, apart from his fervent interest in the University Theatre Club, he was kicked out after the first year, but I suspect this was small beer for him. Another student, from Aberystwyth, became a life-long friend and we have often spent some days at his place in Aberystwyth, or even his cottage in Clegerac, Brittany.

# Chapter Five: Chess and University

I played chess for Reading University Chess Club, and an enjoyable experience it was too. One refined student who had been to public school, M. M. Daube, and I used to play friendly games in his rooms in Whiteknights, which were split about equally between us. Michael Daube came from an upper crust family whose brothers were all prominent athletes; later Mike Daube became the first secretary of the anti-smoking organization called ASH. Whiteknights was not far from St. Joseph's Convent School, on Upper Redlands Road where Marianne Faithfull went to school. They must have had inspirational musical instruction, for Alma Cogan and Sally Oldfield were the only alumni of note the convent has produced, although I am sure there must be several academics and prominent business folk.

One of my acquaintances, for the sole reason that he was a neighbour when I had moved to another hall of residence, was a tall wiry chap from Devon, who was a wild one. One summer, he convinced a welding firm in Reading to take him on during the long summer break, as he had a wife and child to support. Well, that was what he told them at any rate, and at the end of the summer he used the money to buy a new motorbike. Having never driven one in his life before, he got on, started up, drove all the way to Devon and had no idea how to stop his new machine. He crashed the motorbike into a Devonian wall, and gave it away to the first passerby. There was something endearingly quixotic about that as well as revealing the extreme recklessness of his personality. He had an extensive library of books on economics, which I understood he had mostly stolen from the university bookshop. In fact, I don't think he had ever purchased one. Economically, this was the most economical way of obtaining books on economics.

Reading University was a hard slog for me, partly because I was seriously short of funding and lacking in motivation, a problem that was not uncommon with some students in their first year who then dropped out and went on to other things. I did not drop out but continued to the end and got a lower second-class degree. Getting the degree was an essential rite of passage. It was a stepping-stone on which other things could be built, although what they might be at that stage I had no idea.

The Chemistry Department at Reading was a good one, but I did not thrive there. There was too much mathematics to do, which I could not find that interesting. I was a cyclist in Reading too, and felt more exposed to heavy vehicle traffic there than I had been in London. Reading, in Berkshire, is a town most famous for its gaol, where Oscar Wilde was imprisoned and subjected to hard labour, which helped to destroy his health. The centre of Reading itself has been destroyed since those days and replaced with concrete in its multifarious forms, few of which are aesthetically pleasing. Demolition is something of a speciality with Reading Borough Council, hence the vast amounts of new concrete all over the place. The back of the Oracle used to be Reading Town's historic tramway building, and there was an agreement that the council would preserve it and a plaque went up commemorating it. However, another arm of the council pulled the historic structure down and a replacement plaque had to be erected instead, artificially aged to simulate the original. Somehow that epitomized Reading: it lacked class, and what class it might have had went down when all of the concrete went up, while it desperately tried to convince you that Reading was the place to be.

I only really remember the bowling alley and the heavy traffic spewing out black particles of smog as I cycled next to them, which streaked the face as you wiped them. Bicycle preservation could prove costly, as there was a serial thief who prowled around the Reading University campus, stealing any bicycle lamps he could, and having so little money, the replacement was the equivalent of spending sixty quid today, in terms of my gross domestic income, for the replacement.

After my first degree in chemistry, I was lost. There was no path forward. I spent time on the dole: a wonderful thing in allowing time to clear the head, loaf around, read Camus, Sartre, more Dostoyevsky, Turgenev, Henry Miller, Andre Gide, William Burroughs, J. D. Salinger, Dickens (but never Jane Austin), Auden, Knut Hansen,

Miguel de Unamuno, etc etc., find a girl and move on with odd jobs here and there. I worked for a chemical analysis firm on wastewater characterization in High Holborn. Way beneath my degree level, but it kept me going; Clarkson's Holidays, in the days before their cruise ships were banned from all Italian ports, reported gleefully on the front page of the Daily Telegraph, who seemed to have some kind of vendetta against Clarkson's. Eventually they did go bust. Part-time writing for Phillips, or was it Pye-Unicam, with a Scottish sub-editor on the run from alimony payments but longing to get back to the newspaper work he loved. It is all a blur now, but the girl became my wife, Lesley, and we are still together today, fifty years later.

Somehow I got a job as a chemist of sorts with the Counties Public Health Laboratories in Verulam Street, Holborn. My duties were the analysis of water for oxygen content, nitrate content, and the analysis of various products, such as marmite for nitrogen content and various other constituents. The marmite waste feedstuffs were so viscous that trying to get them out of the plastic jar in the 'fridge could bend your nickel spatula like Uri Geller. Some of these nutritious products would even ferment in the 'fridge and occasionally explode. Most were waiting to be given their certificate of analysis without causing trouble. This taste of chemistry awakened the chemist in me again, although the work was fundamentally tedious and I used to spice it up by reading about the chemistry of alkaloids, rubber and synthetic polymers. After my performance began to fall off due to incipient boredom I knew they were thinking of getting rid of me. I beat them to it by tendering my resignation, although there was no job to go to.

# Chapter Six: The Move of the Mind

Just as I was beginning to despair of finding anything to do with my working life, Lesley took hold of the Hampstead and Highgate Express, after I had tossed it disconsolately to one side, and pointed out a small advert for someone to work as a clerical assistant at the Council for British Archaeology. In that apparently insignificant moment, a future was to unfold.

As a 14 year old I had been inspired by reading Sir Mortimer Wheeler's *Archaeology from the Earth*, and had made up, as best I could, a small green suitcase as a travelling lab to lift a Roman mosaic with. The mobile kit was replete with gauze and muslin, scalpels and knives, adhesive and animal glue, test tubes and various acids. I remember taking this with me on the train from Waterloo to Worcester Park when visiting Uncle Fred and Aunt Grace Maude Batchelor in 1962, as a kind of half-realized half-fantasy of such work, but if I had come across a Roman mosaic of modest size, I was quite prepared to roll it up and take it away for study, as I had the muslin, gauze, tools and necessary chemicals in my travelling case. The chapter detailing the conservation work in Sir Mortimer's book had been written by Ione Gedye, of the Institute of Archaeology where the great man was Director. There was obviously something in this inchoate longing that meshed and melded with the fields of chemistry and archaeology which under normal circumstances remained separate and unconnected, or only conjoined by rather privileged folk from well-to-do backgrounds, or at least the middle-classes.

So it was that I began work at the Council for British Archaeology (CBA), which then resided at a marvellous address in St. Andrews Crescent, just off the outer circle of Regent's Park. The great thing about this location was that I could cycle home for lunch or to see my mum and dad at the council flat, some ten minutes away, and could cycle to work from the flat that Lesley and I had rented in Goldhurst Terrace, West Hampstead. The route took me through Regents Park and up Bishops Avenue, to Swiss Cottage and along the road to Goldhurst Terrace. Getting to work was nearly all downhill in the morning, the most magical part of the journey being the slow cycle past the baby emu at the zoo, and the most nerve-wracking, maneuvering the bicycle thought the octopus-like traffic movements around Swiss Cottage roundabout, although it is not really a roundabout more a confluence of organized chaos, which in those days was quite bereft of other cyclists in any number or any sign of a cycle lane.

A Mr. Marchant at the Council for British Archaeology was my immediate superior, while the Director was Henry Cleere, who had worked for the Iron and Steel Institute and was an expert on the Wealden iron in antiquity. Henry Cleere later took his PhD from the Institute and stayed in the field, becoming a stalwart of ICOMOS, international charters and codes of archaeological conduct. Good for him and quite admirable has been his dedication, although his opposition to metal detectorists, while understandable, has proved to be quite unenforceable, and perhaps misguided. Just recently a member of the tribe of metal detectorists (as they are now called), discovered the Staffordshire hoard of Anglo-Saxon jewellery in a farmers field, quite the most important find of recent years, which I was invited to examine recently, in 2015, at Liverpool Museum and Art Gallery.

At one stage, in 1974, when Mr. Marchant learnt that I had a degree in chemistry and an interest in archaeology, he told me that with my qualifications had I ever thought of taking up conservation? I was excited by this revelation: like so many other people, I had never heard of archaeological conservation as a profession. Many of us have stumbled into this field, previously unknown and mysterious and have engaged with it in delight. That applies to folk in all sectors of the large umbrella covered by conservation of our material and immaterial culture. As an exercise in humanism the thought that chemistry could be put to use in the service of archaeology seemed like the least commercial and degraded activity and elevated chemistry to a caring profession, nurturing the past and trying to preserve the detritus of our cultural lives had a noble aspiration to it. Not only that, it might even lead to employment! I paid for a one-year's subscription to Archaeometry magazine, then the most prestigious science-based archaeological journal. It was so long ago that an article by Andrew Oddy, whose path I would later follow, described how the gold content of a small coin could be estimated by a specific gravity determination using an ordinary chemical balance. Back at the council flat, I actually had a laboratory chemical balance purchased second-hand from Lawrence Corner on Hampstead Road, at that time an emporium of wonder to me. Lawrence Corner Stores specialized in government surplus army gear and much American laboratory glassware, perhaps from the Korean war. Most of my pocket money was spent at Lawrence Corner.

I had already received a student grant from ILEA for my degree in Chemistry, but at this time, around 1973-4, there was a discretionary fund available for another first degree, for those whose vocation might lie elsewhere, if the assessment panel of the ILEA could be convinced of the genuine need of the poor applicant. What a wonderfully liberal concept in the best sense of what liberalism might mean for conducting the affairs of state of educative evaluation. The philosopher-rulers of the County Hall committee could apparently see that I was deserving of this additional funding. I only wish I could write to each of them today to thank them for making this award, and it saddens me to think this is impossible, since every member of the panel was about fifty years of age, that would now make them about the same age in 2017 as my mother, 97, or possibly older. True, she was still alive last month, but I think it unlikely that the Platonist philosopher-rulers of ILEA are.

Not all local authorities gave one this opportunity: we can guess which ones were the least generous in this regard: those controlled by conservative party apparatchiks rather than the socialist-friendly old liberals who inhabited county hall in those days. My wife, Lesley and I had forsaken London at this stage, after a few summers working on archaeological sites we decided to move to Wales. Our friend Paul Lambert who owned then an impressive and expensive passenger van took us down to Wales and back quite a few times. On one of our journeys we picked up a pair of Spanish hitch-hikers in London, who chatted to themselves quite happily for four hours, and when we returned to London some days later, we picked up the same two lucky folk in Wales, who repeated their contented conversation as if it were the most natural thing in the world that we should drive them 200 miles to Wales and then the same 200 miles back for free! We were stopped by the fuzz twice: once on the M4 down to Wales. Paul was driving barefoot and when the fuzz spotted his bare feet they made some derogatory remark about his feet and lack of any attire. But when they saw his driving license, HGV Class 1, they were suitably impressed and on we were waived. Then when we got to Wales, we were stopped by the fuzz again, for no reason in particular. I think they were just curious as to how these hairy hippy types were driving around in a new, expensive passenger van. We were waived on again. The only time I got stopped by the police was cycling up Camden Road on a journey from my mum's Council flat to our rented accommodation in Islington. I was going very fast indeed, as I had seventeen years of London cycling under my belt and I was the only cyclist on the road at 9pm at night: an extraordinary thought compared with today's London. A jar of laundry detergent was the only odd item I was carrying, but I resented being singled out and having my extraordinary momentum along Camden Road interfered with, especially as all red lights had been dutifully obeyed, there was no reason for me being stopped. Years later I got my revenge on the very same road. A Police transport vehicle carrying about eight coppers tried to overtake me, illegally, on the inside just past where the bridge takes the railway line over Camden Road in Camden Town. I accelerated the hire car and blocked them behind me, and then proceeded to stick rigidly to the speed limit and stop for pedestrians at every single pedestrian crossing between Camden and the far end of Holloway. One of them bellowed at me out of a side window as they turned off the road. I had my revenge and could travel on in peace, ignoring the speed limit like everyone else: now we were even.

Lesley and I had saved up the lamentable sum of one hundred pounds between the two of us; neither of us could drive at that stage, a few years before the sorry tale recounted above, had no other source of income, no stocks, bonds or shares, no help from our financially strapped parents and no inheritance. We ended up living in rural

Pembrokeshire, at Bwlych-y-Groes, where we shared an old farmhouse with a group of other hippy-like folk. One of them from Devon who attempted to sign on the dole, was unlucky enough to have worked as a TV repair man, and was soon found a job travelling all over west Wales repairing television sets, having to set off to work at an early hour. Not exactly the relaxing time he had imagined. Those of us with a degree in Chemistry were somewhat more useless, and joined the 10% unemployed of the west Wales region. This was a real unemployment rate, unmanipulated, rather than a pretend one that we use today, which we will come back to in a moment.

Well, my chemistry degree might have been of non-utilitarian value, but some were of practical value, such as Richard Kemp's Liverpool University degree, which enabled him to start producing, just down the road from us, D-lysergic acid diethylamide, near Tregaron at Llanddewi Brefi, Ceredigion. An enantiomer of such purity that many notables made the pilgrimage to Tregaron to experience a pure high from LSD unlaced with secondary reaction products or junk, including the Rolling Stones, Jimi Hendrix, and other famous names from the Pop world. The reason Kemp was so skilled at this synthesis was that he had been employed in 1969 by author and magazine editor David Solomon, a fascinating character in his own right. Solomon had served in World War II, and lost both of his brothers in Germany. Like the hero of *Saving Private Ryan*, he was pulled from the front. Knowing Aldous Huxley and William Burroughs, Solomon had an evangelical zeal for mind-altering drugs. From 1964 to 1975, Solomon edited a series of anthologies that provided intellectual, philosophical, medical, and historical perspectives on various drugs from LSD to marijuana to cocaine. The titles include *LSD: The Consciousness-Expanding Drug* (1964), *The Marijuana Papers* (1966), *Drugs and Sexuality* (1973) and *The Coca Leaf and Cocaine Papers* (1975). He created a forum of educated and academic discussion for much mythologized subjects and his works became best-sellers. So this is why Solomon had funded Kemp's LSD work. The end result was that Kemp moved to a cottage in Tregaron around 1974 and began to produce some of the purest LSD in the world, uncut or unlaced. Millions of tablets were making their way around England and the rest of the world from this Tregaron cottage until a disastrous accident happened with Kemp's Range Rover near Machynlleth in 1975. Evidence of hydrazine hydrate was found in the Rover. There was only one reason why this would be found in an ordinary Rover, and that was the essential role that hydrazine hydrate took in the synthesis of LSD. At the time, I was more interested in the chemical reactions of alkaloids rather than hallucinogenic substances, but Kemp was making the money while I was lazying about.

An operation was set up to smash the drugs network. It was run in secrecy by Operation Commander Dick Lee, as a precaution against corruption in the Metropolitan Police and loose tongues in provincial police stations.

A Mr. Stephen Bentley was the copper charged with watching Plas Llysyn - an imposing mansion house deep in central Wales, where Kemp and his girlfriend, Dr Christine Bott, were suspected of producing 90% of Europe's LSD. Bentley, in his book about this dramatic case, *Operation Julie,* which was immortalized in the song by the Clash: *Julie's been working for the Drug Squad*, writes that his work as an undercover agent was responsible for his subsequent addiction to alcohol and hash.

"The over-riding feeling was fear" He writes "I was worried about smoking dope and taking cocaine, but those fears subsided as I took more and didn't end up in the gutter," Despite a total of 120 arrests, resulting in 15 convictions and prison sentences totalling more than 120 years, Stephen Bentley thinks that the long term impact was "negligible", and a waste of resources. He now lives in the Philippines. Kemp was welcomed back to Wales after his sentence. Most unfairly, David Solomon got ten years for what? I seem to recall that some criminals responsible for GBH or Burglary got a lot less than that in jail. I suppose at that time people like David Solomon were seen as a threat to the establishment, while someone doing a bit of GBH was no real threat at all. Even today, in 2019, GBH under section 20 of the criminal code merits five years in jail, so you can see just how dangerous David Solomon was! Twice as dangerous at least.

Well, back when Kemp was earning megabucks and I no bucks at all in 1976, 10% was a real unemployment statistic, apart from the various dog-breeding scams, and unemployable idiots like us, not related at all to the so-called unemployment percentage figures used today, which have been redefined a total of over thirty times by successive Labour and Conservative governments to massage the numbers of the indigent ever downwards.

In an interesting paper on the differentiation between conceptual instruments (a term apparently introduced by an academic named Scott in 1990!) and technical instruments, Yorgos Vournas explains that 'conceptual instruments' is the term used for categories in producing a report on, say, unemployment, while the term 'technical instruments' refers to the specific methods used to collect the relevant information, and never the twain shall meet in any modern parlance of this discussion thread. A first result of manipulation of the definition of unemployment is the discontinuity of the official records: the comparison of the unemployment records prior to and after 1983 are therefore rendered ineffective. In reality, these records measure two different things: registered unemployment and claimant unemployment. In practice, the devil is in the details once again, as researchers compare these records, often being unaware of the fact that they are both discontinuous and unreliable as a consequence of political interference. This is something that should be hammered home by newspaper reporters on the subject, but most journalists seem too lazy to go into the matter in any detail and just quote that today, unemployment is 6.2% or whatever it is, as compared with 10.3% when we lived in Wales. Keeping the electorate selectively informed is in the interest of Government: not adequately and continuously reporting on that matter is the failed hermeneutic of the press.

As Vournas writes: "Thus, the conceptual instruments, which are used to define the categories, should also be continuous. For example, in order to have continuous, comprehensive, and reliable records of unemployment, we need a standard definition of what 'unemployment' is".

Well, whatever definition was used in our case we were the ideal candidates for being completely useless, apart from reading, writing, walking, and hanging about. I managed to link up with the Cardigan Chess Club and they came to pick me up a few times to play in matches for them. I think the standard of the opposition was low and remember nothing of them, but there was one Welsh player from the hills that everyone in our game had heard of, and that was I. C. Jones:

a player of great natural talent. It was said that A. H. Williams, the former Welsh chess champion had once tried to teach I. C. Jones opening theory without making much headway with him. That did not stop I.C. Jones from causing upset even at International events, where once Wales was pitted against the mighty Hungarian team with Lajos Portisch as Hungarian top board, then one of the eight strongest players in the world, at the time of the Chess Olympiad in Nice in 1974.

Due to ridiculously inept French planning, the running of the tournament was made possible only by the volunteer help of many chess enthusiasts who had come to Nice for a vacation, and had been roped into arbiting, typing, serving drinks, etc. Bobby Fischer would not play because no separate building was provided for him, Bent Larsen from Denmark did not turn up because of lack of funding and suitable opposition, presumably because Fisher's building did not materialize, and the East German team chose not to come at all, because they had stated that they could not win, so were not bothering to show up: an example of truly feeble East German communist logic if ever there was one. But that is what happens with chess primadonnas, and even entire teams might be infected with the superiority bug, even if they cannot win by staying away, at least they can't be beaten. Anyway, in the Wales vs Hungary match, Portisch was gradually getting into a very difficult position against Jones, and might even be in danger of losing, which would be unthinkable. The game was adjourned, and with the help through the night of the entire Russian and Hungarian teams, a possible drawing line was worked out. The game was resumed the next morning and Portisch scraped a draw. Score: Hungary 3.5, Wales 0.5.

I used to love the games of Portisch for their strong strategic import and powerful understanding of the openings he played; they seemed to have a solidity and logic to them which I tried to emulate, failing of course. He was reputed to study his game eight hours a day: a true professional.

Before moving to Wales, I had completed the paperwork for a second grant for yet another first degree from ILEA when we had lived in Goldhurst Terrace, Swiss Cottage. I never thought that anything would come of it and when we had moved to Wales we were amazed, some months later to find a letter forwarded from our former landlady in Goldhurst Terrace, informing me that I was being called for interview at County Hall, in two days' time. Almost at that moment, one of our old friends arrived in his car, having driven down from London. By that extraordinary coincidence, I was able to travel back to London the next day, and turn up for the interview at County Hall the morning after. They did seem surprised to see me. I was a long-haired, skinny, penniless specimen living on the dole, but the liberal-minded panel who interviewed me that day changed the course of my entire life, and awarded me the funding for my second first degree at the Institute of Archaeology, University of London, which I already mentioned above.

Looking back on any of these coincidences: the arrival of the letter in Goldhurst Terrance; the trouble and care of the landlady to find our obscure address; the forwarding of the letter onto us; the unexpected arrival of our London-based friend in time to take us back; the travel to County Hall; the successful interview; and finally learning about my award, can make choice in life seem scarily absurd. Not many people who want to study again can look back on the course of their life being decided almost purely by chance with a series of unplanned events of this sort. The reason the reflection is especially worrisome is that there was no logical alternative to life on the dole in Wales. Before this letter arrived, I had had thoughts that the University of Lampeter, not too far from where we were living, would have a chemistry department and I might be able to convince them that I could be taken on to do further chemical study. This was based on complete ignorance: in fact, the University of Lampeter even in the 1970's did not even have a Chemistry Department! So what would we have done? The nervousness of the thought is that I have no idea. No clue at all really, no clue at all.

The area of Wales around Cwrt-y-Brodr near Lampeter, which we were now living, was a remarkable countryside whose farmland, trees, banks and hedges had essentially remained unchanged for many hundreds of years, and it lay enveloped in its own time period, entirely unrelated to the events of the modern world. The hedgerows had trunks that were as thick as a man's waist: proof of their constancy, unmoved and obdurate, for generations. Nothing had disturbed them for centuries. Sheep grazed on a large field, green and damp not far off, covered in the dramatic backdrop of heavy clouds of purple-grey hanging low over the land, while a herd of cows churned up the mud near the stream where we had to get our drinking water from, and there was a tussle with time to get to the stream before the cows in the morning. The stream water was filtered through the hills of Crymmach, which must have a Welsh name. The grandmother of our friend Gerran used to take jars of the water away with her, such was its renown in old myth and mind as beneficial in its natural purity and sweetness.

Perhaps a few farms in England can boast of such medieval hedgerows, but I doubt it. The farmer next door to us stared at me in mild horror when I had eventually plucked up the courage to knock at his door and ask if he had any work for me. He shut the door slowly and that was the end of my local quest for work. The farmer drove around his land in a tractor with a tax disc many years out of date, never used a bank, or any rubbish service, and years later when he eventually had to be taken off to a care home, the money under his mattress, more than 200,000 pounds, was sufficient to keep him going in care for many years. So, he was still independent in his own way of the state, or banks, or the Department of Health and Social Security, or the Tax authorities. Down the road were undeclared dog breeding set-ups, making illegal moolah, and of course there was Kemp and his famous visitors.

An Irishman had arrived in the area decades ago and stayed in a rough stone hovel on the farmers land: no running water, no electricity, no gas, no telephone, no mail, and had stayed for forty-nine years, earning a pittance clearing weeds and roadside ditches, and eventually died in his hovel, independent, unremarked on and unremembered now, over forty years after his death : I do not expect that he ever claimed a farthing from the State, unlike us spongers, the Cwrt-y-Brodr residents who were a couple of hopeless hippies whose social security form had to be countersigned by someone, and as we effectively had no neighbours, I had to forge this to get the dole money sent to me by cheque. Our pace of life was so slow that travelling to the nearest village on foot to buy some food essentially took an entire day! The need to cook one's own food, made sure that day went by in a rustic time-warp, as if we were still living in the 1880's. If we had forgotten something, I would get on the bike and cycle there and back, which took over an hour. When we left for London for a few days, the rats gnawed through our mattress and an owl had managed to fall down the chimney and battered itself to death amongst our meagre belongings, now covered in feathers and blood.

Nothing changed in our area, and probably the only thing that has changed now in 2019 is the presence of more lucrative farm shops and the demise of the dog-breeding scams. No more penniless Irish labourers working for nothing and living in stone cottages like their forebears two hundred years earlier.

## Chapter Seven.  London and University College

We moved to a flat around the Portobello Road area, which we never warmed to, being essentially northern London habitués, of Camden Town, Kentish Town, Hampstead and the 'Heath.  It did for a while as I started studying for my second first degree, this time in Archaeological Conservation.  My teachers were Pamela Pratt, Nigel Seeley, Elizabeth Pye and the just retiring Ione Gedye, whose writing I had read all those years ago.  Kathy Tubb was our skilled laboratory supervisor, who forty years later, was still working at UCL, and has only just retired now in 2017!  There were six students in our year, one of the first years to undertake a degree in conservation rather than a diploma. I was the only male, an imbalance in our profession which has tended to get worse as the decades have rolled by.  Male conservators are now an endangered minority.  I have never been able to understand why this should be, and we will return to that question later on.

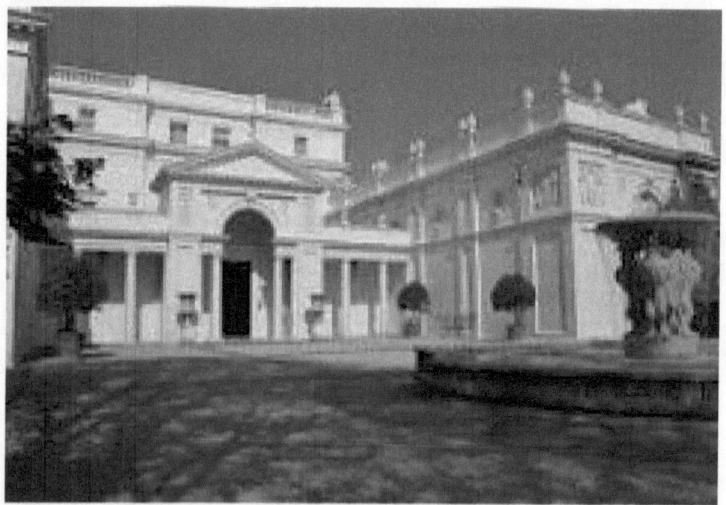

St. John's Lodge, Regents Park. Grade I listed.  Home of the Institute of Archaeology from 1937-1958. What a wonderfully suitable home. Pity we did not have 50 million to offer to the Crown Estates, especially as the footprint of the building could be doubled with no planning problems.

The Institute of Archaeology had originally been even closer to my parent's council flat, being housed in St. John's Lodge in Regents Park itself, some seven minutes' walk at most. The lodge had been so unwanted, incredibly, that it had been used as a hospital during the First World War and in its dilapidated state by 1937 was still, unbelievably, an undesirable location. Hence the Institute of Archaeology moved in and stayed right through the Second World War until the late 1950's. A purpose-built block was built for them around 1958, facing Gordon Square, not far from the British Museum and the former hang-out of St. John's Lodge moved on to other occupants. After the Crown Estates gave permission for the footprint of the building to be greatly extended (in fact doubled), disturbing really since one would have thought it was a grade 1 listed structure, not to be messed with, it was leased to Prince Jefri Bolkian of Brunei for 40 million quid. That is leasehold, not freehold, which means that in 99 years' time, the Crown Estates can lease it out again for another astronomical sum. The great benefit of the English leasehold system: property need never leave ones possession, but can be sold over and over again to the poor buyers over generations, who cannot manage anything better. An old Labour policy called for the abolition of the leasehold system, but that went very quiet around 1985.

In a former life, when the Lodge was occupied by the Marquis of Bute, dramatic murals had been commissioned, restored by English Heritage, perhaps employing a few conservators who had graduated from the same building the Sultan now occupies.

It was a comforting idea that 32-34 Gordon Square, some fifteen minutes from my parents council flat, had been designed solely for the benefit of archaeologists and conservators. This alone made the Institute seem special, which it undoubtedly is, and especially focused on its task, nurturing of the ideal of becoming an archaeologist or an archaeological conservator. It was a kind of Platonic form as far as I was concerned, an abstraction of the mind made manifest in the real world. I thrived at the Institute. My varied background of some archaeological site work, disorganized chemical knowledge, random readings, and interest in art, antiquity and the materials of art, coupled with the hand skills honed by my interests in woodwork and electric circuitry, were the perfect complement to this kind of academic and practical study.

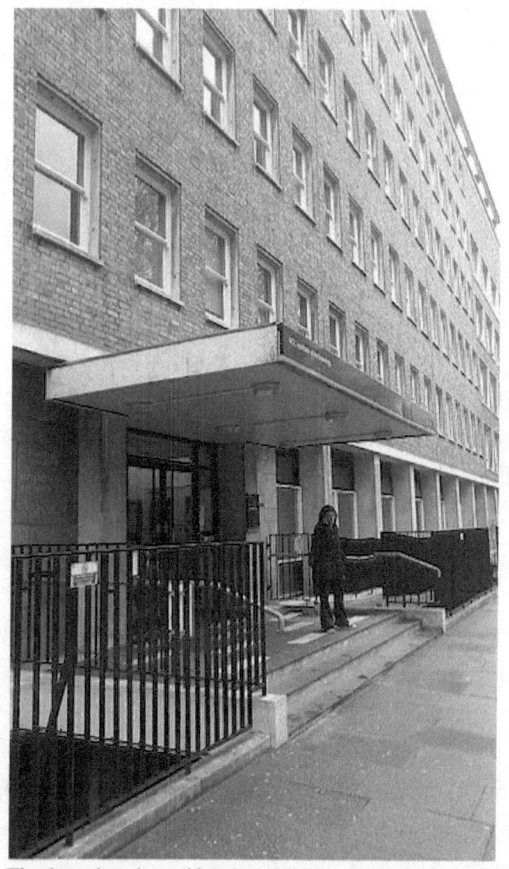

The less than beautiful, but functional University of London, Institute of Archaeology from 1958-2019 and still going. The archaeologists have outgrown the building and are now squeezed in like sardines making this a powerhouse of archaeological productivity.

During this time, from 1974 to the early 1980's, Lesley and I had fourteen different addresses of rented flats, covered neatly by page 45 of the London A to Z, apart from our less enjoyable start near the Portobello Road. North London then: this was our world. I began to take an increasing interest in the structure, composition and conservation of metallic artefacts. The lecturer I felt closest to was Dr.

Nigel Seeley, who had previously worked at New Scotland Yard Forensic Labs, which I was to visit a few times later on. He was an expert bibliophile, had a sharp sense of humour, a gifted instructor, a specialist on the preservation of paper and books, and a fine grasp of the chemical basis of art conservation, including metals, leather, ceramics, frits and glass. His general contributions to the life of the Institute of Archaeology were wide-ranging and subtle, but somewhat under-valued. The only problem with his approach to academic life, was that knowledge became his form of power, as he published very little, the power remained inside his personal realm, and if you wanted to access his precise and accurate store of erudition, you had to ask him yourself. This would become an impediment to advancement, and he later left to become the chief conservator of the National Trust, being greatly involved in the restoration of Uppark, when it had been burned down and subsequently completely restored.

The hardest-working member of our department was Elizabeth Pye, who later in life became Professor Elizabeth Pye at UCL by virtue of her contributions to teaching, management, administration and student nurturing. This was an extraordinary achievement, and UCL were loath to offer the title to her, as her application was rejected on the first attempt by the committee charged with conferring the title of professor on various applicants in the college. The reason for the refusal was that Elizabeth had published little, but the teaching route was supposed to overcome this problem, because it constituted a recognised route to a full professorship. However, the committee apparently could not reach the conclusion that advancement was justified.

I was one of the external letter-writers for the process of advancement at that stage, many years after I had left UCL, over twenty-five years later in fact. There was just one slight problem with this decision of UCL: if Elizabeth Pye could not be elevated to a Professorship via the teaching route, then patently no-one could. Someone in the hierarchy of UCL eventually noticed this absurdity, and Pye was asked to put in her application again. Once again, I wrote a letter of support and this time, the committee reached the only decision that made any sense, and she became Professor Elizabeth Pye and retired with the title about three years later.

The Director while I was at the Institute was Professor John Evans, who in the 1940's and 1950's had excavated important Neolithic sites in Malta. This seemed an incredibly long time ago to a youngish student, such as myself, in 1975 who had only been born in 1948. Evans even worked at Knossos in Crete, the mostly invented site of Sir Arthur Evans, who oddly was no relation of John Evans at all, at least at a level of relation less than five degrees of separation. John Evans seemed a shy and benign presence, indeed he might be seen as ineffectual, but he was a very capable administrator and sheparded the Institute into the fold of University College London, which guaranteed the Institute's stability and financial survival. Professor Evans was completely committed to the Institute and its staff and students. He served for a long time, from 1973-1989, more than enough for most ordinary folk, and out of the question at UCLA where two successive terms of three years each is the norm for most of the professorship, followed by a year's paid sabbatical to recover from the rigors of the six years of toil. Well, Evans toiled for seventeen years, well beyond the call of duty and should probably have been knighted for his services were it not for the fact that no-one in government gives a fuck about academic archaeologists these days. They would rather confer a knighthood on Malcolm Walker, Chairman of Iceland Foods. Now I am quite sure that you would prefer to shop at Sainsbury's or Waitrose, as Iceland's credentials are hardly inspiring, but apparently enough for a knighthood, if you are perceived as a ruthless money-maker selling crap food. Some of our other colleagues are also passed over, such as Dr. Paul Craddock of the British Museum, the doyen of ancient metallurgy over decades of work, with scores of important publications to his name, should have been turned into Dr. Paul Craddock OBE, but I am afraid the chances of that happening are far less than if you work for Sellafield Ltd and are in charge, for the last few years, of decommissioning nuclear waste sites, in which case you are an obvious choice for an OBE.

In a later period the Director of the Institute was the late Professor Peter Ucko, from 1996-2005, who once told the late Dr. Frank Preusser, my director at the Getty Conservation Institute, that his actual salary as director of the Institute was, in fact, twice his published salary. This extraordinary fact is not so extraordinary, for in the higher echelons of British university life, transparency is the last thing on anybody's mind. However much academics bang on about transparency in public life or academic discourse, they are not necessarily very transparent about themselves. Peter Ucko was a somewhat divisive figure in archaeology, noted for the exclusion of South African archaeologists during the apartheid era, where the international community had exercised a boycott on academics from South Africa. An important event took place at the International Union for Prehistoric and Protohistoric Sciences (IUPPS) Congress in 1986. Disagreements over the academic boycott of South African archaeologists led Ucko to denounce the IUPPS and to found the World Archaeological Congress (WAC). This resulted in fame for Ucko, who was staunchly anti-racist. Ucko was an overbearing figure who reorganized everything in his own mold and had his own opinions as to how teaching should be (re)configured and structured: rather the opposite to Professor Evans, although he did eventually come to realize the importance of conservation, although the Metals Summer School I had been teaching at the Institute each summer when I travelled over from Los Angeles, had to be relocated to UCL Mechanical Engineering when Ucko gave the marching orders. A pity, as I used to saunter over to the Institute of Archaeology in July, and the place was practically deserted!

I enjoyed the Institute in the 1975-1987 period, while I was there and loved what it stood for: academic archaeology, archaeological conservation and international research on a wide variety of topics spread across the world. Its illustrious founder was Sir Mortimer Wheeler, a born wheeler-dealer, with charisma and chutzpah. One of his archaeological digs was given a human scale bar which appeared to make his excavation much larger than it really was. Sir Mortimer had contrived this effect by inviting a midget he had met on the train to come over to his excavation and pose for the photographic record of the excavation trench. Now that is chutzpah and also rather cheeky. The Institutes most famous member was Vere Gordon Childe, who used to arrive for lectures with a copy of the Morning Star under his arm, and whose work on cultural diffusion was highly significant. Professor Childe, despite being invited many times to give lectures in the land of the free, was legally barred from ever entering the United States of America because of his Marxist philosophical leanings.

Clearly Professor Childe was a man of great power and influence who had the potential to undermine the dictates of the USA government, which is why the USA had to ban him as an undesirable. Sad: but then much of America is sad. Having reached the conclusion that his contribution to life and academe was over, Professor Childe returned to Australia and threw himself off the blue mountains of New South Wales, not too far from Sydney. He left a sealed letter to our then Director, Professor Evans, which was to be opened some years after his death. Our year missed Professor Childe and other autochthonous occupants of the institute for the most part: it was the second wave of academics who taught us now: Professor Hodson, Dr. Nandris, Dr. Glover, Professor Evans, Dr. Bray, Dr. Brothwell, Dr. Mellart, and others, some of whom have passed on already.

Studying archaeological conservation was delightful: it was of no use in the real world, no real utility, outside of the ambit of its sphere of influence or operation, designed to try to preserve what limited remnants of the ancient world had managed to accompany us into the present and possibly save them for the future. We, the conservators, would ensure that what could be saved for future use, would so be ensured, regardless of how much that might cost you, the public at large. Meanwhile, the rest of the world could do as it liked. We would carry on with our appointed task. It was a calling not a job. There was one former student who had become a priest, but most of us were gainfully employed in conservation work for archaeological sites, local area conservation groups, the Ancient Monuments laboratory, the National Trust, the National Museum of Scotland, the British Museum, teaching posts, etc etc. We are preservation functionaries, our appointed task independent of governments or countries: our allegiance is to artefacts.

I got a First, which in those days was listed in the pages of *The Times*, and our landlady, Mrs. Edney, a regular reader, cut out the page from the paper and gave it to me. Mrs. Edney came from a distinguished line of socialists, who had supported the left in the Spanish Civil War, could remember seeing H. G. Wells walking down the Euston Road, and had an impressive library of orange-backed penguin books in the hallway, which gives you some idea of how old that collection was: all pre-1970.

The First assured that I got an award from the Department of Education and Science, of a full grant to study for a PhD. I was so very happy: we may have had no money between us, Lesley and I, but we lived an easy student existence with no debts, no credit card, no car, no expensive outings to the theatre, no foreign holidays, no expensive restaurants. Some of our friends had led expansive and rewarding lives during the period when we were penniless students, and would remark on this or that concert or this and that film, or club or music scene, years later, to which we had to profess ignorance to 90% of it, as we could not have afforded anything but the Hampstead Theatre Club, the Diwana Indian restaurant in Drummond Street, and the Italian restaurant down Parkway mentioned before, with one bare light-bulb.

My PhD was a successful one, which led to several publications, and was finished on time after three years, since that was one of our main sources of income, while Lesley enjoyed working at the Employment Exchange, Archaeological Digs or Foyles Bookshop and finishing her own degree in Life Sciences at Westminster Poly. Finishing the PhD in three years was unusual, and in the American academic system, impossible, because in the latter system, one has to take languages, preliminaries, some course-work etc, with the result that many PhD's take seven to ten years to complete.

The Institute was full of colourful characters, Professor E. E. D. M. Oates, had worked with Sir Max Mallowan, OBE, the husband of Dame Agatha Christie. Professor Oates had a small area for his secretary, completely lined with pegboard tiles perhaps as a noise abatement effort, to keep any disturbance from his inner sanctum to a minimum. Each Department had a secretary, ours was Wendy Rix, a most efficient and capable worker, who eventually left to become the secretary to the Director of the Science Museum. Sir Max's second wife was the archaeologist Lady Barbara Parker. I had no inkling of any of this when, later on, I became a lecturer at the Institute and was assigned the rather nice room with two windows that was presently occupied by Barbara Parker. I strode into the room with the first of my trolley of books in tow, to find that a rather flustered Barbara Parker was still occupying the space, and had not realised that she was about to give it up. Very modestly she made her exit and I never saw her again. I suppose it had been a grace and favour room in honour of the grand old days of Max Mallowan, Dame Agatha Christie and Lady Barbara Parker, as Lady Barbara never lectured to the best of my knowledge. It was only much later that I realized who I had so unceremoniously evicted.

The rooms of Dr. James Mellaart, the excavator of the famous site of Catal Huyuk, were permanently wreathed in the smoke of expensive cigars which he seemed to chain smoke, and whose fumes wafted down the corridor. The rumour was that Dr. Mellaart had got himself banned from Turkey because it was claimed that a few artefacts had been smuggled back to the UK. There was also a weird problem with the Catal Huyuk Wall Paintings, whose precise form and extent were some sort of issue. Did they actually exist? There were even problems with the supposed early dates for copper smelting at the site from the 6th millennium BC, but the evidence has now been revised again, in favour of Dr. Mellaart this time. Dr. Mellaart was nothing but congenial with a wonderfully dry sense of humour.

Dr. Warwick Bray was our South American archaeologist who managed to cover the entire continent with shelves overflowing with every possible aspect of the pre-Columbian archaeological past, from corn to maize and the Andean highlands of the south to Costa Rica and Panama in the North, from burial practices to goldwork, excavation work to area survey. Because one of his areas of expertise was ancient South American goldwork, particularly ancient Colombia, I ended up doing a Ph.D. partially under his direction. In retrospect, this was both wonderfully exotic for someone who had never really been abroad before and was an under-studied area, but in the world of archaeological conservation and academic status relationships it might have been better if I had worked on carefully excavated Anglo-Saxon grave goods rather than ancient goldwork from Colombia, most of which came with no associated finds and no archaeological site. The reason for that equivocation is that I knew I would remain based in both conservation and in the UK. If my work had possessed a more direct relationship to the earth of my own area, it would have been better integrated in a nexus which was both sustainable and culturally relevant to my attempts to broaden my horizons.

So much of the goldwork of ancient South America is unprovenanced or undated or both, even those superb artefacts housed in the Metropolitan Museum of Art or the British Museum, or the National Museum of Denmark, or even the fabulous Museo del Oro in Bogotá, Colombia. The list is endless. Trade and movement in ancient Colombian gold had become so controversial that Sotheby's no longer even sells the stuff at auction. 2019 is not 1975.

The entire subject of ancient Colombian gold has become mired in contentious issues over the past few decades and is riven with fakes, looted art, and dangerous characters. Exciting stuff, but not ideally suited to the politically correct archaeological world that most other researchers inhabit, especially today. In 1980 one could even buy ancient Colombian gold-working tools at auction.

Through Warwick we had contacts with the Sotheby's South American expert who had shown us the lot before the sale. The date of the sale arrived a few weeks later and I sat in the front row: seated a few rows back in an impeccable light grey suit, was a very suave David Attenborough, not looking at all like the rough field-working naturalist as he appeared on tellie. Bidding started in the hundreds and very soon my limit was reached: the winner of the bid was none other than David Attenborough, who was a noted collector of ancient South American goldwork. Consequently, the tool collection remains unpublished and unstudied to this day: that is the danger of private collectors, they just hoard the stuff to drool over until the day comes to donate the lot to a museum or pass it on to the relatives, or take a cut from the taxman should the Nation decide it wants it. Now, probably no museum could actually take it in, as being unprovenanced goldwork, it is no longer kocha. Professor Warwick Bray topped my story regarding these auctions. His father had once worked in the goldfields of South Africa and had assembled a collection of Asante gold weights. Late in his life, without telling the family, he decided to sell off the lot through Sotheby's. Warwick attended the sale to try to buy them back, but quite soon, the bids were out of his range. And who was the winner of this auction? None other than David Attenborough!

One of the few UK based trusts that might actually distribute a small amount of money to me to get to the USofA for the Museum of the American Indian and Natural History Collections in New York, was the Leverhulme Trust. This had been founded by the will of William Lever, the founder of Lever Brothers in 1925 and it distributes about 80 million a year to deserving research topics such as mine. I think I got about 150 quid, which I thought was simply wonderful!

It was thanks then to the Leverhulme Foundation that I was able to travel to North America to visit the Museum of the American Indian, Heye Foundation at their two locations: 155th and Broadway and Bruckner Boulevard in the Bronx. I used to alight the Pelham Bay Parkway bus in Manhattan in the morning and take the empty bus out to the Bronx. The bus was essential for bringing in the cleaners and maids to Manhattan in the morning and getting them back: hence leaving Manhattan in the morning meant an empty bus. I loved the Museum of the American Indian with its fusty halls, insect infestations, ancient goods lift, large green walk-in safe and dedicated staff. So how did this museum get to move to the Mall in Washington DC, if the entire collection was left in trust to the State of New York? It was all due to Ross Perrot. Mr. Perrot became aware of the disheveled state of the Museum and its benign neglect by the State of New York, and offered to take the entire collection to Texas and build a new 75 million dollar facility to house it. The then director of the Museum, Dr. Roland Force who I had met shortly before, was quite keen on the idea, while the rest of the New York elites were horrified. Clearly, losing the entire collection to a state like Texas was too much to swallow for the New Yorkers, so a deal was struck with the powers that be and the last spot on the Mall in Washington was designated as the new location for the newly (re)named National Museum of the American Indian (NMAI), with the Customs House in New York being used for small displays, as a sop to the intentions of the original George G. Heye, who had stipulated that the entire collection was left in trust to the State of New York. Small samples from this collection, taken back to the Institute for study, proved invaluable in my research.

One of the intellectually exciting additions to the UCL Institute of Archaeology was IAMS, the Institute of Archaeometallurgical Studies, concocted by Professor Beno Rothenberg, with the help of Professor Ronnie Tylecote and Professor Hans-Gert Bachmann. Beno Rothenberg was self-taught, a photographer of the emergent state of

Israel. His family was extraordinarily wealthy: they were in the diamond business which was international of course, and when we might enter Room 210a in the Institute, he would switch from English to Yiddish so as not to be overheard on one of his business transactions. Rothenberg had left Germany for Israel in 1933 and during the war of Independence that the Israelis fought against the British, he had been attached to an armoured brigade under Yitzhak Sadeh. Later his photographic recording skills led to a study of archaeological landscapes and hence to archaeometallurgical remains, slags and sites, and hence to furnaces and metals. One of his important collaborators was Professor Hans-Gert Bachmann, who had worked for Degussa, and spoke some Turkish along with German and English. Bachmann was a talented and careful scientist, who became an expert on archaeological slags, which you might think of as relatively unimportant in the extraction of metals, but you would be wrong. The function of slag is to remove the impurities and other components which are present in the ore, leaving pure copper behind as prills or cakes. These can then be remelted and traded as ingots of copper or shaped into tools and weapons, mixed with some tin, they can then be cast into useful halberds, palstaves, axes, chisels, fish-hooks, awls and needles, beginning the advanced set of tools which we rely on today, and taking us out of the Stone Age into the Bronze Age and beyond. Hence studying ancient slags can be very revealing of how our ancestors made copper and bronze, and how they smelted the initial components, where the ore came from, and ancient trade routes in metals, ingots and finished goods.

At some stage, Professor Rothenberg had told Hans-Gert that if he was ever stranded anywhere, to give his name to the Israeli desk and a military plane could be arranged to whisk him to his destination. The time came when Hans-Gert was stranded at Frankfort Airport due to a strike by air traffic controllers sometime in the 1980's. Hans-Gert decided to give it a try: he marched over to the Israeli desk, gave the name of Professor Rothenberg, and sure enough, an hour or so later, an Israeli military jet took off, en route for Geneva with one passenger.

Hans-Gert arranged for us to get an old Siemens wavelength-dispersive x-ray fluorescence spectrometer decommissioned from a

Degussa factory, and Nigel Seeley spent some time getting it working. The Degussa factory had walls made of rubber, so that in the event of an explosion, the walls would just wobble about and remain standing, protecting the rest of the invaluable equipment and personnel.

It was a marvellous old Siemens machine, used by us in art conservation long before energy-dispersive x-ray fluorescence spectrometers became a commonplace in museum conservation labs all across Europe and the US, some forty years later.

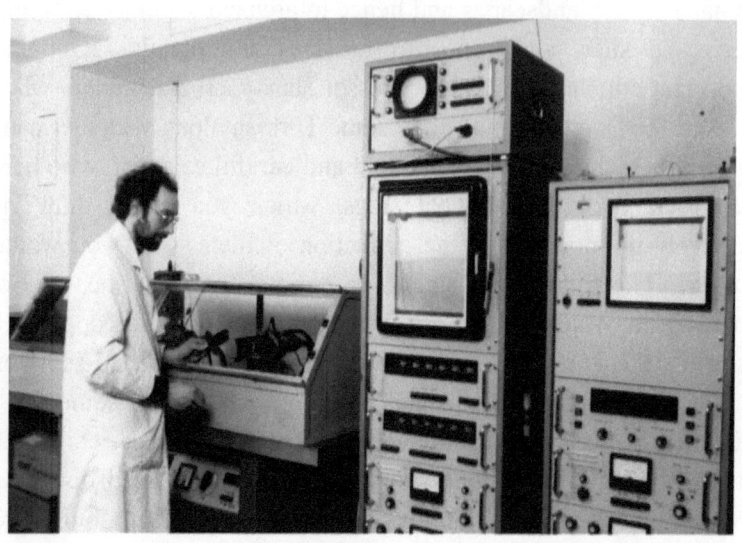

Dr. Brian Gilmour operating the Siemens Wavelength Dispersive X-Ray Fluorescence Spectrometer in 1978. The safety precautions in operation then would today be judged as totally inadequate! But we all survived and the machine was incredibly useful as even small objects could be placed in front of the x-ray beam. Sometimes the generator would cut out if the Institute electricity supply wavered in the winter months, as it was very power-hungry. This machine became in time the energy dispersive hand-held XRF unit now commonplace in Museum labs.

For the cognoscenti there is a difference between energy dispersive and wavelength dispersive analysis, the former assigning identities to elements based on the energy of atomic transitions, which is fundamentally more difficult to keep together in a sharp peak for characterization, whilst the latter uses certain specific crystal reflections of astounding accuracy with an impressive table of reflections for the metallic and sub-metallic elements of metals we were interested in. Wavelengths win for accuracy, especially in 1978, and wavelength machines are even now more expensive than their energy-loving rivals. The person who had worked out the crucial transitions at atomic level was Henry Gwyn Jeffrey Moseley, who was twenty-seven when he was killed. When the Great War began, Moseley left his research work at the University of Oxford to volunteer for the Royal Engineers of the British Army. Moseley was assigned to the force of British Empire soldiers that invaded the region of Gallipoli, Turkey, in April 1915. Now, you might think that this was just another stupid Great War death statistic, but in fact it was a disaster. If Moseley had not died in battle, he might well have been awarded a Nobel Prize in Physics in 1916. This is how terribly stupid the whole thing was: the authorities could just send an Oxford genius off to die like you and me: quite democratic really, even if the military logic was fundamentally flawed and had simply regarded him as another specimen for cannon-fodder.

So, no further advances were made in x-ray fluorescence spectroscopy in many ways, until after the Second World War, some thirty years later, when an Oxford numismatist was chatting idly to a physicist in the senior common room and wondered how he might be able to analyse his coins without taking a sample. Well, replied the physicist, we could build you a machine that could do that, it is called an x-ray fluorescence spectrometer. So, a machine which took up an entire room was built, and spectra from the surface of the coins could be obtained. In 1953, Professor Teddy Hall of Oxford used X-ray fluorescence to show that the bones of Piltdown man had been stained with potassium dichromate to make them look fossilized. The Piltdown forgery caused havoc in the decades before, with the entire confection convincing many that the Sussex creature had been an early man, rather than an outrageous fake. The Sussex confection has generated more books about the forgery than books on our real human ancestors until DNA studies began in earnest and now the Sussex fake is dead history.

Hall was inherently wealthy and never took a salary. He grew up at Shipton Court, a Jacobean manor house in Shipton-on-

Cherwell, which sold for six million around 2010 (worth about nine million today), where he used to keep a laboratory in the shed and outhouse. The Oxford research laboratory, housed in a building in Keble Road, Oxford, was important for us in art conservation in the UK and internationally for its work in radiocarbon dating, Egyptian frits, pottery, thermoluminescence, and a host of other developments. Thermoluminescence is important for dating fired pottery, but because of a huge fandango over ceramics from Mali that the lab was dating for private clients, it had to be hived off as a separate business venture in the end to protect Oxford from the problems of dealing with unprovenanced or possibly looted ceramics from across the globe. We depend on the Oxford Dating Lab a lot: they are timely, professional and trustworthy, and we have used them both from our days at UCL, and later the Getty, and even from UCLA.

Because Professor Hall took no salary, Oxford could afford to hire Martin Aitken as a senior researcher, and he did some great work in dating and physical research. When Teddy was due to retire, the University of Oxford, of course, decided that it had no money, so a public appeal was launched which raised a million pounds to endow a Chair, saving the lab. Professor Mike Tite, from the British Museum Lab, took over and stayed happily researching ceramics and frits for many years.

Despite his incredibly privileged life, Professor Hall was a firm supporter of the Old Labour policy of no university entrance fees. He was an old liberal, one of a faded generation whose political views are totally out of step with today's political elites, especially as it was the Labour Party itself which introduced Tuition Fees, and particularly the Liberal Party under Nick Clegg, which had promised to not raise tuition fees at all, and then raised them to 9,000 quid with the Tories triumphant at this wonderful coup, as the Liberals reneged on their promises and were subsequently destroyed at the next elections. Nick Clegg, former deputy Prime Minister lost his seat at the election and was out of the Liberal party elite and out of Parliament. He is now out of the country having left us for Silicon Valley and pastures, or rather deserts new, a long way from his former phone-in on the radio, where he answered questions from the listeners on political topics of the day, as if his word meant something, as if it had an import, which now it has ceased to be.

The last time I saw Professor Hall, was on a subway in Ontario where we both had attended the Archaeometry Conference, in 1991. We had a pleasant chat and then went our separate ways. The Oxford lab was one of the premier institutions that solved the problem of the dating of the Turin shroud, as not dating from the time of Christ.

Having been in America for some time at the moment that New Labour first introduced tuition fees, it was all too obvious what would happen: that the level of fees introduced by New Labour would just keep rising and rising, inexorably, as had happened in the USA, until something in the public psyche in the UK began to question the whole idea, which, sure enough has begun to happen in 2019, even afflicting Lord Adonis, the daft Labour politician who helped to introduce them in the first place. It is the mountain of debt that has become the problem, with fees, apparently, in need of being reduced!! They should never have been introduced in the first place: the authorities should have followed the example of Germany who pledged never to introduce tuition fees.

Unlike Scotland, which must of course be an extremely wealthy country, because they did not introduce Tuition Fees either, the UK must be comparatively poor. Student debt is now, we understand, becoming something of a major problem. I detest England for introducing tuition fees: there is no other word for it but detestation.

Let me get back to Professor Hall for a moment to dwell on x-ray fluorescence analysis, because it has become so important in art conservation, from its putative beginnings as a room-sized monster to a small hand-held instrument modeled on a Star Trek machine held by Dr. Spock, which now exists in the real world and can be carried in a suitcase to study a Caravaggio, Rembrandt or a Giambologna, a Hockney or a Bacon, in whichever country they may reside. This is thanks to the research of Dr. Bruce Kaiser, who has spent a considerable amount of time in his later years instructing us conservationists in the finer arts of hand-held x-ray fluorescence machines, whose utility is currently going from strength to strength.

It is true that we still need to take a tiny sample from the Rembrandt when it is undergoing restoration, but this we can do from an edge under the frame, causing no visible damage to the painting at all. The more non-destructive our techniques become, the more we are allowed to probe into the secrets of artist's techniques, the substructure of paintings, and the composition of ancient metals.

Professor Ronnie Tylecote, the pioneer of the study of ancient metallurgy, which we call archaeometallurgy, had published a seminal text on Metallurgy in Archaeology around 1962. He was the leading exponent of the subject for decades. He stayed put in Room 210a, being made an honorary Professor at UCL, since his previous appointment was at Newcastle. He wrote, researched and did a little teaching, until 1990, after I had left UCL for the Getty. I was fond of him. It was a good time for archaeometallurgy, the beginnings of the sub-discipline were past and solidified, and new discoveries lay everywhere for researchers to uncover. Controversies lay ahead and exciting fieldwork across Europe, China, Peru, Colombia and the Near East in particular.

After finishing my Ph.D. in ancient metals, principally based on Pre-Columbian goldwork from Colombia, I was appointed to a teaching position at the Institute, and began to teach the conservation of ancient copper, bronze and iron; elementary conservation to the archaeology students, ancient materials to the first year archaeology students, and some practical supervision in the lab for the conservation students. The salary was something less than 14,000 pounds per annum, which with a wife and child to support in inner London was a hard proposition. Lesley had somehow managed to save about 3,000 pounds and we were able to move to 53 Hargrave Mansions, off the Archway Road, a two bedroom, tiny flat, on the third floor of the Victorian block. Our first purchase: hardly inspiring, but for us an amazing step: the flat cost 27,000 pounds, and a great deal of the work renovating the flat and making it habitable had to be done by myself, including plumbing, woodwork, electrical work and painting. After an exhausting morning I remember mentioning to Nigel Seeley that I had had to plumb the toilet overflow pipe back into the waste pipe. "You can't do that" said Nigel, clearly unaware of the extreme lack of finance we had, "That's illegal". Yes, exactly: well since those days in the early 1980's, I think the law might have been broken thousands of times as new bathrooms became designer units rather than plumbing exemplars. We even managed to purchase an old Austin 1300 car, as I had passed my driving test at the age of about 30. It cost 800 pounds and keeping it going was also a financial strain. To pass its MOT I had to trawl around Kentish Town and Camden Town to find the cheapest possible quote for a spot of welding for a rotten sill; the cheapest axel rod repair under the arches off of Kings Cross. That job I had tried to do myself in the carpark of the Institute of Archaeology, but I could not get the thing to budge. When I went to pick up the Austin from the Kings Cross cavern, the mechanic pointed to a thick metal bar some five feet in length "That's what we had to use" He said. That made my own pathetic efforts seem not so bad, that the professionals had had to resort to major trauma work to get the axel off and replaced.

Many autobiographies are very reticent. This one is no different, but being relatively poor, there is no need for reticence about our financial lives. We were on the breadline or close to it. A bill for the repair of the car over 200 quid would have taken it off the road. When Margaret Thatcher took office, the salary for Judges was raised, but the salary for University staff was frozen for that particular year: 1982. The Thatcher administration was of the view that the professorate and the rest of the university staff were a spoilt bunch of left-leaning bastards, who were in no need of any salary rise: this affected us greatly in 1982-3, as we were in dire need of a rise of even one or two percent, but that was denied us by the Conservative Government. According to them we were sufficiently well-rewarded already.

Not much has changed since really, as Labour and Conservative administrations come and go, for Lord Justice Gross, who earned 200,000 pounds a year in 2017, noted that no-one goes into the Judiciary to make money. But there comes a point when the pay of judges is so far out of line with the private sector market that it endangers recruitment, since 200,000 a year is such a miserable salary. This is because judges are not swayed by market forces, apparently, where they could make perhaps, as much as a University Professor in 2017, around 70,000 a year. What a load of crap: try making one of these judges live on the salary of a full professor in London and see how happy they would be.

Since 1982, the pressure of work on academics in the UK, the number of students, the tiresome administrative work, the endless need to publish and the research assessment exercise, which is like a needlessly bureaucratic burden dreamed up by the public equivalent of the Ministry of Magic in Harry Potter, has altered their academic lives considerably and many now have their nose to the grindstone or are subject to dangerous repercussions from the research assessment exercise. I will give you one example: a Lecturer at the University of Exeter in our field, an expert on the archaeometallurgy of Sri Lanka and much else besides, was told by the assessment exercise committee that her work was not of international significance and that, as a result, she was going to be demoted, on the advice of a panel who knew absolutely nothing about the archaeometallurgy of ancient Sri Lanka.

I was one of a number of USA based scholars at that time who wrote letters to the Vice-Chancellor of the University of Exeter, and whose words were rebuffed by the Chancellor's office, when they demeaned themselves to actually answer our letters, to say that they were simply following the results of the assessment carried out by a panel of distinguished UK academics, which of course they had to abide by. I followed up with another letter, to which I never received a reply. In the meantime the Lecturer had threatened to take the University to a sexual discrimination tribunal and they quickly caved in under the pressure and promoted her instead, having come to the conclusion that the assessment exercise must, surely, have been in error. We tried to exercise our own magic, but in the end she had saved herself, truly a Potterish tale, and she still teaches there to this day, although she did once characterize to me the administration of the University of Exeter as "Stalinist".

There is even less justification for such a large pay differential now between judges and professors than there was thirty years ago, given the amount of work that professors in the UK actually do these days.

An intellectual epiphany for me took place around 1981 as I stared at a small box of corroded Iranian bronze fragments that had been brought back from the Iran Bastian Museum in Tehran by one of our former Iranian PhD students. In 1979 Lesley and I were all set to travel to Iran in the summer recess to work on the conservation of finds for the Bastian Museum, but that was the year when the bomb went off in a cinema in Tehran, killing many, and signaling the start of the Iranian Revolution when the Ayatollah Khomeini returned from his Parisian exile to assume power, and the Shah and his western backers was toast.

Our Iranian friend was arrested. He had married a Baha'i who was a classical guitarist, her guitar was smashed up and she had to flee the country, ending up in Canada, while he was under house arrest in Iran for nine months. Nigel Seeley warned us not to try to communicate with him at all during this time, as it could be dangerous to have any international liaisons. Our Iranian friend was then allowed to travel to his office, but he was not actually allowed to do any work. This went on for some time, about a couple of years, until the authorities began to realise that the kind of elite work on artefacts which us conservators and conservation scientists perform, was obviously important for the Iranian state, whatever the colour and creed of its practitioners, and work began again on conservation in Iran, which was sorely needed. Our friend, now Head of the Iranian Conservation Center, regularly speaks to the Minister for Culture, and we have been invited over to Iran, but so far have not had the guts to accept.

I began to realise that I had become enraptured by the subject of ancient bronze, the corrosion of copper alloys, and the microstructure of copper alloys, especially tin bronzes, and that I would greatly enjoy learning more of the subject on which I was already quite familiar. It was clear to me that the complexity of the corrosion of ancient bronzes had been under-researched by 1982, as I stared at the Iranian fragments, and a lot remained to be done. And this has come to pass: over those last thirty-five years huge strides have been made in patina characterization and analysis by a large number of researchers from across the world.

I began to teach my Summer School Course in the Microstructure and Metallurgy of Ancient and Historic Metals in 1983, and it is still being taught this coming year in 2019 to a full house and is already booked for 2019! Extending my intellectual tentacles into the subject of copper and bronze, their corrosion and conservation, their authenticity and history, was a natural step, and could encompass a wide geographical spread, from Jordan, Ireland, Iran, Peru, Ecuador, England, Austria, Hungary, Switzerland, Greece and Egypt, in terms of microstructure, authenticity and corrosion.

I should add here that the summer teaching was made possible by the Summer Schools Programme that had been initiated by Jim Black in 1983. Jim Black had taken over from Pam Pratt when she resigned in 1976. He was fit, an excellent squash player, with a varied intellectual set of interests, from excavation to conservation, and wide-ranging abilities, which struggled to be contained in the role of a lecturer in archaeological conservation. He began to branch out: first a series of summer schools on a variety of topics, including mine, then publications resulting from the summer schools, and finally the launching of Archetype Publications Ltd, which has become one of the major publishers of books and monographs in the field of heritage and art conservation. What a wonderful achievement, and where would we be without Archetype Publications? We would be a lot less satisfied with the publishing industry that is for sure.

# Chapter Eight.  Leaving UCL for the Getty.

I enjoyed the teaching at UCL, but as a lowly lecturer the chances of being promoted were slim and would take some years.  Meanwhile the salary never seemed to actually go up to keep pace with inflation. The intellectual life of the Institute rather marginalized conservation as naturally enough, simply providing conservators to attend to finds at archaeological digs.

I began to think about making a move and had connections in the National Museum of Denmark, Copenhagen, who were looking for a conservation scientist at the time.  We made the trip with our eighteenth month son, Daniel in a buggy to the snowy city of Copenhagen in November for the interview. I did not know at the time, but another eccentric and talented conservator, Tim Padfield, had moved to the Smithsonian Institution in Washington, DC, and was quite homesick for Europe or the UK. His retort stand, visible from a side window of the lab at the Smithsonian Institution had a hand-drawn Union Jack flag attached to it.

No jobs in the UK, so he too had applied for the position in Copenhagen, and as he had more experience than me, the Danes offered the job to him, leaving me stuck at the Institute.  He was to occupy that position in Denmark until he retired twenty odd years later, back to old Blighty.

This was a blow: jobs were few and far between and at the intermediate level I had reached in the profession, they were generally not that remunerative.

A lot happens by word of mouth, and my friend Steven Weintraub, had recently been hired by the Getty Conservation Institute in Los Angeles in 1986.  Frank Preusser, the Head of the Scientific Department, was looking for a museum scientist with an expertise in metals to head up the Museum Research

Laboratory: I had already done some authenticity work for Sotheby's and Christie's and was a reasonable, although not outstanding choice for this role. We took the plunge, took the job and moved, now with two young children to Los Angeles in 1987: Lesley was not that happy with the choice but we lived with it: in the end we lived with it for nearly 30 years. We had been flown out to LA at the Getty's expense, business class, and the interview took place, with Luis Monreal, the Director of the Conservation Institute, and Frank Preusser in the Museum in Malibu over a couple of Greek antiquities and a Romanesque aquamanile. Luis Monreal, was not to last too long as the Director: within a couple of years or so he had resigned and was off, leaving America, never to return, ending up as General Manager of the Aga Khan Trust for Culture in Geneva. Luis was charismatic, clever, mercurial, self-described as a conservation specialist, art historian and archaeologist. Wow! Now to be all three of these things at once is quite an achievement: a claim which may make one wonder if it is really possible. However, look at the list of his positions: Secretary General of the International Council of Museums for UNESCO (1974–1985); Director of the Getty Conservation Institute (1985–1990); Director General, 'La Caixa' Foundation (1990–2001); followed by the Aga Khan Trust, and apparently the author of numerous works as well, although they are hard to spot on Amazon in any number. The problem with folk as Europeanly cultured as Luis Monreal is that America is too small-minded to accommodate them: indeed, as he resigned Luis complained that the tax codes and bureaucracy of the American system hamstrung things. When he left he was supposed to become coordinator of Cultural Heritage Programs for UNESCO, but as the then Director of UNESCO was himself Spanish, Frederico Mayor, the political reality was that this was one person from Spain too many, and the La Caixa foundation had to do instead, although exactly what this foundation did never made it across the Atlantic or the Pacific, so we never heard of Luis Monreal again.

Back in the Malibu lab I stuttered to say something meaningful about these objects, which must have been passable, although the only emotion I recall, in front of Frank and Luis was embarrassment. Later Frank asked me what my salary was at the Institute of Archaeology. I thought: what would Frank imagine my salary to be, so I inflated it to a level which seemed appropriate for the level they were thinking of, and said "20,000 pounds" "Yes" said Frank "That is more or less what we thought" So, I was offered 50,000 dollars, which I accepted.

But even in 1987, Los Angeles was not cheap for those folk with only tiny downpayments like us poor saps. The ambience of Los Angeles at the time was strangely still laid-back and somewhat sedate in a dusty and polluted air. Diners were relatively empty and quiet, even if getting a cappuccino coffee might be hard to find. No-one sat out on sidewalk cafes in those days. One used to wonder why.

One reason for the iconic LA is the absence of rows of terraced houses. You can have large buildings of multiple occupancy but these too sit on their own plot of land. Detached single story wooden framed stucco houses with a backyard and parking at the front or side down to the garage were pervasive. Variations with one bedroom or two or three or even four, and with one or two or three bathrooms: that used to be ninety percent of the LA housing stock. Down Redondo Blvd in the still dodgy Adams area, the small houses have wide grass verges at the front. Very wide. This is where the kids used to play while the adults hung out in the back garden or yard in the 1940's - 1980's. Our two bedroom wooden house had been erected in 1925.

I say erected because it was decidedly not a craftsman wooden bungalow of the type now much admired in the city. It may have served as a farmhouse since in 1925, our entire area was surrounded by cauliflower and broccoli farms. It had only a modest frontage and back garden with a four hundred square foot garage. The house itself was about 1100 square feet and with the five of us and one bathroom it was not long until the garage became a third bedroom with extra bathroom and laboratory cum workroom for me, which I built myself over a period of years. For a middle-class American family it is almost unthinkable that five people would have to share one bathroom or be crammed into a two bedroom house for years. The house came with an alley at the back, most useful for the rubbish bins and occasional temporary car parking for cleaning or repairs. No overnight parking or impeding the trash collection down the alleyway.

The garage conversion was completely illegal, according to our old-time Californian colleagues at the Getty who had no need of such illegal conversions as they had lived in LA thirty years before when such things were unheard of, prohibited, or not needed. The garage saved us really as for some years we were in negative equity thanks to what? Was it the savings and loan scandal? The LA riots? The fires? The floods? The loss of jobs in the engineering and defense sector? The police corruption? The earthquakes? Or all of these things that left LA depressed with itself? Luckily in Los Angeles County hardly anyone by the 1990's bothered a jot about garages turned into living space. Over in prissy Santa Monica there could be problems. One of our acquaintances had an artwork studio in her garage and had to turn it back to a car house. In fact, most cars were happy on the drive or the roadway. They really didn't need a four hundred square foot detached structure for themselves. In the past, many bands had started off in garages. The garage lined with old carpets. There were plenty of those a bit before our time for the most part. There is a photograph of Crosby, Stills and Nash sitting on an old porch seat somewhere in Hollywood with the typical wooden stuccoed old house behind them. The porch. Even if modest in size what a useful thing to have, and why don't all houses have porches to embellish them? The old wood framing of our house, like many, rocked and rolled in California earthquakes, ours having survived the Long Beach quake around 1933, the Whittier Narrows quake of 1987, and the 1994 Northridge quake, along with many others too small to have been given their own name in history.

Although cooled by the Pacific Ocean breezes so in the 1990's we never needed air conditioning or even heating for more than about 20 to 40 days in the year, the dust that settled from the air was black. Black due to car pollution, which often seemed to accumulate in a few days into a filmy deposit. We lived on busy

Walgrove Avenue, still a sleepy neighbourhood when we moved in in 1990, and relatively speaking, not busy. We were the first to build a wooden picket fence and turn the crab grass into a front garden. As the years rolled by, we were caught up and overtaken by massive expenditure on gardens and newly revamped properties in our areas of Mar Vista and Santa Monica as the new occupation of the area began until by 2019, our busy street boasted the most expensive property on the Mar Vista market at 3.5 million dollars. By then the traffic was stationary by three in the afternoon down Walgrove, forcing one to leave our front drive by reversing very slowly into the traffic and becoming an expert in alley driving, until everyone else was doing it too so there was no escape from driving tedium. Amusing to look at out of the window, as the cars just sat there, but as ludicrous as the commuters looked as they just sat there too. No choice, they had to get to work but their daily commute now took hours. Los Angeles was always a monster out of control.

On the Doors Song of *LA woman* the line goes "The cars hiss by my window like the waves down on the beach". They used to do that too on our road back in the early 1990's. But overbuilding in the city became the new normal so the hissing turned into chugging engines. When the glass and steel modernist monsters began to go up, zoning changed in Santa Monica to allow less sidewalk and more building. Less driveways leading to garages now, and who cares about those old chestnuts on occupancy rates when even a tiny Venice house could set you back two million.

Steel framing and less wood took hold, so that when the 1994 earthquake hit, 15,000 steel framed buildings failed at the welds in LA including several welds at the putative Getty Center. Try to keep that quiet as much as possible. More research clearly needed even as late at 1994, so the Getty was one of the sponsors of work at the University of Florida, which resulted in the new standard of hot-welded steel triangular plates being used at each vertical join. The Getty was behind schedule, of course, so huge holes could be cut through eight inch concrete floors or ceilings to get at the steel members without too much disturbance as the artwork had not yet moved in: just a few more million dollars in costs.

In 1990 our neighbors on Walgrove Avenue were a rental on one side and a Hispanic installer of security systems on the other. Luis had installed the security system for Liz Taylor's house in Beverly Hills. His family owned the small house on a half sized lot. He was also an expert on brakes. Lu used to advise me on brake repairs back in the day when money was so tight you had to do it yourself.

I recall one Saturday morning when I had the front wheel raised up on our Toyota passenger van and the tire off. Lu had the knowledge: he looked at it solemnly. He began to explain the problem to me. "Well Dave" He began "in the old Toyota system the brake fluid is controlled from one master cylinder that distributes the fluid to the four brakes. This creates uneven fluid distribution leading to poor braking capacity. That's your problem. You need a new brake lining on that as well as pads because it's too grooved. If you go to Carter brakes and linings in West Adams you can get it redone for twenty bucks." I was the professor, but he was the professor of car brakes and regularly did his own. So in my old Ford van, our second car, I travelled down to Adams and was the only limey there. So with new pads as well, the Toyota van was on the road again.

Our renter on the other side did design work some for USC and other jobs but he was underemployed and left LA for a good design position in Denver a few years later. We were there for 28 years, our wooden shack selling for a million dollars. It cost about 10,000 dollars when built so had increased in value one-hundred times; an extraordinary increase not that uncommon. Back before the modernization of the city, Los Angeles had empty, calm, surface streets and cheap rents. You could rent a good three bedroom house on Superba in Mar Vista with the usual yard, front garden and side parking and garage for 1500 a month. Days long gone. I do not miss what Los Angeles became but the generosity of the space of the city and freedom for easy driving meant traveling around locally or even further afield could even be pleasurable if not a joy. I remember visiting the

Southwest Museum on a Saturday. The entire area seemed deserted. Not a soul to be seen. About twenty visitors, perhaps, in total over some hours. The sense of place is intimately associated with its architecture and atmosphere. Los Angeles had a sad but intriguing atmosphere to me as if what had been built had been part of a neighbourhood with its character you could still sense and roam through, taking in an intangible essence of what this region of Los Angeles was and what it had become and survived, that you were now observing. Now many of these talisman of the minds journey do not exist, the lower middle class ambience which gave it such unpretentious space, cheap parking and cheap housing was gone. And part of the mystique of Los Angeles is or was, the empty streets and the car free to drive where it will: after all, it was built with the motor car in mind. If you think back to those Raymond Chandler movies, where the car headlights flood the empty road ahead and behind is only darkness, that was Los Angeles. Part of the peace of location is lost if instead it took Chandler's characters two hours to drive to their Malibu bungalow from downtown LA. The roads belonged to everyone, on an equal footing, able to drive and park anywhere, often without charge, or for a dollar charge for two hours or a day, which everyone could afford.

When a Colombian colleague was giving a lecture at the Bowers Museum, I was convinced she needed to see the beauty of the Getty Villa where I worked. I drove from Mar Vista to the Bowers Museum in Santa Ana, picked her up, drove to the museum in Malibu, then back to the Bowers Museum and then from the Bowers back home to Mar Vista. Today such a journey would be totally impossible, as impossible as renting a house on Superba for 1500 dollars or finding a place to park right near the Beach in Santa Monica for free. Those easy days, when some of the parents at our Santa Monica school lived in small back houses not far from the beach and sported long pigtails of blonde hair under broad brimmed hats are no more. One of our acquaintances sold up his desirably located Santa Monica house and left for Hilo on the Big Island. "I didn't leave Santa Monica"

He would say "Santa Monica left me". Years later, even folk who had lived on the Venice Canals could stand it no longer. They were trapped in by the beach traffic that had never bothered them thirty years ago, but now getting anywhere was becoming ridiculous. They sold up and found a Classy residence in Ventura County, part of the rich flotsam of escapees from the city of lights, responsible for the trebling of house prices all the way along the coast as far as Montecito and beyond. We were often down at the beach, station twenty-six. In fine weather with the folk from the Santa Monica Alternative School, SMASH for short, we hung out there. But it was always a good feeling getting back to the house from road trips. Not that sinking feeling as in London when you drove in, hemmed in by the suffocating history of the buildings on your way to our tiny second-floor flat in Archway. The air clogged by so much brick and traffic like an old party you should have left a while ago with its stale atmosphere.

As one of our friends remarked "America is not for cissies", we unfortunately came into the class of folk who could be so easily labeled "cissies" and therefore were never going to be able to become Americanized or undergo "Californication" in anything but a superficial sense. We were not ideal transplants as so many Brits have proved to be: many become American in mind and body, they create new roots, new spaces, new habits, assume new accents, American wives, or American attitudes. They don't complain about the political life of the US, about death penalties, racial injustice, incarceration rates, military spending, the lack of any decent national health service, the discrimination and extermination of the original inhabitants, the North American Indian, the appalling treatment of mental health patients in LA prisons, the dumping of impecunious Hospital patients, some in their operating gowns, on the streets of downtown LA, appalling Police corruption, or the ready availability of guns and assault rifles. I used to complain and occasionally send emails or even write.

It is an advantage to the new immigrant to the US that, apart from when a new President is going to be elected, no-one even mentions politics in polite conversation, so one's ignorance is never on view, and neither is theirs. Gradually however you realise that Americans are so poorly served by their own media that they have no fucking clue what is going on most of the time. This is fine with them: they can just stay content in their house in the San Fernando Valley, languishing in the pool while oblivious to the rest of American life, and go the gym or play golf or take a dip in the Pacific Ocean. In any case, they are kept busy working, repaying student loans, repaying the mortgage, shelling out for private school fees, taking the kids to baseball practice, paying the co-pay for the doctor or dentist, getting two weeks holiday a year (some days might have to be deducted from the 14 days if you are off ill), and no maternity leave and, of course, paternity leave would be close to a sick joke: so what time do they have left for reflection and demonstration?

One of our friends of a friend had a ninety-five year old father who regularly attended church on a Sunday. She dropped him off and returned to pick him up a couple of hours later. No sign of him. Getting rather worried she made more enquiries and ended up touring the local police stations to report him missing and asking if there had been any sightings of him. Nope, nothing at all.

What had actually happened is that our 95 year old, getting rather desperate for a pee, and finding nothing in the church or outside, had relieved himself against an exterior wall and had been spotted by a LA Police patrol car. Having nothing better to do, the LA police arrested him for public urination and he was carted off to the police cells. Our 95 year old had a spotless record, not even a parking ticket. Someone at the police station must have told the stupid officers to get rid of him, and they drove him around and dumped him not far from the church the following morning, so he had spent a whole night in the cells. He made his way to a phone and eventually his daughter got him back. The dishonesty of the LA police, in denying that any such man was in custody, coupled with the gross insensitivity in arresting a 95 year old in the first place are archetypical attitudes and behavior of the LA police force.

Another friend of ours, living on Superba Avenue in Venice, had a Dutch neighbour who had come to LA specifically to study Reichian therapy. One day, he needed to get his car off the drive to attend a meeting, only to find it blocked by a LA City Police Car. He asked them to move it. Presumably because he was Dutch, he must have imagined that this was a reasonable request. Some sort of verbal disagreement ensued, the end result being that the Dutch mature student, an ex-lorrydriver, was arrested, taken away, and spent the night in the Culver City Police cells. He was so angered and upset by this, that he cut short his Reichian training and returned within the week to the Netherlands. I think in Holland, these things are settled more amicably. The general ambience of life in Holland does make one feel envious at times for everything that has been lost in England over the last forty years or so and what has been kept in Holland. There is decidedly an edge to Los Angeles, in being a Police State. Sorry, but that is the case compared with life in Europe. In the new buzz concerning everything LA, you will not find these unsavoury facts mentioned very often.

Well, of course, life at the Getty is much more desirable than life working for Walmart, and we Getty employees were a privileged lot in many ways: we were not that noble, we were still taking the American dollar for our income, so let's not kid ourselves entirely, while we complain like the old liberals that we are, even if we were not quite champagne socialists, we come a close second.

At the time I left UCL for the Getty, the Getty was in a state of euphoria, bubbling with excitement and ecstatic about all the possible outcomes for the new infant: the stirrings of a putative museum with apparently boundless sums of money to spend on art. Outsiders were worried that the Getty millions would distort the art market and snap up everything in sight for inflated prices. After Getty's death, the J. Paul Getty Trust was formed with a group of impressively connected Trustees. Nancy Englander and Harold Williams, were the prime movers in deciding exactly what to do with the billions Getty had left. Williams, a former UCLA Professor, and Director of the Securities and Exchange Commission more or less told the Trustees what do to and a great deal of credit for what the Getty became belongs to Nancy and Harold. A long period of gestation began with liaison and listening: many voices descended on them in those early years, giving counsel, advice and persuasion, among them the international conservation community who would prove so vital in persuading the Trustees to form the Getty Conservation Institute (GCI). It was becoming obvious that while archaeologists, architects, art historians and planners paid lip-service to the need to conserve and preserve, no-one had the money to put where their mouths were, and no-one had the intention of doing so.

The Conservation Institute was a natural outcome on a blank slate, in the same way that forming a Conservation Institute at a University such as UCLA in 1985 was totally impossible. There were no blank slates at such Institutions waiting to be filled up. Even today, in 2019, academic conservation in the UK struggles with the competing demands of excellence in publication, excellence in teaching, the award of suitable grants and external funding, suitable numbers of students, management of laboratory facilities, enough summer placements for students and conducting research at the same time, sufficient to fulfill positive external evaluation of achievement, all on a budget the size of a pea compared with the budget for the Getty Conservation Institute, some 11-15 million dollars a year. At least the GCI existed and was not going to be taken down based on the criteria listed above. Money brings largesse and more degrees of freedom to choose what actions to take and when. No pressure on publications here! Get a trip to ICOM or an IIC Conference in an exotic locale and present a paper there or even go and listen to others: that will do perfectly well. No-one at the Getty Trust could appreciate the need to publish that us professors are faced with.

So who was Jean Paul Getty and why had he built this beautiful museum in Malibu? Getty was described by one biographer as: spectacular lover, absent parent, philandering husband, social snob, hypochondriac, Hitler sympathizer and the richest man in the world. At one time, around 1930, Getty, along with a string of other dwellings, bought 641 South Irving, aka 10086 Sunset Boulevard, a faded Gothic monstrosity created by entrepreneur William Oscar Jenkins, although Getty never lived there, this was the set for Billy Wilder's Sunset Boulevard. Getty had a similar approach to his magnificent new museum in Malibu which he designed from his Tudor mansion, Sutton Place: a re-creation of the Roman Villa dei Papiri in Herculaneum, He only visited the Museum a handful of times: he never lived there either, and never showed up, even to the grand opening of the Getty Villa.

Always something of an art collector, Getty took the advice of Norris Bramlett, one of his long-time associates and tax expert, to form a non-profit institution, which would prove very advantageous taxwise and keep more money out of the hands of the IRS. That formed the real beginnings of the Trust. Getty had purchased the property in Malibu, the Ranch House, some years before, around 1953, an area supposedly agriculturally zoned. Clark Gable used to keep his horses up at the back and ride down the small canyon to the ocean on horse-back, before the Museum was built on the grounds. I met Norris Bramlett only once, over a dinner at the Getty Villa around 1992, where he seemed sharp and incisive still.

The Ranch House, aka The J. Paul Getty Museum, lodged in a favourable canyon whose mouth faces outward to the Pacific Ocean is cooled by the gentle littoral breezes and nestled among Eucalyptus trees, in an idyllic spot contiguous with the Pacific coast. The Getty Museum, now known as the Getty Villa Museum, was a recreation of the Roman Villa mentioned above, which went down with the Vesuvius eruption in 79 AD. With the insatiable curiosity that characterized the famous Roman writer, Pliny the Elder, he visited the eruption and unfortunately went down with it. Some of his writings are also lost, but at least the ten volume Natural History, a wonderful mine of information on ancient Greece and Rome survived the Dark Ages to come down to us, and a compendious source of information it is.

On one of his rare visits to his Museum, Getty asked the few employees what they would like in his will. One probably said a small car; another a gold ring, and so on until Getty got to the loping African-American gardener, Mr Batch. "I don't want nothing" said Mr. Batch. "All right" Replied Getty "You can live here rent free for as long as you like" And Getty built a couple of small wooden houses, one of which Mr Batch, and Minnie Batch, lived in for over thirty years, rent-free, in Malibu.

When the Museum was being built, Minnie Batch used to travel over to Sutton Place to update Getty on the state of play on the ground and how the building was actually getting on. It is touching now to think of this amiable African-American lady turning up at Sutton Place and carrying out this important task for J. Paul, since he was effectively marooned on the British Isles.

Minnie Batch performed the function of badging new arrivals to the Getty in 1987, and I remember being inducted by her, into the mystery of keys and protocols and forms. Minnie Batch had the staff entrance road named after her when she eventually retired to Arizona, Batch Lane, a nice touch which, of course, did not survive the later corporate entity that the Getty was to become, and her name is now only lodged in the memory of older Getty employees. Batch Lane no longer exists. That applies to a lot of things about the Getty, mores the pity.

While it is all too easy to poke fun at J. Paul Getty, one overlooks the fact that the man must have had special characteristics to be one of the richest men in the world, and to maintain a real interest in art, especially antiquities, partly because they could be purchased inexpensively in the post-war period. Getty would sit up in bed at night at his English mansion, Sutton Place, and go through the accounts of his museum in Malibu, the Villa. One month Getty noticed that expenditure on light-bulbs had practically doubled compared with the month before. Getty rang his London lawyers for an explanation. The London lawyers rang the then Museum Director, Stephen Garrett, and Garrett asked the conservator, Steve Coulton, if he knew anything about the light-bulb expenditures. Coulton explained that they had to keep climbing up on high ladders over the priceless French furniture, to change the light bulbs, which posed a certain amount of risk, so long-life light bulbs had been installed. Garrett reported back to the London lawyers, who relayed the situation to Getty, who made a hand-written emendation to the accounts "Long-life light bulbs installed" That is how cognizant Getty remained for the slightest costs associated with his Museum, from a distance of 6,000 miles and a few light bulbs! There is a foresight, concentration, and thinking presence, a logical positivism, behind the man in the best American tradition. Getty would have made a good chess-player, because he could see opportunities and consequences where lesser business men had not really worked through the reality of what was to come, Getty saw it with clarity and purpose. Even with paintings, Getty could bother to do technical research of his own, when confronted by the art historical opinion that his painting was not a Raphael but an old copy, he persisted and would not give up immediately. Of course, paintings in general were even then too expensive for Getty to consider purchasing, given his parsimonious attitude to excessive expenditure, and the second-rate works he did acquire were later quietly resold by the Getty Museum through the art market without even any newspaper reporter noticing the event.

The Getty Museum, as it then was in 1974, a controversial replica, housing an extensive collection of Greek and Roman antiquities, Italian Renaissance and Netherlandish baroque paintings and decorative arts. Using records from an 18th-century excavation of the villa, as well as Italian Government archives, a team of Los Angeles researchers, architects and craftsmen worked for three years to assure Mr. Getty that his museum was as authentic and opulent as the original villa, to the last detail.

Getty, of course, never attended the opening of his new museum, and it had been three years previously, that he had announced to his startled associates one day in Sutton Place, that this was what was going to be built on the land adjacent to the Ranch House in Malibu, which Getty had purchased from a retired judge some twenty years before and which had opened as a small museum in 1953. Over the years, this decision to build an ersatz Roman Villa in Los Angeles, costing some 17 million dollars, (in 1974 dollars), met with derision and ridicule from the architectural fraternity. I am sure that the Smithson's would have had something derogatory to utter on seeing it. Even Joan Didion wrote in 1974, that there is something about the place that embarrasses people. According to the reports in the New York Times for 1974, regarding the opening of the Getty Villa, one critic remarked that the Museum "outstripped any existing monument to expensive, aggressive bad taste, cultural pretension and self-aggrandizement south of Hearst Castle." Architectural critics now tend to keep these kinds of opinions to themselves, too well aware of being politically correct, and Didion's sense of discomfort has abated with time and is not now an emotion with any traction.

Getty could be seen by outsiders as a parvenu oil billionaire, creating a kitsch offering to an ignorant LA public, who might prefer the stark brutalism of modernity to a Roman replica. Like Getty, I essentially hate brutalism and all my sympathy is with Getty's architectural taste. Criticism of the Getty Villa is heavier in New York than Los Angeles, which is all part of a cultural tension between the two giant cities, which has continued for decades. Doing down LaLa land has been a New York pastime for generations. It is true, of course, that those working in conservation, conservation science, or curatorial positions, who have left LA for New York rarely, if ever, return. The cultural depth of the Big Apple is hard to compete with and moving to New York is still considered a step up rather than a step down.

Now that the Getty is an even more powerful institution in 2019 than it was in 1974, any criticism of the Getty Center, the new museum built to complement the much smaller Villa, is very muted in the East Coast press, and the same goes for the Getty Villa too in contemporary discourse, as it underwent a 250 million dollar retrofit in 2005 conducted by Chicago architects

Rodolfo Machado and Jorge Silvetti. Silvetti visited the site, just after one of California's routine forest fires, which came fairly close to the Malibu property. Ashes from burnt buildings and trees were still descending, swirling in the air around the Villa, which Silvetti took to be a sign that he would invoke the spirit of the Villa rather than imitate what had been already present on the site as his model. What a load of crap: the end result being unfinished concrete rendering, French doors replaced by modernist versions, toilets exterior to the Conservation Laboratories, whose heavy doors did a loud double-click every time they were opened, and as they could not be kept open, because of the stringent security concerns for the site, one just had to live with this totally unnecessary noise in the background. I could go on with a host of other petty design failures. However, there is always another side to a coin, even a debased one, and the user just had to be grateful that the building was provided in the first place for our conservation training programme which I was to head up, later, in 2003. However, imitation being the sincerest form of flattery was definitely the way to go in any redesign of the Getty Villa, but that would be too much for modern architects to swallow. Imitation of something that was itself an imitation of a Roman Villa would be one imitation too many, and the architects would almost certainly have been subject to ridicule, a mirror-image of the criticisms of Getty's original decision. So, no criticism in 2019, at least not in public anymore!

# Chapter Nine:  Getty Villa to Getty Center

Sometime in the 1890's to 1950's period, great new buildings had gone up in Los Angeles, such as the LA County Museum of Natural History; The University of Southern California; The University of California, Los Angeles (UCLA); The Norton Simon Museum, the Southwest Museum; and the Los Angeles County Museum of Art (LACMA).

Apart from a few jobs at LACMA, there were practically no senior roles for conservators in Los Angeles at all: it was a backwater compared with what was happening on the East Coast of the USA. Even recently I was shocked to see someone at the San Diego Museum of Man, sorting out a box of human remains on a couple of sheets of old newspaper.

Los Angeles had lost its way, floundering about with riots, police corruption, earthquakes and little new investment and nothing much of inspired construction in the arts had happened since the 1970's, and certainly not for us art and archaeological conservators. Even in the 1990's, during another recessionary episode, the only conservator at the Los Angeles County Museum of Natural History was laid off: really quite disgraceful, but the American way is to think positive under all circumstances, never to protest or complain, so no-one even mentions this sordid fact.

One of the largely unsung triumphs of the Getty, under the umbrella of the Research Institute, is to have created, in a few short years, a major art and conservation library of international significance. Treating art conservation as a subject in its own right has been a major boon for us, both in research and teaching, since in many libraries there are complex problems with the subject falling through the cracks or else being dispersed into myriad sectional regions: it does not fit well with the Dewey system or most other attempts at categorization.

The Institute of Archaeology at London had its own library, and so much of our conservation research could be undertaken there too without stepping out of the building, it was quite marvelous. But if one needed to go to the main library at Senate House, of the University of London, that was a whole different can of worms. Senate House used to issue a six-page guide for the collection for those involved in art conservation. What a nightmare. Great bibliographical and geographical skills had to be developed to extract the books one wanted from the library holdings: would Arthur Lucas's seminal book on *Ancient Egyptian Materials and Industries* be housed in Egyptian Art; Art Materials and Techniques; The History of Science; A special section on old Art books; Conservation Science or Art Conservation? These categories were all on different floors of the library. Never mind, I got the book and no-one would recall it for years. When I left UCL for the Getty, and returned it, I photocopied the entire book.

At its inception, the Getty Conservation Institute too had its own library housed in Marina del Rey, and it was excellent, even in the early 1990's. We could peruse the stacks and wander around for hours in the unlikely presence of Glencoe Avenue. This was impossible when the library was taken over by the central GRI library years later: what a drag, and what a real impediment to browsing research. Actually, this was the fault of the Getty Conservation Institute (GCI) senior staff, then under Miguel Angel Corzo: the architects had provided a large space for a library to be housed, but at the eleventh hour, this was aborted by the GCI and they used the space for a meeting room instead, the books being sent off to the Getty Research Institute, which housed the main library. A sign of bad planning by the architect, the imperious Richard Meir, and bad judgement on the part of the Getty Conservation Institute as to whether they even needed a meeting room: it was unclear why, in the planning process, costing millions in itself, that this could not have been foreseen.

Joan Didion's embarrassment no longer exists: the Villa is a much loved location, and now, since it is dedicated to Greek and Roman antiquities, it is ideal for the kinds of art currently on display, which is entirely appropriate for it.

The new Getty Center is another matter: Getty would have hated the vast expanse of glass and concrete that characterizes the hill-top monster, and would have never countenanced its existence or its exorbitant cost. But when I joined the Getty Conservation Institute in 1987, based at my lovely laboratory at the Getty Villa, the Getty Center was still a long way off in the future.

If Getty had chosen to leave all his money to fund a new museum in the UK, the loss to Los Angeles would have been immense. As far as conservation was concerned, the Getty created a new life in Los Angeles which could have never existed without it. Los Angeles is not a city which has shown much interest in its own past, and that has been reflected in the lack of art conservators, and LA's ability to embrace the new and trash its history: especially the history it would rather not acknowledge or remember. After all, in a city of a mass of immigrants from around the world, who has the collective memory of the past life of the place? Only a very few such memories still exist. Getty had been brought up in LA, on Wilshire Boulevard, and must have retained a fondness and attachment for the city which he rarely came to visit in later life. Getty's gift has meant that, despite all the criticisms of what he achieved, that the cultural and neighbourhood diaspora which Los Angeles has now become is the major beneficiary of his billions, something that even Getty himself could not have foreseen the scale of.

Getty had opened his museum, without entrance charges, and so it endured until the Trustee bureaucrats took over and found a way of circumventing the free entrance to the museum: by ring-fencing the cost of the parking structure and charging visitors fifteen dollars to park their cars there. Since Los Angeles is still umbically tied to the motor-car, most people have to pay this "entrance fee", which, I like to think, Getty would never have endorsed. He was quite adamant that no entrance fees should ever be levelled on a population which he saw as in dire need of the civilizing influence of classical art, especially that of ancient Greece and Rome. In one of his books, *As I See It*, Getty writes "...it was my intent that the collection should be completely open to the public, free of all charges – be they for admission or even parking automobiles. Nothing of this sort could be insured if the museum were under the control of a city, state – or even the federal – government..." Getty saw this gift to the public in terms of his intense business acumen, that if he had wanted to make money from the collection then he would have sold it off instead. His fiscal perspective was to regard the museum as a public gift, a deliberate act of his own volition, as a monetary principle of his own choosing. Those with less interest in the finer points of Getty's intentions are now in control of the Getty Museum, and Getty's statements are now regarded as historical peccadillos of an eccentric founder, rather than a clearly perspectival vision that Getty had ensured and instituted.

What happened to the Getty billions and how were they spent? After the wise counsel of Nancy Englander and Harold Williams, several different entities were created: the J. Paul Getty Museum: the Getty Research Institute (GRI); the Getty Conservation Institute (GCI); the Getty Education Institute, the Information Institute; the Getty Leadership Institute; and the Getty Grants Program (GGP). Not all of these entities have survived into 2019: the most obvious and useful survivors are the Museums themselves, the GRI, the GCI, and the GGP. In fact, since 1982, the coinage of the GCI has become increasingly recognized internationally, because conservation had been so marginalized in the past, that recognition of the efforts of preserving heritage properly are long overdue. Of course, given the Getty environment, a great deal of time and money are wasted in meetings, discussions, travel, consultation documents, strategic plans, etc. etc. I give just one example: when the Getty Trustees were due to have a meeting in London, senior staff of the GCI had to 'scope out the terrain beforehand to make sure that everything went exactly according to plan, because the Trustees are so fragile that waiting for a while for a meal at a Jamie Oliver joint might put them over the edge. This involved several business class flights to London and a lot of staying in an expensive hotel and sampling quality food. Well of course, one would have to do that, since no-one has ever had experience of elite food and accommodation in the UK capital before. What tripe: Getty himself would have been horrified and the tens of thousands of dollars involved accomplished what exactly, and that does not include the cost of taking all the trustees there and back.

You have to remember that, despite being one of the richest men in the world, Getty used to save money by washing his own socks in the hand basin when he was operating his business from a hotel room. Getty travelled economy class whenever he could, and you could see how this was consistent with his own business philosophy. Well, in the early days of the Getty Museum, Getty had heard that some museum employees were travelling business class for Getty-related projects or meetings and consequently he wrote them a memo. The memorandum said: *"It has come to my attention that staff are travelling business class. This practice must stop. I always travel economy class and what is good enough for me and my family is good enough for the rest of the Getty staff. Sincerely, J. Paul Getty"*.

In later years, one of the Museum Directors, Bill Griswold, kept a framed copy of this memo on his desk. I do not expect it is still there today. The Getty is a great stepping-stone: and many of us have gone onto greater things with a Getty employment record under our belt: so it was with William (Bill) M. Griswold, who seemed to be at the Getty for quite a short period of time. He ended up as Director of the Cleveland Museum of Art. While at the Getty, he was lodged in Scholar Housing. This is one of the many perks that guest scholars have when they are selected to spend three or six months at the Getty, and I would strongly recommend it to anyone: a wonderful experience awaits, devoid of the many vicissitudes and petty complaints, rules and restrictions, meetings and strategic crap which the ordinary employee might have to put up with. Griswold had a dog, and pets are not allowed in Guest Scholar Housing, so Griswold used to smuggle the dog in and out in a large suitcase, much to the annoyance of the then warden of the Guest Scholar suites, Karen Sexton-Josephs, but as he was the Museum Director, he was above reproach and there was nothing Karen could do about it.

But this is the Getty: there are so many thousands of dollars which might be needed to be spent on a series of meetings, that no-one would even raise an eyebrow on expensive travel abroad, and at a cost several times greater than the orange juice or umbrellas that Barry Munitz was reputed to have needed to be flown out to him on his international business meetings, one of the factors that ended in Dr. Munitz being sacked. Barry Munitz was one of the most eloquent and loquacious speakers that I have ever heard. But he had his own way of doing things, which did not always meet with approval from either the Trust or the employees themselves. Apparently, Munitz had spent Getty money on first-class travel with his wife, approved various grants to friends and lobbied for a raise while ordering budget cuts and staff sackings (these are called layoffs in the US of A). Orange juice and umbrellas were just the final straw and Munitz had to go, followed by the State Attorney General moving in to undertake investigations as to whether Munitz had compromised the Getty's non-profit status. Munitz had been on dining and wining terms with 95% of LA's elite, such as Eli Broad, Pete Wilson, Grey Davis and Sherry Lansing, so his fall from grace was doubly astounding. Barry Munitz still had the imagination of a chess-player in his mind, so that I once sent Jill Murphy of an interesting chess set (as he still collected them) for sale in a junk shop down Venice Boulevard, and when I left the Getty for UCLA, he gave me three giant chess pieces as a leaving gift, which I kept at UCLA for several years.

House styles of conservation tend to become ingrained and one day during a conference the conservator from the British Museum went round the collection and announced that they would have had many of the bronzes off display for treatment. I was perplexed by this revelation. Exposure of the bronzes over time has not tended to confirm this conservators opinion, as virtually none of them have given any real trouble. What did look incongruous at the Villa was some of the French furniture and the more modern of the paintings, especially the *Entry of Christ into Brussels 1899* by James Ensor, squeezed on a wall space far too small for it, as if it had escaped from an Alice in Wonderland world where it had grown far larger than it should, too large now to be able to get through the door.

My assistant scientist was Michael Schilling who was a remarkable and talented laboratory worker. Between us, with back-up from the Getty Conservation Institute, then housed in an industrial building in Marina del Rey, we dealt with Renaissance pictures, Decorative Arts and Sculpture, Antiquities, Gemstones, and later some photographs.

Dr. Frank Preusser, our boss, was an interesting character, gaunt and intense, a chain smoker and possible alcoholic, who had been the former head of the Doerner Institute in Munich, and had big ambitions for his new Scientific Department in Los Angeles, of which the Museum laboratory was just a small part. The entire premise of this integration of the Museum lab within the Getty Conservation Institute was fundamentally flawed, since what we needed was partially archaeometric, while archaeometry was not supposed to be an activity undertaken by the GCI, under the parameters dreamed up by Frank. Therefore an inner tension existed between the demands of the museum and the mission of the GCI in terms of projects and strategic goals that never underwent a Hegelian spiral into a new synthesis.

I have known several men who are both chain smokers and alcoholics, all rather thin since they are less interested in food and more concerned with drink: there must be something in their talented compulsive brains, that gives them no rest, a drive which they tend to inflict on others, less capable, less fanatical, less dedicated, in their work than they are themselves. Such was life working with Dr. Frank Preusser: he would extemporize on his past achievements and projects, as exemplars to the rest of the senior staff, Neville Agnew, Jim Druzik, Steve Weintraub, Bill Ginell, Charles Selwitz and Shin Maekawa, and myself during senior staff meetings which went on and on along the same lines as a result and were in danger of consuming the entire time for the meeting.

William Seaman Ginell, was a remarkable man, who had worked on the Manhattan Project in the 1940's, at Columbia and Oak Ridge. He had been charged with investigating gaseous diffusion, an essential part of the atomic bomb project. I like to think that some of his reports had been microfilmed by Donald Maclean, at a time when Maclean had free access to all Los Alamos files, and had made their way to Russia where scientists had been busy, pouring over Bill's diffusion equations. All those files were essential for Russia's atomic bomb development, thanks to Donald Maclean and Kim Philby. One of our Los Angeles friends, Susan, had been brought up in Washington DC, and had played with Kim Philby's children. Sir Anthony Blunt had been on the management committee of the Institute of Archaeology in London, and I had written about Eric Hebborn, the famous British forger, who often relied on Blunt to look at some of his "antique" drawings. It is a small world, the world of informed information, and the academic world smaller still.

Bill Ginell had retired early, at the age of sixty. He had been charged by Frank with purchasing the myriad equipment that a conservation science laboratory might need: ellipsometers, infra-red spectrometers, x-ray diffractometer, UV spectroscopes, balances, glassware, distillation equipment, metallographs, hot-plates, environmental weathering chambers, computers, electron microprobe analyzer, glass dishwashers, petri dishes, chemical store, chemical supplies, benchtop microscopes, and whatever else might be needed. He was assisted by Frank Lambert, a subtle retired chemist, who interviewed potential staff, and who made the wise decision to hire Michael Schilling in the first place. While an extensive personal interview exists with Bill Ginell which can be accessed on line by typing into Google *Manhattan Project Voices – William Ginell*, the Getty have, as far I know, no such personal video archive from these pioneers of the Getty Conservation Institute, which is fairly par for the course. Why would anyone be interested?

Frank's megalomania clashed with Miguel Angel Corzo, and Frank was effectively sacked in1993. At the Doerner Institute, before he had left Germany for the USA, Frank had built up some expertise examining art objects brought in for evaluation, and he returned to authenticity evaluation to keep him going for a few years. It was a cruel fate for someone who had thought that he, himself, should be running the entire Institute, and who had taken the rash decision to move into the directors office before the Trust had made an announcement concerning the new head: but it was not to be Frank, but Dr. Miguel Angel Corzo. When Frank Preusser had been working away independently for a few years, Dr. Mark Gilberg, just appointed as Head of Conservation at the Los Angeles County Museum of Art (LACMA) took him on in 2005: a tribute to how hard Frank had worked in the meantime to keep himself afloat, and he ended his days in 2017, working feverishly on the Watts Tower Conservation Project, dying in the saddle a little before its final reports. He is much missed for the unique personality that he was, and the passion he brought to his work. Nothing mellowed or changed him: not even being sacked from the Getty Conservation Institute altered his mental attitude one jot, and his wide-ranging knowledge made him indispensible at the LACMA Conservation Department.

Like Luis Monreal before him, Corzo was highly educated, charismatic, talented, and urbane, with an all-embracing Mexican smile.  Educated at a tiny French private school run by the famous Madame Tron, he then attended the Lycee Francais of Mexico City, followed by a degree in Engineering from UCLA and a PhD from the Technical University of Munich and a post-doc at Harvard. Corzo took over from Monreal, until sacked by Dr. Barry Munitz, the new CEO of the Getty Trust, who took over from the retiring Harold Williams in 1998. So why did Corzo get sacked? The whole of the upper management of the GCI was tainted by association with an independently-minded Mexican of great talent, too large for the Getty Trust to deal with, and too much at odds with the way Dr. Barry Munitz, the Trust CEO, who wanted to take control of the individual Getty entities, so Corzo had to go. There was a sense of evangelical zeal in the GCI higher echelons at the time when Corzo was in charge, in the mid-late 1990's admirable, but not Trust-authenticated, and

Munitz seemed to think that the Trust had to authorize or approve of all activities, not to everyone's satisfaction.

All the time this was going on, the Trust was planning to build a much larger Museum, since some of the artwork looked decidedly out of place at the Getty Villa.

John Walsh went, our handsome and experienced museum director, into a happy retirement just a few years after the new Getty Center was finished, keeping the Trust-purchased house, as his base in LA, while his own house was purchased in Arcadia, California. His log cabin LA house in one of the most exclusive canyons in LA, had been used as a movie-set for some silent movie way back in time, in the 1920's or 1930's, and had been taken apart, the logs numbered, and moved to its present highly desirable location. I liked John Walsh very much. The last time I was at his log cabin house, around 1993, I was introduced to Sir Dennis Mahon, whose personal art collection; left to the Nation was later to be valued at over 100 million quid. I extended my hand to shake with his and was alarmed when Sir Dennis raised his arm and presented it to me to be...what? Kissed? That was the high position of the proffered hand. Taken aback, I took hold of the hand rather limply and shook it. The conversation was strained since at that time my knowledge of early Italian art was quite limited, Sir Dennis had no interest in antiquities, and I had no idea who Sir Dennis Mahon was apart from knowing that he was an art historian. I know now, and revere his accomplishments in resuscitating the reputation of Giuseppe Maria Crespi, Ludovico Carracci, Luca Giordano and many others who no one else thought worth a fig. The art collection that Mahon assembled is now worth hundreds of millions of pounds, so the nation got a real bargain.

John Walsh, something of an expert on Dutch art, still gives lectures at Yale on the subject, but in the wider field of scholarship does not seem to have published a major volume on the topic, perhaps too relaxed to really exert himself, and too talented and too comfortable to bother.

It was a timely departure for Dr. John Walsh, as the writing was on the wall for the Getty Museum due to the controversy about to erupt over its dodgy acquisitions, especially those antiquities that could be traced back to Italy. Walsh escaped from it all, but not from the fall-out due to the "resignation" of Dr. Marion True, Head of Antiquities Curatorial a little later on. The turmoil at the Getty simmered on for years. Deborah Gribbon, who had taken over in an acting capacity from Marion True, also had a major disagreement with Munitz, took a multi-million dollar settlement and left the Getty forthwith, prompting Walsh to describe her "resignation" as a "black eye to the Getty Trust"

During this time, around 1997-2001, I was writing one of my books, *Copper and Bronze in Art: Corrosion, Colourants, Conservation*, and I had a sophisticated designer at the Getty Publication Department. He ensured that the book was a high-class production and the intelligent eye of Marta de la Torre chose the cover picture from one of my pictures in the book. It was published in 2002, has sold over 2000 copies worldwide, been translated into Chinese and Persian, and won several awards, including the major award from the American Association of Publishers as the best Scholarly/Art book published in the USA in 2002, and I was supposed to travel to Washington DC for the award ceremony, but never had the time and someone from Getty Publications picked up the award for me. The book is still in print, some eighteen years later, now in its second edition and is the book I am most proud of, out of the nine I have written. It was a book that I wrote in spite of the Getty rather than because of it. The reason for this is that the GCI were project-driven and writing a book on copper and bronze conservation, pigments and corrosion was never a project per se, it was just something that I was determined to write, and given the extra degrees of freedom afforded me by virtue of being head of the museum lab, I embraced. One of my poignant memories of writing the text is watching two of my children ice-skating in Culver City, while I hunkered down with a small notebook and wrote out a few pages of text, later to be typed up on my laptop. The subjects of pigments and metals are usually dealt with in different sectors of our profession. Pigments is often the preserve of paintings restorers and metals the concern of the archaeological conservator. However, intellectually we know that pigments are minerals and that the corrosion products of metals are minerals. Many pigments are made by the deliberate corrosion of copper, iron, tin, mercury, lead, arsenic, or bronze.

All of this extra-mural activity was to serve me well when I resigned from the Getty to take up the position as the new director of the UCLA/Getty Conservation Training Programme; I had many publications and a couple of good books under my belt. Dr. Barry Munitz took over the running of the Museum as well as being the CEO of the Getty Trust, an arrangement which the art critic of the Los Angeles Times, Christopher Knight, described presciently as a "recipe for disaster" The strange thing is that the Trust was peopled by very intelligent and elite folk who apparently had no inkling that such a situation was indeed potentially a disaster. How this was even possible, when it was patently obvious, one simply would not know, except for the fact that they were not really museum-savvy folk.

Dr. Nicholas Turner, the Curator of Drawings at the British Museum, was another important hiring by the Getty Museum, which promised much, but the sharp and experienced eye of Dr. Turner thought that five of the drawings in the Getty Collections were forgeries by that talented English faker, Eric Hebborn, who had had his skull smashed in on a Rome street a few years before. Needless to say, his killer has never been brought to justice.

Turner was sure one of the drawings, a pen-and-ink study of a female figure attributed to Raphael, was a forgery. Another was a portrait of an infant attributed to Fra Bartolommeo, whose most important work is the great altarpiece at San Marco in Florence; and another was the only surviving drawing by the Italian sculptor Desiderio da Settignano. Indeed Settignano and his school was one of the artists who Hebborn liked to imitate, and he makes mention of Settignano in one of his books on his own fakes. In our lab at the Getty Villa, my assistant scientist, Dr. Arie Wallert, a great expert on Renaissance art and drawings, apparently detected titanium in one of these suspect drawings, which if proved correct would condemn the work as a modern forgery and vindicate the opinion of Nicholas Turner. We shall never know if this is correct or not, as the rumour was that it was the backing board, a modern support, in which the titanium had been present, but as no further work has been carried out, there is no way to know. I wrote a memo on the subject to the Getty Department of Drawings and Manuscripts around 2004, but not surprisingly received no reply.

The only way to tell if some of Hebborn's work is actually fake or not is by art connoisseurship, and Dr. Turner was one of the best there was. The reason for that equivocation, is that in his best work, Hebborn only used old paper and old inks. He had been known to buy an entire 18th century watercolour set, just for the bistre ink, so hard to imitate today even using the original recipes of the time.

There were just one or two problems which conspired to produce a whirlwind of circumstances: George Goldner the previous curator of drawings, who had had an affair with Deborah Gribbon, threatened to sue if acquisitions he had made were to be dismissed as forgeries by Turner, and the Getty were very unwilling to ever admit that something they had bought could possibly be a forgery. The secretary Nicholas Turner had begun an affair with at the Getty had turned nasty, as he had ended it, and she was harassing him. It was all too much: Turner resigned and then sued for sexual harassment. The Getty, very eager to settle out of court, paid Turner a six figure sum to go away, probably in the order of $500,000. Then the catalogue, which the Getty had promised Turner, would be published which would clearly express Turner's view that these particular drawings were forgeries became stalled and so Turner sued the Getty again. Once again, the Getty was very keen to settle out of court for another six figure sum. Turner returned to England, reputedly to run a pig farm, and was never seen in the Getty environs again. The suspect drawings seem to be always in storage, which is a Museum-honoured method of dealing with possible fakes: just keep them out of the public gaze for a few decades, and everyone will forget they ever existed.

Dr. Barry Munitz was an interesting and charismatic character, who I saw from time to time, and I enjoyed my limited time with him, because he had installed his remarkable and extensive chess library of well over a thousand volumes, in his Getty office, replete with numerous chess-sets and a few giant chess pieces in his small balcony, which I could see from my laboratory office across in the Getty Center Museum, and we would occasionally chat about chess when we met.

It turned out that Barry Munitz had gone to the same Brooklyn High School that Bobby Fisher had attended, Erasmus Hall High School. Munitz was one of the organizers of the Erasmus Hall School Chess Club, so he approached the 16-year-old Fischer, who at that time had just won the United States Chess Championship and asked him if he would like to play for the school club!   Fischer looked at Munitz and told him to "fuck off".   Well, Barry Munitz remained entranced with chess, and although his chess library was not added to over time, it had been his father's chess library, it was a magnificent chess repository, which I browsed in, from time to time. Barry mentions to me the New York Chess Club, where a bag lady shuffled in to watch some prestigious team match, opened her bag and took out a chess computer and plugged it in.   She followed the match, making comments, a true kibitzer.   Munitz had practically all of the games of Capablanca and Alekhine, and some of my old favourites from Akiba Rubinstein to Edward Lasker.   Quite wonderful, although one suspected that Munitz had installed his chess library at his Getty Center office to baffle and disorient the typical visitor, who would not even recognise the name of Akiba Rubinstein if it came at them in the face.

Munitz used to go on summer holidays with Ray Riordan, the Major of Los Angeles at that time.   Ray's only interest in the holidays was to play chess, and Munitz related how his father had been born on the same day, same time, as Sammy Reshevsky (a very prominent US grandmaster). Somehow the opportunity came to invite the then World Chess Champion, and chess genius, Garry Kasparov to the Getty Center to give some kind of simul and educative talk. One of the Getty security guards at that time had once been the US Women's Chess Champion, and she and I used to meet with Jill Murphy, Barry's assistant, who it was reputed he had met when she was a waitress.

The meetings progressed until Garry Kasparov and his business manager, a former South African tennis pro, flew over from Florida for a meeting with the three of us, the security guard, myself and Barry. Garry Kasparov and his manager had hired a stretched diesel Mercedes, a rare and exclusive vehicle, to take the World Champion to the Getty Center from LAX, where, unbelievably, despite Munitz's express instructions, they were shown to underground visitor parking rather than to the elite top-of-the-hill parking! This had the incongruous result of the World Champion squeezing into a packed tram surrounded by school-kids and other passengers who had no idea who he was, and I nervously met him at the top, anticipating some kind of blow-up from the World Champion, who however, seemed quite unperturbed. He was not Bobby Fischer! Garry Kasparov had been the only visitor to the Getty that had impressed Munitz's father as someone worthy of attention.

We showed Garry around the Getty Center, the manuscripts and historical silverware, while Kasparov embarked on an exposition of the weird theories of a group of Russian mathematicians who had worked backwards in time from the present and come to the conclusion that the dating of ancient art was quite in error. I tried to explain to Kasparov how we arrived at the dating of artworks, of TL, of radiocarbon, of isotopes, of dendrochronology, but I think it made no impression.

Over a light lunch before we went to Barry Munitz's office for the meeting, Kasparov asked me what my FIDE rating was. I had been playing correspondence chess at that time and had advanced to 2120; quite a respectable grade for me, but one that was equivalent to a possible imbecile as far as the World Champion was concerned. He made a face, as if such a lowly grade could surely hardly be possible for someone who called himself a chess-player.

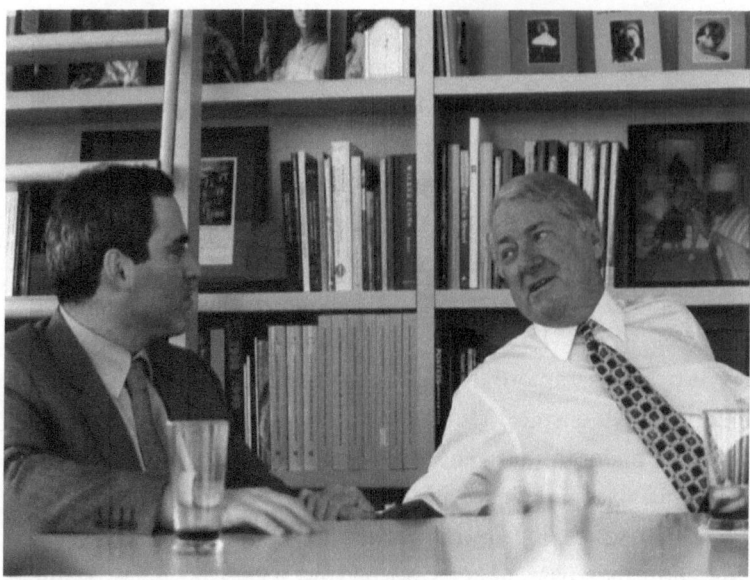

Garry Kasparov, Chess World Champion, with his South African business
manager, Owen Williams, at Barry Munitz's Getty Trust Office on 16th April
1999. The books in the background here are mostly Getty Publications. Dr.
Munitz was at that time the Director of the J. Paul Getty Trust.

Kasparov intimated that he was thinking of going into politics, in
Russia, which seemed to me very ill-advised, but he was quite
unstoppable and the last time I saw him on television, he was
being bundled into the back of a police van and taken away from
some demonstration or another in Moscow around 2008. Of
course, being world-famous, he was soon released and continues
to take an interest in chess and politics.

Back at the Getty, the arrangement to get Kasparov to the Getty
stalled: I never really knew why. The loquacious Dr. Munitz was
beginning to run into trouble.

The end result was his resignation, the write-off of his severance
package and the repayment to the Trust of $250,000 for various
semi-authorized or un-authorized expenditures on first-class air
travel, staying at five-star hotels and a using a leased Porsche
Cayenne. It had a touch of irony, since it was Munitz himself
who had brought the Trustees from a rubber-stamping collection
of business folk to a group more involved with the running of the

Trust as a whole, as compared with Harold Williams, who more or less told the Trustees what was going to happen. John H. Biggs, the very proper Chairman of the Board of Trustees, told the LA Times that Munitz had "really done a terrific job," though he added that he had warned Dr. Munitz about travel expenses, including yacht trips with Mr. Eli Broad in Greece and Eastern Europe for which Dr. Munitz was partly reimbursed by the Getty. For those not in the know, Eli Broad is one of the most important art collectors of the age and his collection of modern art is unsurpassed in private hands. He is also a billionaire, so money hardly matters to him if it is a Getty funded yacht trip or not, some of his art might even have made it to the Getty Center if things had been different.

This entire imbroglio was taking place against another backdrop: this time the problem of antiquities and what to do with them. For the last several months, the Getty had been under siege on several fronts. Its former antiquities curator, Marion True, was hung out to dry by the Trustees and faced trial in Italy on charges of trafficking in looted antiquities, while the Trust assumed no guilt or responsibility whatever: it had all been the fault of that evil woman, Marion True. She resigned her position, having been responsible for so much of the re-design of the Getty Villa, that the entire vision of it was hers: even the staircase, installed in a honey-coloured stone to take visitors to the second floor was her idea. Marion True was a frequent visitor to the Museum lab, so I knew her quite well and liked her very much, since she was at least, a true scholar.

Deborah Gribbon took on the task of directing the Museum, but as Munitz saw himself as the overall director of the museum, there were many sources of conflicts. The management structure, however, required Gribbon to report to Munitz and they clashed repeatedly over the direction the Trust should be taking, particularly whether the emphasis should be on art or, as Munitz insisted, on other activities such as grants, scholarships, conservation and education. That was good for the Getty Conservation Institute, and helped to up its image overall, but not so good for some potential Museum acquisitions, such as

Raphael's *Madonna of the Pinks*, which went to the National Gallery, London rather than to the Getty. The natural consequence happened, and Deborah Gribbon resigned with a handsome pay-off and was replaced by William Griswold. As she left, Gribbon said ""I leave the Getty believing as passionately as ever that museums best serve the public by collecting, exhibiting and interpreting works of art of the highest quality. J. Paul Getty left a great legacy to the people of Los Angeles and to the world, and the Getty has extraordinary potential. I remain optimistic that this potential will be realised."

I think she was right and that, despite its daft problems, that the Getty has realised this potential, but no outsider could begin to appreciate the costs associated with achieving that aim, and the various stupidities that the Trust has managed to commit over the past forty years.

The *Madonna of the Pinks* has an interesting back-story. One day, in 1991, Nicholas Penny was taking a stroll to the WC in Alnwick Castle, Northumberland, when he noticed on the wall of the corridor a dingy painting that, when he looked closer with the experienced eye, under the heavily discoloured varnish, seemed to be a work of high quality: not one of the several copies of Raphael's work, but quite possibly the original! It was a *pentimenti* that did it: the landscape ran through a tower in the background, and such alterations in a copy are highly unusual, unless the work is a modern sophisticated fake.

Taken to the National Gallery, London and cleaned, all experts agreed that this *Madonna of the Pinks* was indeed the lost original and not a copy at all, and worth about 35 million quid! The infrared reflectogram revealed an underdrawing typical for Raphael. When we see a characteristic underdrawing in any panel painting, that is a good sign for the material authenticity of the work. This was a nice little earner for the Duke of Northumberland. The Getty played an important role here, as the sale of the picture to the Getty had been agreed at a price of £34.88 million. Now, the treasury decided that in order to help poor owners, such as the Duke, to sell their works to National Collections instead of rich institutions like the Getty, that they were in need of an additional financial inducement, given the suitably obscure name of a douceur. A douceur, in effect, a private bribe between the tax authorities and the individual, gives the seller a tax sweetener above the level of remuneration they would have got if they had sold their painting abroad. You can see why they decided to call this arrangement a douceur. No austerity requirements imposed here! The douceur was not affected in level of remuneration while the rest of us were getting hammered. The National Gallery gets the sale price net of tax. In this complex arrangement the National Gallery gets 75% of the tax benefit and the Duke 25%.

By my rough calculations, this saves the Duke about a quarter of a million! In an attempt to justify the massive expenditure, a problem created by matching the sum the painting would have obtained had it been purchased by the Getty, the poor Madonna was sent on a nationwide tour across the British Isles.

After this triumph, a dissenting art historian, Dr. Caruzzi, published, maintaining that the work is a copy and that the case in favour of authenticity made by the National Gallery is incomplete. Often the owner proposes a number of stipulations before the sale to the effect that no destructive investigation is allowed to be carried out, and indeed, the Duke so stipulated this restriction before the sale, so any probing scientific studies had to be carried out afterwards, so to speak.

The late Brian Sewell also thought the work of low quality and possibly a forgery, since Madonna's right leg seemed to be disconnected from her body. James Beck, in his posthumous publication, *From Duccio to Raphael: Connoisseurship in Crisis* additionally did not like the work. One of his principal arguments, and there are many, is that old engravings of the work show a more expansive space around the central figure and that one shows the second knee, hidden in the National Gallery version, because it can be seen on the infra-red reflectogram but not on the picture. This raises a doubt: how can the engraving show something that is now invisible on the work itself? It suggests that there may have been an original that did show the second knee, but in the National Gallery version it was hidden either under later layers of paint, or perhaps the work is a workshop copy with an underdrawing in the style of Raphael close to the time of the master. There are apparently fifty-five copies of the *Madonna of the Pinks*, a daunting number to unravel. Part of the problem here is that Raphael ran a very large workshop, where assistants would work from the master's underdrawing, or perhaps even copy the master's underdrawing and continue to complete the work, or perhaps the face or hands were finished by Raphael himself with assistants competing the work. So how would one ever know outside of a deep art historical connoisseurship? Professor Beck takes the argument further and maintains that the underdrawing is in a much later 18th or 19th century style and that the Madonna is a fake. It is true that the early engravings of this picture, showing a more expansive space around the Madonna and child appear more composed, serene, and naturally spacious, while the smaller National Gallery painting has a somewhat cramped appearance. The strange thing is that the National Gallery painting has not been cut down in size, which is a bit unsettling. Given the very small size of this work and the fact that a clear provenance for it cannot be taken back further than about 1850, the decision to value the work at 35 million quid is perhaps over-generous.

As with Rembrandt, there are extraordinary subtleties in deciding whether, for example, the Polish Rider in the Frick Collection, New York is actually painted by Rembrandt or not. In 1998 the Rembrandt Research Project concluded that Rembrandt was not the only artist to have worked on the painting and that another hand was evident. These kinds of pronouncements have serious monetary implications: if dismissed by the Rembrandt Research Project, the value might drop from 600 million quid to something like 15 million at auction. All of these scientific and connoissuerial issues add spice to our lives in the art world, and variants of them continue at every major museum, including the Getty.

Well, back at the Getty, Deborah Gribbon was succeeded by our new CEO, James Wood, aged 68, who managed to die in the saddle, or rather the sauna quite soon after his appointment, and so Wood was succeeded in turn by James Cuno. David Bomford, one of the leading lights of English art restoration and the conservation of pictures was appointed as acting museum director by James Wood as they had got on well together, but he did quite have what Cuno was looking for.

David Bomford, Anne Moncrieff and myself had met every month for some years, as we were the triumvirate of editors in change of the flagship journal, Studies in Conservation, so we went back to the early 1980's, some twenty-five years earlier than the events recalled here. I had continued in this editorial duty while Ann Moncrieff slowly disappeared and David Bomford went onto other things, some higher up in the IIC, some higher up in the life of the conservation profession.

I still recall some of the polished and eloquent speeches that David made at that time at the Getty Villa. But Bomford was not the favourite to take over the Museum directorship, as James Cuno, wanted his own man, Timothy Potts, to take over at the Getty Museum, and so Bomford was sacked. In a press statement, Cuno stated that Bomford was going to return to the UK, since "As a scholar of distinction, it is understandable that David would want to return to research and writing and to do so in England where his family resides. We will miss his many contributions as Associate Director for Collections and Acting Director and we wish him all the best in his new endeavors" This was news to David Bomford and his wife, as they had not known that they were to depart for England at all, as Cuno seemed to imply!

Sarah Staniforth, the Head of Conservation for the National Trust visited, and David, Sarah and I had a sneak preview of the Bronzes from Pompeii exhibition then just coming on at the Villa. This, just a few weeks before Bomford was sacked, as in the photograph I have of the three of us together, taken by Jerry Podany, Bomford is still wearing his Getty Museum identity badge.

When the Trust decided around the early 2000's that it was in financial trouble, although its trouble would have been untroublesome to any normal institution, the Trust announced that each entity had to sack some employees. David Bomford refused to get rid of any of his staff: not a move to endear himself with the crusty Trustees, while the more compliant departments, such as the Getty Conservation Institute set about getting rid of staff. The scientific department, it was decided, had to get rid of two employees. This was a disaster: the unwholesome task fell to Dr. Giacomo Chiari, at that time our Scientific Director. Giacomo mulled it over and decided to sack Cecily Grawycz and Dr. Eric Doehne, both of whom had given solid performances at the Getty for over twenty years. Cecily was personable, a good worker, with an excellent team spirit who was responsible for several types of equipment and environmental monitoring, while Dr. Eric Doehne was a geologist with advanced skills in computing and the principal operator of the Electron Probe Microanalyser, a serious bit of kit which cost a million dollars, and which needed a highly trained operative to get the best out of the beast. I relied on him often in my analyses of Getty Museum objects and samples. Very few of such machines exist, they are so highly specialized and expensive that even the annual service contract costs about $35,000. Skilled operators are akin to artists in coaxing the best out of the sophisticated machinery of the electron probe microanalyser, which can be recalcitrant for the beginner to operate.

I should explain here that the forced ending to a career at the Getty Conservation Scientific Department might entail serious problems in being immediately re-employed in Los Angeles in an equivalent position, and such was indeed the case, neither of our fellow scientists was able to find similar positions, one had to move to Washington, DC, to work in environmental monitoring, and the other tried his hand as a scientific consultant who ended up doing some teaching at Scripps College, and in one sense, their careers had ended and had to be redefined. Not having an experienced operator also had serious repercussions for our electron microprobe machine, a thoroughbred that demanded great experience to get the best out of it, and without that the machine languishes, in mourning for an operator matching it in terms of sophistication.

As work on the deterioration of stone or the analysis of metallic samples began to dry up, especially following on from the time I had left the Getty to take up my Directorship of the new UCLA/Getty Conservation Training Programme in 2003, the writing was on the wall for the wonderful electron microprobe itself, a machine many others would have given their eye-teeth for. Soon after, it was disassembled into a number of sad crates and was donated to some department or other at UCLA, where I never saw it again. The last I heard of our million-dollar marvel, it was still languishing in its crates somewhere in storage in Earth Sciences. What a waste in more ways than one. For me, a very serious waste of resources.

Natural staff wastage at the Getty is already so extraordinarily high compared with UCLA that all the Trustees had to do was wait for a couple of years, and the forced redundancies that they had carried out would have occurred anyway through a natural process of folk moving on, so the painful excision of important staff members was nothing less than a fucking waste of time, resources, and skills. Thereafter, Dr. Chiari had a large photograph of Dr. Eric Doehne operating the electron microprobe installed on the wall outside of his office at the Getty Center. One can guess his feelings about what he had to do, hence the large and prominent photograph on view to all who passed through, to remind them of their stupidity was the only course of action Dr. Chiari could have taken.

Knowing the two institutions of the Getty and UCLA intimately, I can say with some authority that an electron microprobe operator at UCLA would never have been sacked. In fact, the chap who operates the current electron microprobe at the Department of Earth Sciences, partially works as a lecturer too, as an Associate Professor, while at the same time having to work the machine for idiots like me, once I have prepared my sample, in this case an ancient Chinese bronze mirror for the research I was then doing for Lloyd Cotsen's wonderful private collection of ancient Chinese Art, which was published in two lavish volumes by the UCLA Cotsen Institute Press. That alone gives you an idea of how esteemed the electron microprobe operator at UCLA is.

One of the staff members at the Getty, Chris Wheatley, a talented communicator, facilitator, and instructor, who had been responsible for many activities in connection with the building of the new Getty Center and the rehabilitation of the old Getty Villa, was one of the folk declared surplus to requirements. When he got the notice that he had been sacked he remarked that he felt that "He had been disposed of like a used handkerchief". Well, such an obvious talent was immediately hired by UCLA where Chris still works today. The old Villa was the subject of an NBC television programme, given by the famous commentator, Hewl Howzer, and Chris was the obvious choice to show him around the site for the programme. Now, Chris is happy at UCLA and I have never seen him at the Getty Villa again, apart from one special party we had there, to say "goodbye" to several folk who had come and gone over the last few years, such as Mahasti Asfar, Rona Sebastian, Michel Bishop, (He was actually sacked from the GCI too and went to work at the Los Angeles Zoo, and I could never appreciate why). Some of the lecturing folk, who were taken on at the Getty in management or curatorial positions, such as Kara Cooney and John Papadopoulos, also ended up at UCLA and while neither of them enjoyed their time at the Getty, both benefitted from, at least, being kept in LA while their real job openings became available at UCLA where they are very happy. They will not be returning to the Getty anytime soon, except as a rest as a guest scholar or distinguished visitor.

# Chapter Ten: Work and Research at the Getty

Back in 1987, the Institute was composed of the Scientific Department, the Field Work Department, with Miguel Angel Corzo, a Training Department, under Marta de la Torre and a library. One of the first jobs Michael Schilling and I did ourselves, outside of the Getty Museum, was to be summoned downtown by Miguel Angel Corzo to Siqueiros House, where we were non-plussed to learn that we were about to climb onto the roof and inspect the ruined glory of a major work by David Alfaro Siqueiros, *America Tropical*. The Mural has as its centerpiece, a cross on which a Mexican peasant is hung, being shot at by confederates. Completed in 1932 the mural was heralded by the Los Angeles Times as a great work of art in progress. That was before Siqueiros sent everyone away and, working under floodlights by himself, he completed the crucified peasant that night. When the mural was unveiled, the authorities were aghast and the mural was quickly whitewashed over.

The 1930's was a period in many major American cities when the so-called 'Red Squads', special police units, roamed LA rounding up Mexican immigrants and packing them into railroad cars like animals and deporting the lot to Mexico; they broke up union meetings with violence, held communists in jail on trumped-up charges, and ensured that racially biased trials sent African-American men to prison, some for life on hearsay evidence. Yes, welcome to America: the land of the free: just as long as you are not Mexican, African-American, a Socialist, a Communist, or a Union organizer. This is the cultural backdrop to *America Tropical*. There is, to the best of my knowledge, no detailed historical work, which gives an account of the activity of these 'Red Squads' in Los Angeles, apart from a 1990 publication by Frank J. Donner, called *Protectors of Privilege : Red Squads and Police Repression in Urban America*. Even *America Tropical* itself was forgotten outside of the Chicano community for fifty-five years. LA County officials had once considered even the *Watt's Towers* as a suitable case for demolition, as a safety risk, that is how imaginative they are!

Michael Schilling and I determined by microscopy and XRF, that there was indeed some original paint of the Siqueiros masterpiece under the whitewash and on that basis, restoration work could go ahead. This report was crucial for the hundreds of thousands of dollars that was then spent on bringing back a perceptual reality to the work over many years, and millions of dollars later, there is now an observation center at Olvera Street where one can view the work. All credit to Miguel Angel Corzo, who is now a forgotten name at the Getty, as he was sacked by Barry Munitz, the CEO, who took over from Harold Williams, as mentioned above. A nice trail of events there: Dr. Frank Preusser, Head of Scientific, was sacked by Dr. Miguel Angel Corzo, Head of the Getty Conservation Institute, who was sacked by Dr. Barry Munitz, overall Director of the Getty Trust, who was himself sacked by the Getty Trustees a few years later.

Lower down the ladder, in the Scientific Department, we just got on with the work, bemused by all the chaos. Luis Monreal and Corzo had begun to work with the Egyptians, and the Tomb of Queen Nefertari was selected as the project focus. Michael Schilling took an active part in this project and travelled to Egypt to take colour recordings of the tomb wall paintings, some of the best and most aesthetically pleasing of all ancient Egyptian art. An international team of conservators and conservation scientists was assembled to work on the conservation and restoration of the tomb, over a period of five or six years, which cost in excess of 11 million dollars. Frank did a lot of management for this project, the late Shin Maekawa, a real gentleman, and Neville Agnew, a lot of environmental monitoring and Dusan Stulik and Herant Khanjian a lot of inorganic and organic analyses, and Paolo and Laura Mora's group from the Istituto Centrale del Restauro in Rome, Lorenza d'Alessandro, Giorgio Capriotti, and many others, a great deal of restoration work on the surfaces of the wall-paintings. The project and the work carried out was a triumph of conservation and preservation. It was 11 million dollars well spent and while supposed to be a model of treatment for many other tombs, the reality is that the Egyptian Antiquities Organization needs serious outside help to make the preservation a reality. Michael Schilling's colour measurement work was groundbreaking, in the sense that it seems to have rarely, if ever, been equaled, due to the many hundreds of measurements that Michael made. As a consequence interesting inferences could be made about the paintings in the different rooms. Dusan Stulik was charged by Frank to develop new methods of organic analysis for binding media determination, and Michael, who by this time had moved to the GCI HQ and forsaken the Museum Lab, was one of the principal architects of the project which was resoundingly successful, and the papers which he wrote on the topic with Herant Khanjian or Dusan Stulik are classics of their kind and much quoted in the art conservation literature.

Xunatunich, an important Mayan site in Belize was another major site preservation effort by the GCI in conjunction with Associate Professor Richard Lowenthal from the Cotsen Institute at UCLA. Dr. Dusan Stulik was the principal scientist for another major project based at Prague Castle on the St. Vitus mosaic, which had formed the Golden Gate of Prague. At one time the dilapidated mosaic had been cut away from the wall of the castle and placed into storage. Dr. Stulik organized, controlled and directed the entire conservation effort which was a major accomplishment and which took years of work and research in order to devise a suitable coating, which would survive the Prague winters and summers without material degradation. Even the cleaning of the tesserae of the St Vitus mosaic required a series of ingenious research work by Dusan, ending with the use of a glass bead peening process using fine glass beads, softer than the mosaics themselves but hard enough to clean the deteriorated crust of the glass decomposition products from the tesserae themselves. The whole project was a triumph for the GCI, cost several million dollars overall, and for Dusan a personal triumph as no-one else could have done it. One of the reasons was the proximity of UCLA and the polymer research group of Professor Mackenzie. This group came up with the sol-gel technology used for the coating on the St. Vitus mosaic and has not been used on any other project to the best of my knowledge. This is partially due to the costs involved, the sophistication of the technology, and the relatively modest literature dissemination of the entire project itself. Dr. Stulik did not find writing in English that easy, and therefore the story was not repeated numerous times, as many scientific reports are in different contexts, or split up into several parts, as some other major works are to squeeze the maximum number of publications out of them. The entire project, and the science behind the accomplishments deserve to be better known.

# Chapter Eleven: Objects and More Objects.

One of the first objects I thought odd at the Getty was indeed the Romanesque aquamanile, referred to above, but fortunately I was asked to examine a small Greek bronze statuette of a fallen youth, from about 480 BC, which had only recently been purchased in 1986. This period, around 500 BC, was one where the arts in ancient Greece flourished, with many masterpieces in stone and bronze being made, few of which have survived to our present era. Mostly we know about this artistic apogee through the host of Roman copies and fakes. Luckily, there could be no reasonable doubt that this fine bronze casting was authentically old. It had a strange patch with different corrosion on one of the upper arms where it must have been in contact with something in burial, for which there was no diagenetic evidence, since this particular piece arrived with no exact provenance. This is the trouble with trying to form a major collection of Greek and Roman art in the latter decades of the 20th century: it is impossible if the strictures thought necessary by purist archaeological colleagues on only obtaining artwork from known excavation sites were allowed to hold sway. Unprovenanced artwork cannot even be published anymore in the *Journal of Archaeological Science*, in an effort to prevent looting and to appear PC. The forces acting upon the world in the early 21st century are such that the amount of artwork that has been looted or stolen is so great, that the restrictions imposed by the *Journal of Archaeological Science* have little or no discernible effect, apart from an ethical posturing, and preventing some areas of the archaeological world such as ancient Colombian goldwork being reported at all. This is because vast amounts of the stuff held in museum collections across the world, is also unprovenanced. This allows us a subterfuge: we can quite legitimately state that the goldwork is housed in the collection of the National Museum of Denmark, Copenhagen, while omitting to mention the fact that the goldwork was smuggled out of Ecuador in empty toothpaste tubes in the 1930's, ostensibly for recycling the metal toothpaste tubes in a Danish recycling plant, but in reality for the magnificent gold and platinum objects they concealed.

When I arrived at the Getty there was a huge fuss about the *Strozzi silver basin* from Genoa, an Italian masterpiece, dated to around 1620, with scenes based on the life of Cleopatra, after a design by Bernardo Strozzi, possibly made by Francesco Fanelli, a noted silversmith and probably executed by some unknown Dutch or Flemish master silversmith. The basin was first exhibited in the modern sense of the word, at the Esposizione artistico, archeologico, industriale aperta nelle Sale dell'Accademia Ligustica, and the Museo dell'Accademia Ligustica di Bella Arti in Genoa, in 1868.

These fancy basins were originally used for washing the fingers of the right hand before eating, which is what we all did in the west before the 14th century AD. Like Arabic countries, we used to dip the fingers of our right hand into a bowl of clean water, perfumed with rose petals, before eating. Fashion then changed and knives and forks came into general use; many of the silver basins were molten down at this time to be turned into silver cutlery: fortunately a few survived.

One of the Getty Museum conservators of the Department of Decorative Arts, Billie Milam, was convinced that the *Strozzi silver basin* was a fake. This was because traces of silicon rubber had been found in interstices of the basin, suggesting the thing was produced in a mould. Strange, small bubbles on the surface of the silver greatly troubled Billie Milam, and could be further proof that instead of being heavily worked silver, the basin had been cast into a mould or was an electrotype copy, which would tend to produce small areas of bubbly surface. Then, traces of cadmium had been found in a sample of the silver, analysed, a few months before my arrival, using the sophisticated and normally reliable electron microprobe machine, based in the GCI lab at Marina del Rey. Now, Renaissance silver cannot have cadmium as an impurity, and therefore the entire basin must be a forgery. We tend to reply on the fact that when we detect cadmium in silver and gold objects, it is a very bad sign. Cadmium is an impurity in modern silver, often associated with early 20th century solder and its reuse, not an ancient component, and no antique or Renaissance silver artwork has been found with a cadmium content sufficient to make it useable for characterization of ancient silver, unlike traces of iridium or platinum which might be.

What a mess to have walked into: it could hardly have been a worse beginning, having to deal with a potential major forgery case as soon as I had arrived. The late Peter Fusco was the curator, and he used to come round to the Museum lab, demanding answers. I prevaricated as best I could, which only confirmed the suspicion in the curatorial mind that all of this scientific stuff was just a complete waste of time which muddied the waters and gave no clear answers to a comparatively simply question. What was their problem if science gave equivocal answers? Otherwise one might just as well do without it and use art historical intuition instead a la Bernard Berenson.

I cut out a small sample of the basin from underneath a shield, which could be detached, so that no visible damage could be seen from the front when the shield was screwed back in place. Looking at the microstructure, I thought it very unlikely that this masterpiece was a forgery, because there was so much disturbance of the silver at the surface where it had been heated and shaped. Oxygen is rather soluble in hot silver, and this can disrupt the grain structure of the silver. In more ancient silver objects, where a little copper has been added to harden it a bit, we also have a special kind of precipitation which occurs at the grain boundaries of the metal, which is only associated with very old silver, called discontinuous precipitation, hence by microstructural study alone we can often state with some certainty that the silver is old rather than made last month in Genoa. This we cannot do with many other alloys: you can't tell how old a piece of iron is from looking at the extent of corrosion. Gradually the puzzle began to unravel, not to the satisfaction of Peter Fusco, who obviously could not understand how science had tied itself up in knots and couldn't answer his demand immediately as to whether the basin was authentic or not. Another analysis of the silver found no cadmium content. This was a great relief to me, and removed a major stumbling block in proving that the basin was indeed authentic. The problem had been that the previous analyst had mistaken a small subsidiary silver peak in his microprobe study for a peak for cadmium, which overlapped. He proceeded on the assumption that the machine, which had presumably labelled this peak as being generated by cadmium, to report the presence of a trace of cadmium in the basin, where none existed. So that cleared up that problem, even if the logic behind it proved an embarrassing lack of acumen on the part of the GCI scientists. How about the traces of silicon rubber? It transpired that the previous dealer in Italy, longing not to give up the original completely, had made a series of silicon rubber casts of the basin, presumably to produce a wax copy to then cast in silver as a replica for himself. The bubbles on the surface are what is known in the trade as "orange-peel effect" and are due to the overheating of the silver while it is being worked and annealed to shape. Oxygen is absorbed by the hot silver during annealing, which is then released back to the atmosphere when the silver cools down, but one consequence is that small protrusions or bubbles on the silver can be left behind, creating the "orange-peel effect". So now there was a rational explanation for the bubbles, the silicon rubber, and the traces of cadmium as well: the *Strozzi silver basin* was resuscitated as a masterpiece, and I could now write the internal memo to Peter Fusco that he had been impatiently waiting for, to conclude that the Getty purchase was indeed authentic, and the basin could return to display once more. It is still on display today at the Getty Center Museum as one of the prized objects in the Decorative Arts and Sculpture Collection.

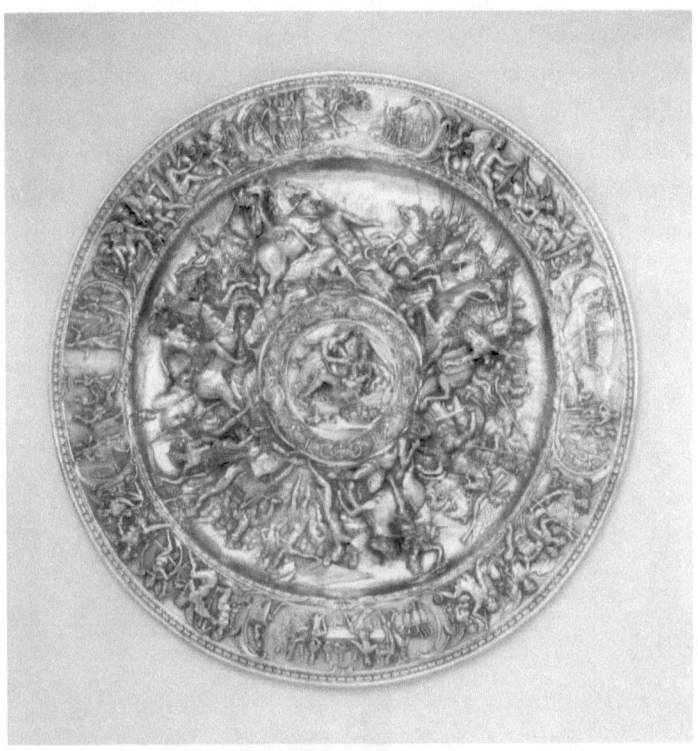

Strozzi silver basin with scenes from the life of Cleopatra. From a sketch by
Bernardo Strozzi (1581-1644) possibly modelled by Francesco Fanelli (circa
1590-1653). Probably made by unknown Dutch silversmith. Genoa, Liguria,
about 1620-25. Museum number 88.DG.61. Dimensions 75.6 cm. This is a
masterpiece of Renaissance silver-working. Parts cast separately were modelled
in the wax and then cut away for lost-wax casting before being reattached to the
hammered silver basin with silver-copper alloy solder. Photograph by courtesy
of the J. Paul Getty Trust. Purchased from Carlo Montanaro of Panama and
Geneva (Choose the best tax-free locations?). On the shipping invoice is "Ex
Christa Brenner Bonini, Geneva" This seems to be a non-existent person. The
seller had taken silicon-rubber molds to make a copy for themselves.

I was able to publish the basin in one of my articles later on. In
the meantime, I took the opportunity to see a few other examples
of Renaissance silver basins in other museum collections, from
New York to Liverpool. There was only one conclusion from
this small study: the *Strozzi silver basin* purchased by the Getty
was of the highest quality artistically and the best example in the
world of a Renaissance silver decorative bowl.

The other issue at that time which would not go away was quite daft, and that concerned the painting by Dieric Bouts, *The Annunciation*. The problem was that several art historians, especially in the UK, thought the Bouts picture a fake. The *Annunciation* had been painted in Louvain around 1450. Bouts sometimes painted in distemper rather than oil.

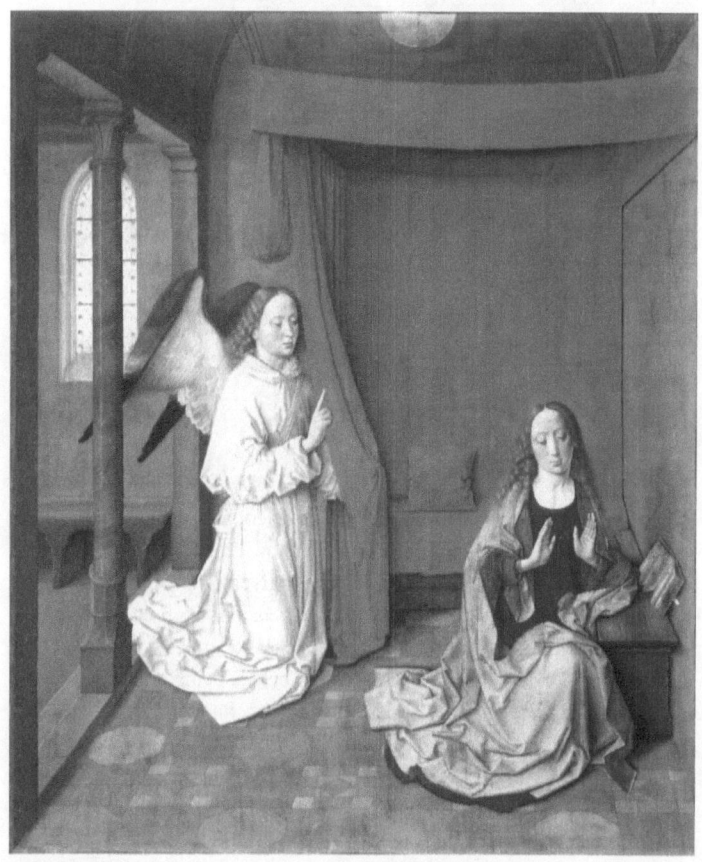

Dieric Bouts, The Annunciation, Bouts lived from about 1415-1476, in the Netherlands. The painting was made in Louvain, Belgium, about 1450-1455, Distemper on Linen, Museum Number 85.PA.24. Dimensions 90 cm x 74.6 cm. Photograph by courtesy of the J. Paul Getty Trust. Purchased from Artemis Fine Art, London; Harari and Johns Ltd., London and the late Eugene Thaw, New York.

What is distemper? Well, essentially it is painting in a glue medium, but is that all there is to it? Not quite, as the National Gallery London, distinguishes between the techniques of glue, glue size, or glue-tempera. The National Gallery has a Bouts painting, which is said to be in glue-tempera. Now tempera is an egg medium and usually made from egg yolk after careful separation from the white. Tempera and glue mediums go back a long way into prehistory. Glue is a cheap medium so perhaps that is why Bouts used it; although it often has to be applied warm otherwise the glue or glue-tempera mixed medium gels too quickly, so it was never tremendously popular with Renaissance artists. One of the problems, which art expert Alain Tarica, quoted in Duvet-Robert's article of 1986 in the *Connaissance des Arts,* points out, is the strange amount of red used for the drapery in the Getty picture, which he regards as a fake. Michael Schilling examined this red and it proved to be a vermilion pigment perfectly acceptable for the time of the 15th century AD. We could find nothing wrong with it, nor could Andrea Rothe, our chief Paintings Conservator. The Getty work by Bouts is an authentic masterwork. This is the problem of evaluation of a work of art by one international expert: in art history there may be as many opinions as there are art historians. Some felt the problem with the Bouts was excessive restoration, and others, that there was no problem at all, while some thought it a forgery. In fact, the Getty *Annunciation* forms part of a polytych which includes the *Adoration of the Magi* (in some unknown German private collection); an *Entombment* (National Gallery, London); a *Resurrection* (Norton Simon Museum, Pasadena) and a *Crucifixion* (Musée Royaux des Beaux-Arts, Brussels). It is depressing how the elites of Europe and America have carved up our artistic heritage between them, dispersing masterpieces which deserve to be seen together, instead of greedily grasping them and never letting go. The market forces act to prevent major works of art ever being seen together again, except for some temporary special exhibition when they might be allowed to rejoin their fellows for a few weeks.

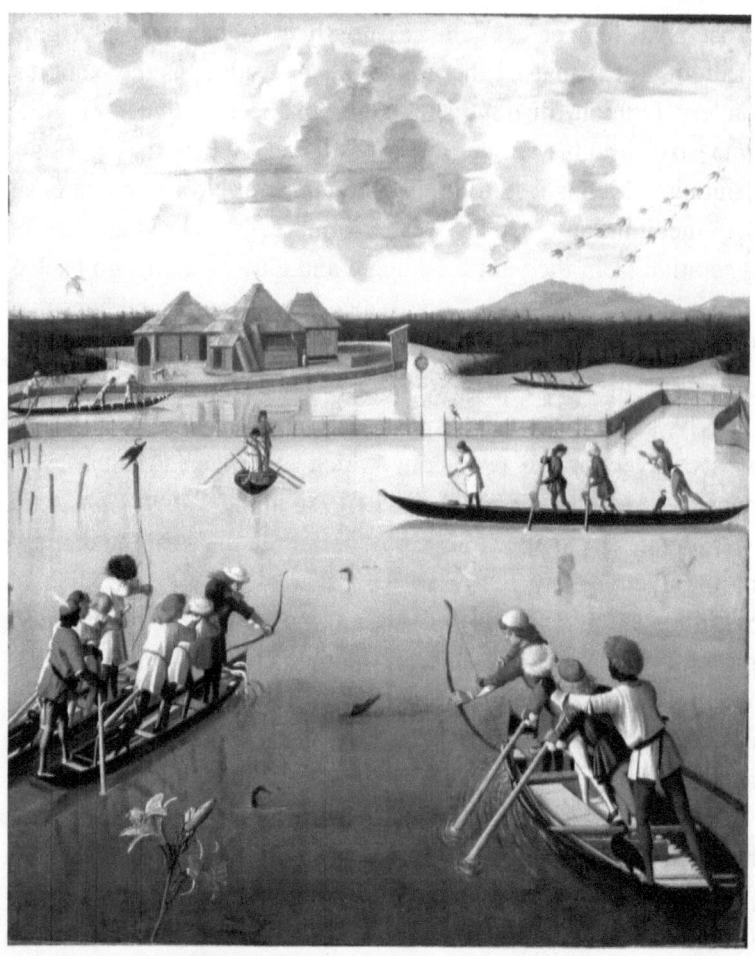

Vittore Carpaccio (circa 1469-1526) Hunting on the Lagoon, about 1490-1495. Oil on panel, Museum no. 79.PB.72. Dimensions 75.6 cm x 63.8 cm. Probably a decorative cabinet door, cut in half, the other half in Venice. An interesting scene of stunned cormorants.

Museums are not keen on presenting a series of panels to one side of their paintings which would make clear what the other paintings look like or where they are, or how they are related or even what the others add to the pictorial unity of the whole work. Sometimes the Predella of a painting is in one country and the principal painting in another: sometimes even the Predella has been dismembered into five separate small panels. Drawing attention to all of this in a museum setting is held to be inimical to artistic appreciation. I contend that this is rubbish, and that the public would be entranced to learn more about the complete work of art and not have to travel to Pasadena, Germany, London, Malibu, and Brussels to understand better the entire conception of which the Annunciation is a part. That is a tension between the awe one is supposed to feel in front of one unique work as opposed to having the experience degraded by looking at a large illustrative panel with all five works reproduced in high quality to enable one to better appreciate what Bouts achieved. Some paintings have even been chopped in half, such as the marvellous Carpaccio, *Hunting on the Lagoon* in the Getty, the other half of the painting being in Venice.

This painting, or the half of it in the Getty, has an amusing aside, as a previous restorer had painted in an arrow that one of the Nobles on the boat was shooting at a cormorant. Except that there was no arrow. When Andrea Rothe was cleaning and retouching the work it was discovered that a small ball was actually being fired at the cormorant, and no arrow. It was a small terracotta ball, designed to stun the cormorant, which would then be taken to a recuperation shed by the attendants, and more cormorants released onto the Lagoon for the aristocrats to shoot at. Andrea Rothe painted over the arrow and revealed the terracotta ball. The cut half of the painting in Venice shows bored-looking women with their dogs, probably having to sit and watch for hours, who are actually observing the lagoon scene from the balcony, while the men play with their lagoon cormorant shooting below. Even here, no effort is made by either museum to have a full-sized replica of what the completed work would actually look like on display, which in the case of this painting by Carpaccio, which is of modest size, would be easy to do, given the superlative digital copies that can be made nowadays.

At the same time at the Bouts controversy was quelled, or perhaps a little later on, another major controversy erupted concerning the *Getty Kouros*, a standing striding figure carved in a dolomitic marble of dubious provenance and dubious authenticity. Fortunately for us, the GCI had chosen to hire a famous geologist, the late Stanley Margolis, to examine the patina of this previously unknown marvel, rather than rely on Michael Schilling and myself, as we might have been out of our depth. Margolis used power x-ray diffraction and determined that the patina was of calcite, and that a process known as "dedolomatization" has occurred, taken the magnesium out of the patina constituents and leaving calcite behind. As a result, an impressive array of experiments was set up at the GCI with the aim of showing that dedolomatization of dolomite would result in a patina of calcite. Jerry Podany conducted a series of experiments to see what effects a variety of chemicals would have on marble and dolomite coupons. Frank Preusser was intensely interested in the experimental work which had been constructed at the GCI, and Luis Monreal, the charismatic director of the GCI at the time, used to bring important guests around the labs for them to gawp at the fascinating array of vials, tubes, flasks and bubbling gases. These experiments went on for some time, with totally inconclusive results.

In the meantime, we had purchased our own x-ray powder diffraction unit at the Getty Villa, where we used to run samples which still needed a darkroom, special 35mm film and the usual washing and drying of a strip of film which then had to be read by hand. My God, it was laborious compared with what we can do with powder x-ray diffraction machines today in the digital world, when a complete study might take five minutes.

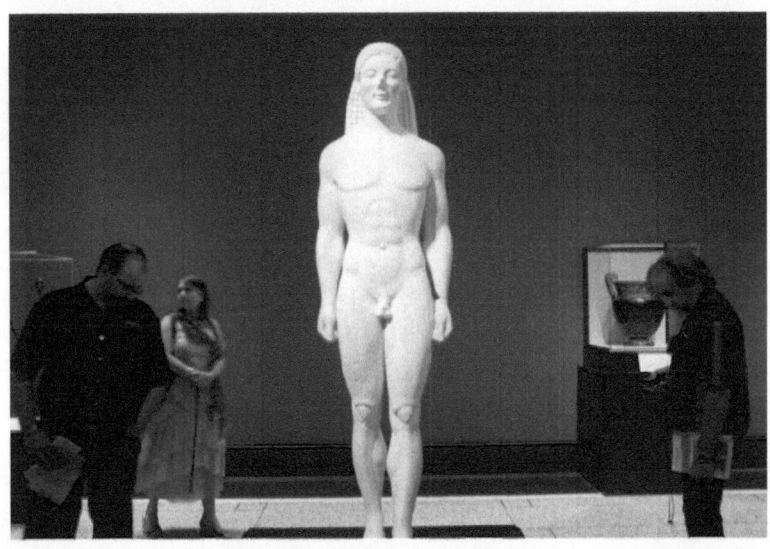

The Getty Dolomitic Limestone Kouros. On display at the Getty Museum in 2017 shortly before its demise into a storage box. A full scientific study awaits, but not anytime soon as the current Getty curators believe it to be a forgery. This needs to be corroborated, Purchased in the 1980's for 9 million dollars, about 22 million dollars in todays money. Note how museum visitors are keen to read the explanatory labels.

Anyway, we had taken a sample of the *Kouros* patina and ran that in our diffraction machine: several hours later, to our surprise a complex series of lines were obtained, far too complex to be calcite. We worked out that this was, in fact, calcium oxalate, aka whellewite. The entire premise on which the GCI dedolomitization experiments, costing hundreds of thousands of dollars, had been based, was completely false. So how had this disaster come about? The problem was the confirmation of the calcite crust by that blasted, wonderful, electron microprobe machine again. What had happened was that the beam current used by the same operator as before was too high and had decomposed the calcium oxalate crust into calcite, thereby confirming the completely erroneous result of Professor Stanley Margolis, whose work had even formed the basis of a much-lauded article in Scientific American, which we had showed was completely wrong.

171

What a shame that the work was so flawed. Now, another series of experiments were doggedly pursued by Jerry Podany and Eduardo Sanchez at the Conservation labs to try to match the complexity of the oxalate crust. Meanwhile, Jeffery Spier, not a great admirer of the scientific method, had discovered another dolomitic *kouros* in Switzerland which bore a resemblance to the *Getty Kouros*.

International consternation followed, especially at the Getty Museum, since it had been discovered that the provenance data for the *Getty Kouros* had been faked. It was not looking good. Faith in the science began to ebb away when the art historians heard that the patina was not an example of dedolomitization at all, but was an oxalate patina, which is a common alteration product on ancient and historic stone artefacts. We call that kind of patina the *scialbatura*, especially that found on Roman Imperial Marbles.

Jerry Podany was able to show that a simple acid bath had been used to try to age the feeble version found by Spier, and was nothing like the *Getty Kouros*. Nevertheless, the Getty purchased it for study purposes and it made its way to Malibu. The great strength of the scientific method is that it is able to question or reassess evidentiary matters to arrive at a new conclusion. This may entail the evidence itself being questioned and hence the scientific connoisseurship of the artifact or art object can advance another stage further

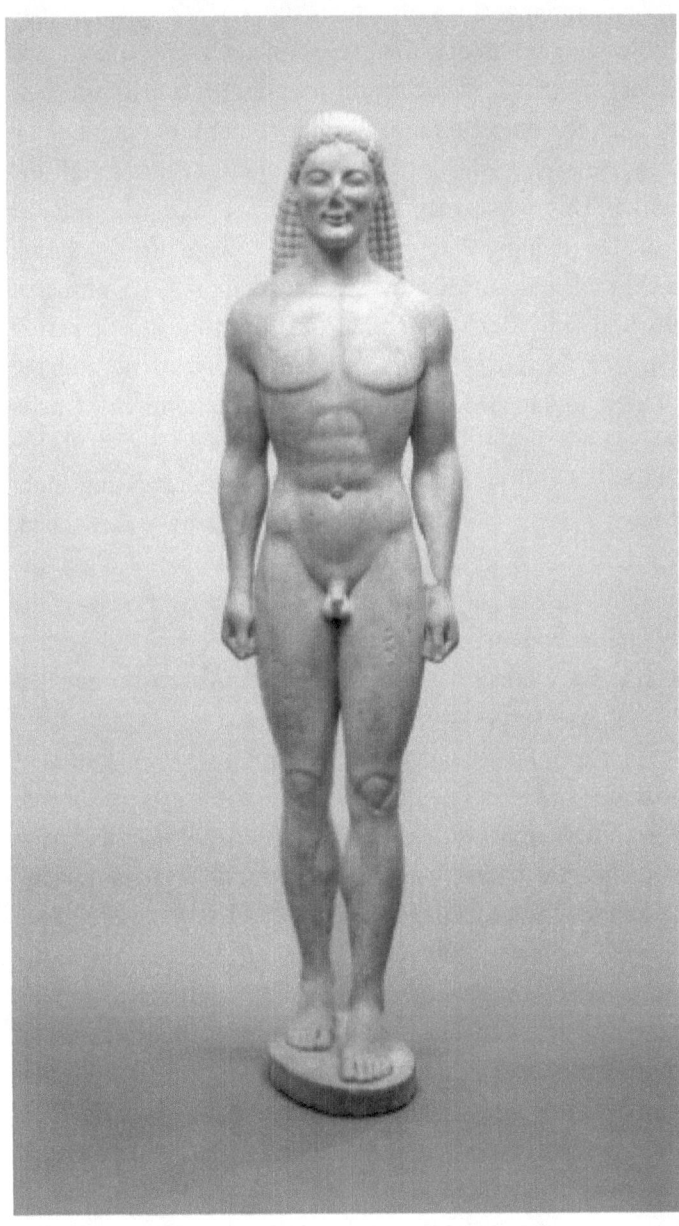

The Getty Kouros. Dated from 530 BC or possibly not. No-one knows for sure. Purchased for 9 million dollars in the 1980's. Now on view by appointment only. That means with considerable difficulty.

Art historians fared even worse than the scientists, since they were unable to agree among themselves if the *Getty kouros* was authentic or not, and some of these disagreements will never be resolved. Just to complete the miserable picture, the publication devoted to the *Getty kouros* was inadequate, insubstantial and inconclusive. This was partly the fault of the GCI who left the writing of the complete report of many years to Dr. Frank Preusser. Frank had already overextended himself in virtue of his duties and activities in running and directing the Scientific Department of the GCI and its numerous projects around the world, which included the restoration of the tomb of *Queen Nefertari*. Frank simply did not have time to do justice to the kind of detailed and precise report-writing encompassing eight years of work that the *Getty Kouros* story would have demanded. Perhaps there was a tinge of embarrassment in revealing the errors which had occurred in the scientific work, and the difficulty Jerry Podany and Eduardo Sanchez had in getting anything like the oxalate patina found on the *Kouros* to develop on their laboratory samples.

No full explanation of the error in determining what the patina of the *Kouros* was has ever been made, which did leave one or two percipient art historians asking what or why or when it had been discovered that the patina was of the common oxalate variety, and what had the science actually revealed? That was 1995 or so: time to revisit the entire subject in 2019, but whether the Getty has the guts to do it is debatable: the simpler solution is to take the striking statue off display and consign it to the oblivion of museum storage. That is the preferred strategy of the museum world: remove the fakes from exhibition, pack them in their storage boxes or crates so that they can only be opened or moved by professional preparators, and take them to the basement to languish in the hope that after several decades, the world will have forgotten their existence, like the (in)famous Boston Throne. The museum visitor or even specialist will have moved on to other problems, deflecting further criticism or ridicule of the museum concerned. This is what happens across the world: at the National Gallery, the Louvre, the British Museum, the

Berlin Museums, the Metropolitan Museum and the Getty Museum. Some works are reputed not to be allowed to be seen by outsiders, even if they are scholars, such as the magnificent and huge Etruscan warriors, once the pride of the Metropolitan Museum, on display for decades, which were discovered to have been made by two quite young Italian restorers and fakers, sometime before the First World War. The works had been authenticated by Dietrich von Bothmer and Gisela Richter at the Metropolitan Museum, two of the foremost scholars of their generation, but their opinions were mistaken: the Etruscan warriors were outright fakes.

The *Getty Kouros* story is not quite finished: the problem is that it is very hard to resuscitate the reputation of a work of art once it has been condemned by the experts. Time will tell, but time is mitigated by further work on the problem and comprehensive publication, so we may all have to be very patient as my memos suggesting the need for another international meeting on the *Kouros* question has fallen on deaf ears: too many red faces in the offing. The next round is therefore being quietly pursued by the indefatigable John Twilley, who used to be the scientist at LACMA before he resigned and went into private practice on the East Coast. Yes, that was another excellent scientist the West Coast managed to loose. We shall have to wait some time before a concerted effort, costing hundreds of thousands of dollars is made again for the sake of the *Kouros*.

An interesting case arose with two remarkable silver plates, unique in the world, which were reputed to have been found in the sea off the coast of Gaza. These large silver plates, the *Fisherman plate* and the *Philosopher plate*, currently on display at the Getty Villa, dating to the early centuries AD, had strange surfaces depicting in the case of the *Fisherman plate*, an aged fisherman removing his catch from a hook, with accompanying fishy detail of lobster pots and fish. The philosopher plate shows two philosophers engaged in a debate on the nature of the world, with a globe on a tripod stand between them, egged on by female accomplices. One is Hermes, putting forth a mystical interpretation of reality and the other is Ptolemy, arguing for a rational explanation. Both are fabricated in apparently worked and hammered silver on the front, with completely flat surfaces on the back. Now, if one hammers and shapes silver to produce raised or depressed areas for the design on the front, then the rough indications of that process, called repoussé, can be seen on the back. So how come the back is flat? There are three possibilities: the silver plates are cast to shape; they are of double construction of two sheets of silver adhered or soldered together, or they are worked and shaped from the front by carving or hammering on a flat anvil. To try to answer these questions a small sample was cut from the edge and we used metallographic examination to get some further answers.

I should say that I had become something of an expert in the subject of metallography and have run a Summer School in Ancient and Historic Metals in a variety of university and museum sites since 1983, including Lucknow, Washington DC., New York, London, Le-Chaux de Fronds, Padua, Hastings and Los Angeles, and am still teaching this in my retirement in Hastings in 2019, to a full house and now again in Hastings in 2019 and for the foreseeable future.

The folk who attend are occasionally Professors themselves, or Ph.D. students, mid-career professionals in conservation or conservation science, or metalsmiths and occasionally art dealers. I have built up, through my own research, donated samples from others, those which have been begged, found, made, or borrowed or bought on eBay or through private contacts or dealers or museum scientists, the world's greatest collection of mounted metallographic samples, from the Tower of London to the White House Library, From Sandal Castle in Yorkshire to the edge of Alaska, from Thailand to Panama. My geographic spread encompasses: Ecuador, Colombia, Peru, North America, Japan, Java, China, Hungary, Egypt, Greece, Jordan, Iran, Iraq, Switzerland, Austria, France, Ireland, England and Germany.

Anyway, back to this particular problem with the silver plates. The mounted metallographic sample showed that the silver had not been cast to shape, nor was it of double sheet construction. That left the possibility that it had been carved to shape on the surface by principally cutting away the silver with chisels from the front. Further detailed work was undertaken using x-rays to penetrate through the silver to take a look at the entire structure of the object and see how it was joined to the ring foot. A detailed chemical analysis was carried out together with a full comparison with the exiguous and comparable silver plates which were only shaped by working at the front: the Mildenhall Treasure at the British Museum, and a *Neptune Plate,* in New York. Things seemed manageable and tranquil, when suddenly art historian Anthony Cutler announced that the Fisherman plate was a forgery and that the Philosopher plate had to be Renaissance not Byzantine from the early centuries AD, as the Getty had thought. How the hell had he arrived at these conclusions? Well, he insisted that the depiction of the Fisherman's rod had a reel, which was unknown until centuries later, and in any case it was a forgery; the Philosopher plate depicted a book with a closure, unknown before the Renaissance, the globe was also unknown in the early centuries AD, the subject matter could only have been depicted in the Renaissance, and clearly the entire plate was only possible in the later Renaissance. We had an exchange of views which went on for a while: at one conference where Cutler and one of the female Getty Conservators were present in the early 1990's, Cutler asked her "Has that David Scott seen sense yet?"

He and I continued to trade opinions, with one of the issues of the Getty Museum Journal containing a 40 page article by Cutler, setting out his view on the two plates, and a 28 page article by myself, setting out my own view. The idea that the Fisherman plate was a modern forgery was totally absurd: the whole thing was heavily corroded, in quite a state of advanced decay, and we never find this kind of corrosion in a large silver object from the Renaissance. There was some bromine present, from the time of its sea burial, it was gilded in parts, had been carved to shape, had no known parallels, had not cost a fortune, and could not possibly be modern.

The silver grains of this plate were so embrittled by the precipitation of copper at the boundaries, that they were disaggregated and separating by themselves. A sign of real age, real corrosion and real burial: there was no way this silver object could possibly be a forgery. By the time the Renaissance comes round, the working of a precious metal such as silver had become fairly standardized. The thin plate would be worked over stakes or anvils, beaten and raised, but never carved to shape and treated like a piece of carvable stone.

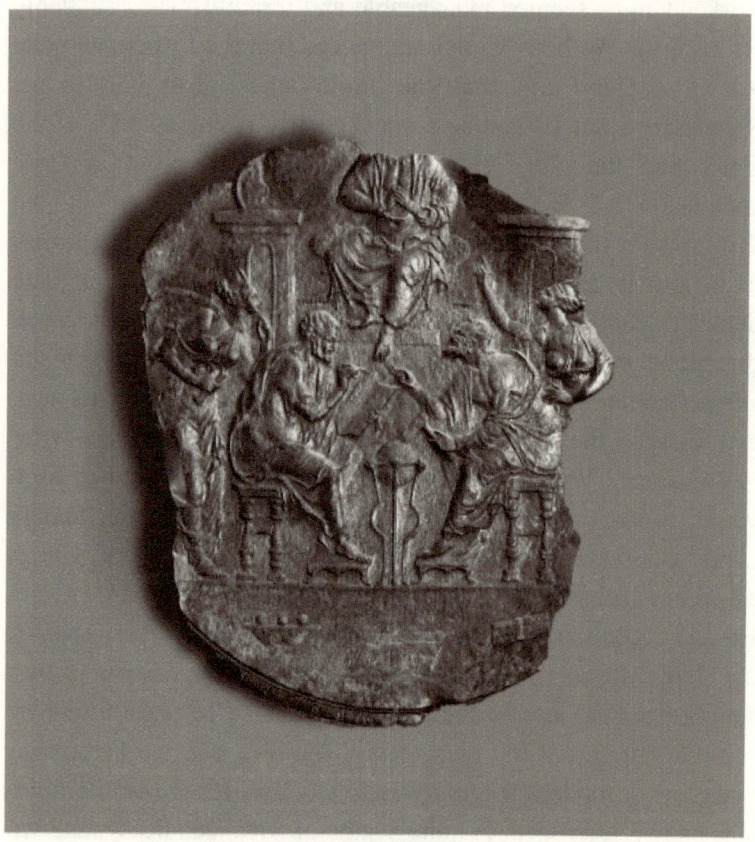

Philosopher Plate, Byzantine, Eastern Mediterrean, 500-600 AD, Museum Number 83.AM.342. Dimensions 45 cm x 28 cm   Weight 5.6162 lbs. Inscriptions:  name of Hermes, Ptolemos, Skepsis, in Greek.  Secondary inscription is of a group of five Greek characters along the edge of the rim. Photograph by courtesy of the J. Paul Getty Trust. Obtained from the Galerie Nefer, Zurich, in 1983.

This is the problem of making judgments concerning authenticity solely by style. True, there can be problems going purely by science: one only has to read of the acumen of the highly talented conservator and art restorer, the late Hubertus von Sonnenberg at the Doerner Institute, who recognised that some German expressionist works were fake, when the rest of his scientific staff could find nothing wrong with them, and we are talking here of highly trained art scientists, but von Sonnenberg was proved right. Von Sonnenburg arranged for some genuine works by the artist to be displayed in the Doerner Institute along with the works he felt were fakes. The scientists gradually noticed that the feel of the fakes was slightly rougher and slightly dirtier compared with the genuine works. Von Sonnenburg was proved right, as he usually was about these things. He published, and the forger, a Mr. Goller came forward. Mr Goller said that he could fool any scientific test the Doerner Institute scientists could use, and that if he had wanted the lead isotope signature to be correct, he would simply have made his own lead white from ground up clock weights of the right age. An interesting story recounted by the late Thomas Hoving, the former director of the Metropolitan Museum. Scientific connoisseurship, which is essentially what is needed to evaluate the scientific facets of art objects, is not the same as invoking a purely scientific empiricism. Pure scientists, expert in their own field have too narrow a perspective to really grapple with art objects in any comprehensive way. They are useful when a detailed isotopic analysis is required, for example, but it is the scientific connoisseur who then puts that in the context of the different lead isotopic signatures for lead white grounds in Italian or Dutch pictures, and combines that information with the frame, pigments, ground, media, varnish, restoration history and labels.

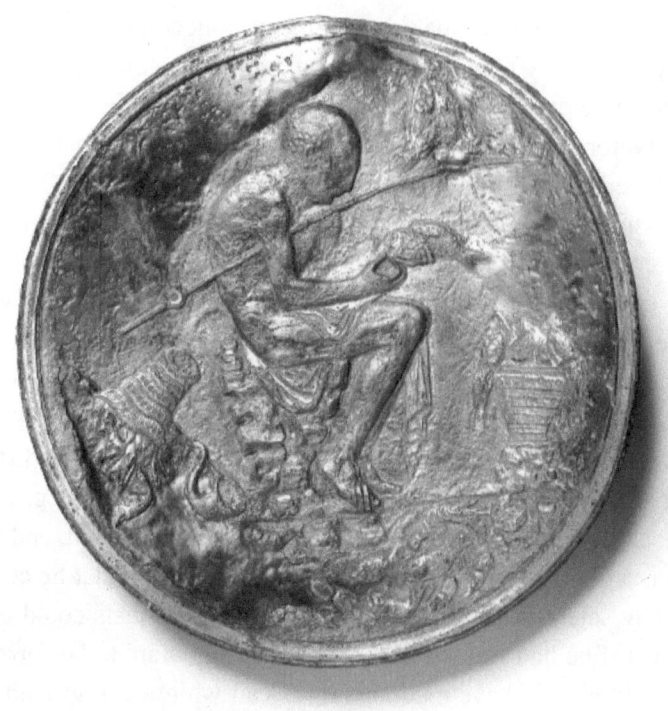

Silver plate with cut decoration showing an ancient fisherman removing his catch from a hooked line. A forgery according to Dr. Anthony Cutler. Byzantine according to most other experts. Eastern Mediterranen 500-600 AD. Silver with gilding. Museum No 83.AM.347. Diameter 41.3 cm. Unique in the world. Obtained from the Galerie Nefer, Zurich 1983.

The connoisseurship which is essential for judgement consists in: a knowledge of the pigments, binding media and varnishes of old paintings and how to characterize them; what kinds of characterization make sense for the case at hand; what impurities have any significance in ancient metals and why; what corrosion products can be expected and how to analyse them; the chemical composition of metals and how they were extracted and made in different historical and geographical areas. Additional areas include: how to date wood, what can be expected from a thermoluminescence study of pottery, how radiocarbon dating works and much else besides.

However, trying to authenticate 20th century German expressionist pictures, which is obviously a tricky number, is not the same as deciding if a piece of silver is old or modern. We have so much more to go on with silver that is old. A postscript to this story is that, a few years later, one of the conservation graduate interns in Getty Antiquities Conservation, employing zeroradiography, found the traces of a floral pattern on the back of the *Philosopher plate* which is invisible to the naked eye. A very careful drawing was made of this design, and it was sent for comment to Anthony Cutler. He pronounced that the plate could not then be Renaissance but must have been recarved, which is absurd, as the corrosion and surface features of the plate are not in any way suggestive of recarving, and besides carving in itself makes no sense as far as silver is concerned for these later periods. OK, sometimes we scientists get things wrong, scientific connoisseurship is not infallible by any means, but I think this postscript shows that we were the ones on terra firma here, not the art historian.

It is the ignorance of some art historians concerning the limits of scientific evaluation which leads to the inane conclusion that science is of no use whatever compared with the eye of someone like the late Hubertus von Sonnenberg. Not that this genius met with much approval from his fellow Bavarian art historians with lesser insight, when he pronounced a couple of pictures on display in the Bavarian State Museums to be forgeries. The refusal by the Bavarian authorities to investigate further may be one of the reasons why von Sonnenberg left the Doerner Institute and returned to the United States to become Head of Paintings Conservation at the Metropolitan Museum of Art, where he sorted out another couple of complex potential forgeries. To have this degree of dedication to rooting out problems of this kind is unusual and is not now encouraged in museum work: the quiet life is an easier option with the museum administrators these days and much more PC.

Even some authenticating bodies such as that for the works of Andy Warhol in New York, refuse to even look at suspect works presented to them because of the legal ramifications if they get it wrong: safer to just work with museum collections of known provenance and history rather than be sued for 60 million dollars by some disgruntled collector.

Working as Head of the Museum Services Laboratory at the Getty Villa was a plum job. I had the idea to begin to invite interns and researchers to come to the Getty Villa Lab, and a few years later, our CEO, the Head of the Trust, Harold Williams, sent out a memo requesting proposals for projects that could be directly funded by the Trust that would bring two of the various Getty entities together. I think he was concerned that there was too much internecine rivalry between the various Getty entities rather than collaboration between them, and he had a point.

I proposed a collaborative research project on Renaissance bronzes, which would be between the Getty Conservation Institute and the Getty Museum, and much to my surprise I got a memo from Harold Williams himself to say that the project, with a budget of 200,000 dollars had been approved. This was very exhilarating: now I could hire a researcher based at the Getty Villa lab who would be dedicated to this interesting and under-researched topic. Francesca Bewer had still not finished her PhD from my old home at UCL and so she was the obvious candidate, since she had been working with the V&A on a casting project of the God Mars, by Giambologna. We were able to borrow several Renaissance bronzes from the collections at the Huntingdon as well as the Getty, and a fine piece of work was eventually completed by Dr. Bewer, although to my regret, she has still not published the full account of everything that was achieved: it languishes in her PhD thesis, which you would have to go Senate House library of UCL to read in a restricted area. Stringent measures are taken with these unpublished PhD theses to keep them in libraries under wraps, although if they are made available as on-line documents, which many American PhD's are, then so much the better: it does not advance scholarship to have all of this stuff secreted away.

Through Dr. Lynn Schwartz Dodd at USC, I had also begun to train a few students of hers at the Getty lab in the analysis of artefacts from the small museum based at USC, in the Department of Religion. Dr. Arie Wallert, a talented paintings and dye expert from Amsterdam had joined me, and Joris Dik, also from the Netherlands had begun a serious career change to art scientist, and he was working in the Villa lab too, as was Ran Boytner, finishing up his Andean dye project work for his PhD. At this time in the 1990's, the GCI took in no students and no interns: When I asked why that was, I was told that the staff at the GCI HQ in Marina del Rey were too busy working on projects to waste time dealing with the kind of students and researchers I had working at the Villa Lab. I just sagely nodded agreement with the senior staff view at the GCI while thinking: what a load of crap. You can imagine the surprise of a visitor from the GCI HQ, when they anticipated seeing a couple of GCI staff members working at the Villa, as they entered the door of the lab to be confronted with an African-American USC student, Dr. Francesca Bewer, Dr. Arie Wallert, Dr. Joris Dik, Dr. Ran Boytner, myself, a part-time secretary, and another intern all beavering away in a lab where only two GCI staff were actually employed! Yes! A part-time secretary! When I had started at the Museum Lab back in 1987, Dr. Frank Preusser only had Michael Schilling and the secretary down at the Getty Villa, so when I joined, I had the luxury of secretarial assistance as well. Our secretary was Ruth Feldman, something of an expert on documentary film production, which may be why she had ended up in Malibu from New Jersey. She had a rent-controlled apartment on 11th street in Santa Monica, so was only eleven streets from the Beach. Her rent was about 180 dollars a month, so she could easily survive well on her part-time Getty employment and live in Santa Monica into the bargain! This is not that long ago, and she stayed there until around 1995. It is extraordinary, given what has happened in the UK that both New York and Los Angeles still have rent controlled apartments going for such tiny rents! Try finding a one-bedroom apartment in Brighton for a rent of 140 quid a month. They are about 900 quid a month, and I chose Brighton, as it has the young flavour that Santa Monica has now, by the sea. Now who would have thought that the US of A would display more socialist principles than the Brits, given that there are still hundreds of thousands of rent controlled or rent stabilized properties in the big apple?

This socialist streak for subsidized or cheap housing which has lasted in North America since the 1920's in one of the most expensive cities in the world, is still going in 2019, practically one hundred years later. One of our friends in Venice, California, is still living in rent controlled housing a couple of hundred yards from Abbot Kinney Boulevard, a feat increasingly rare if not impossible if you think of repeating that event a couple of hundred yards from Bond Street, the nearest UK equivalent that springs to mind.

Back at the Museum lab, the management would not have been happy about all of this work going on, especially as the GCI spurned interns at this stage, to discover that David Scott had created some sort of mini-empire giving work to students, education for researchers, opportunities to experiment with under-used equipment, getting money from the Trust directly, and being involved with various projects connected to microscopy, dyes, metallic microstructures and mineral corrosion products.

This is one of the problems of the Getty: it is all about the careful management of resources, endless meetings, planning documents, project design and strategic goals. The kind of organic growth that I prefer could not be tolerated, and which began to lead to subtle conflicts with the establishment, for that is what happens to organizations like the Getty. There is so much money going around and so little need to actually produce anything, that the whole circus can rotate by itself, spinning away, and sending out messages about further planning meetings and focus groups or retreats that might have to be held off-site at an expensive hotel or resort. Meanwhile, publications streamed out of our lab at a unit cost a fraction of that spent by GCI HQ. I did run into trouble with some private work that I began to do at this time, and this had perhaps taken things too far, although there were some interesting scientific enquiries that one simply had to undertake, such as telling nutty Americans that they did not have a brass plaque which proved that Sir Francis Drake had landed on the American shores: the Drake plate was a phony.

There is one external request that I never regret having said yes to: I got a telephone call from a collector who said he had a bronze plaque from Argentina and could I authenticate it for him. Now, these cast plaques from preHispanic Argentina are among the most under-valued masterworks of ancient South American bronze castings. Go to Google and see if you can find one of the type I mean with raised and recessed intricate geometric design, intaglio and repoussé if you like, the only examples made in ancient South America. I told him this was impossible as they were extremely rare and seldom seen outside of Argentina, and that his piece must be a fake. He persisted and said he had obtained it himself in Argentina: I relented and he brought it in for me to evaluate. I was astonished to find that the more I studied the plaque, the more authentic it seemed: there could be no doubt. I reported back to the delighted collector, and since that day, sometime in 1993, I have never seen another in the flesh or ever heard anyone singing the praises of this superlative work of the preHispanic Indians of Argentina which are truly artistic masterworks in bronze.

Some of this additional work was connected to Getty interests in one way or the other as well, since a few of the Trustees were themselves art collectors, and I was involved in looking at one or two of their private artworks during that time, and giving them advice or carrying out a thermoluminescence dating for them, so it was not clearly delineated as to the limits of our activities.

There were strange connections between all of these events. I knew of Dr. Roxanne M. Brown because of my brief acquaintance with the Markell's art gallery on La Brea Avenue, an archetypical Los Angeles road, traversing several neighborhoods from Pico to Beverly Hills. At the Gallery I was shocked to be shown a tibia with two or three typical Ban Chang bronze bracelets still in situ. Apparently this was all due to the activities of a Robert Olson, who for years had imported a container of Thai antiquities and works of art which would be sold to local galleries or museums. Probably when he started, no-one gave any thought to the problems created and even august figures in the Museum and Universities of the area, were reputed to visit the container, to see for themselves the latest trawl of artworks from Thailand. My occasional TL dating work for Getty Museum Trustees and Galleries had brought me that day to La Brea avenue, not long before a tragic turn of events would result in the death of Roxanne M. Brown, alone and having died in great pain, on the floor of her detention cell in Seattle. Who was Dr. Roxanne M. Brown? She was the Director of the Bangkok University's Southeast Asian Ceramics Museum, and a much-published international expert on Thai ceramics who had lived on a pittance in Thailand for decades, and she was getting worried about her monetary situation as she was getting older with a son to look after. In 2004, encouraged by Professor Bob Brown (no relation), Roxanne enrolled for a PhD from my own home department at UCLA, the Department of Art History and graduated in 2004, a year after I started at UCLA. Due to Robert Olsen and other nefarious importers, the FBI raided, on 15th January 2008, the Los Angeles County Museum of Art, the Pacific Asia Museum, in Pasadena, the Bowers Museum in Santa Ana and the Mingei International Museum in San Diego. Brown was charged with wire fraud in May 2008 after arriving at the University of Washington to present a lecture on Thai ceramics. Considered a flight risk, this international criminal mastermind (sic) was incarcerated in the Federal Detention Center in SeaTac and, being denied any medical attention, died in agony in her own vomit and excrement. Her heath was so fragile, she should probably never have been detained at all. The few relatives of Roxanne sued the Federal Government who admitted liability for flagrant neglect and settled the case for $880,000. If Dr. Brown was responsible for any wire fraud regarding the authentication of Thai ceramics or their appraised value, the total monetary benefit involved for her was way less than $100,000!

So let me see, the needless death of Roxanne M. Brown ended up costing the Federal Government eight times or more of the total amount of alleged wire fraud. And what happened at the various museums which were raided by the FBI? As far as one can tell, nothing happened at all to the curators and administrators. The return of much looted material to Thailand did take place as a result of these raids, about which the various museums have been completely silent. In 2015,Jonathan Markell was arrested and sentenced to 18 months in federal prison. So that was the end of that saga. But the entire area of Thailand, Laos, Cambodia and Vietnam is one rife with stolen and smuggled art of every description, and now, thanks to eBay, huge numbers of fakes, replicas, and forgeries, all of which helps to protect the real antiquities from continual looting. For some of these high-end ceramics, who can tell the difference between the genuine antiquity and the sophisticated forgery? The answer is that perceptually there may be no difference as the correct clays and even old straw tempers have been used in the fabrication of some ceramics in old molds That is the subject of another story, to which the interested reader is referred to my book "Art: Authenticity, Restoration, Forgery".

We would also look at things for other museums from time to time as they might send us a special request, or as part of some wider project. The museums that we advised included: The Museum of the American Indian, Heye Foundation (later the National Museum of the American Indian); the Dean and Chapter of St. Paul's Cathedral; The Royal Collection, Windsor Castle; The National Art Collection of Romania; The Cleveland Museum of Art; Los Angeles County Museum of Art; The San Diego Museum of Man; Santa Barbara Museum of Natural History, and even the Metropolitan museum once sent me some contentious solid cast Greek silver statue for my opinion, to see if it backed up the view of their experienced and very knowledgeable Museum scientist and art connoisseur, Dick Stone, who had to look at scores of potential acquisitions for the Met every month. Dick Stone had been taken on to do a PhD degree, which he did not finish because he then started another one, which also was never completed, but what an education he contrived for himself in the process. He wrote little, but two or three of his papers are minor masterpieces which have been highly influential.

One of the interesting projects I did get involved with was the Infinite Column by Constantin Brăncuşi, his masterpiece at Tărgu-Jiu, Romania. Why Tărgu-Jiu? The answer is the extraordinary dedication and desire to memorialize the elders, women and children who died defending the bridge at Tărgu-Jiu from the advancing German army in October 1916, when the Romanian government had switched sides from the Germans to the Axis. The reasons for that are all very complicated and connected to the power of the old and interesting Austro-Hungarian Empire. At a high human cost, the Romanians did manage to halt the German advance, by which time many of the children were dead. By the 1930's the mothers of the dead had raised enough money to buy a strip of land in the town and they had the inspired idea to ask Brăncuşi to design a monument in honor of their dead. Brăncuşi would accept no money for the commission himself. So, how many contemporary artists in the UK and the USA were asked to produce commemorative monuments to the war dead of the First World War by a group of mothers or other individuals and who refused to accept any money, creating in the process an extraordinary modernist work of art which stretched through the town? I am guessing none: all of the monuments were either state, county or government funded, sometimes a depiction of toiling soldiers, perhaps an inscription of the names and regiments of the dead, sometimes the battle they fell in, and their age, if the latter is mentioned at all, or at best a *Victory of Samothrace* with wings lofting the departed heroes to an unlikely Greek embrace with the Goddess Nike, the Greek Goddess of victory.

Brăncuşi, on the other hand, conceived of a tripartite sculpture through the town, from a *Table of Silence*, through a *Gate of Kisses*, to the *Infinite Column* beyond, linked in a Pythagorean geometry in a right-angled triangle formed from the table, to the gate, and the *Infinite Column*, one mile in the distance and nearly 100 feet in height. Amazingly, Brăncuşi had first proposed a series of twelve sculptures, of which the three mentioned above were completed in the late-1930s. If the twelve had been possible, that would really have put Tărgu-Jiu on the map! The *Gate of Kisses* is an impressive limestone arch composed of highly abstracted versions of embracing figures, and is a masterpiece befitting the superlative infinite column.

The tripartite work is a poignant reminder of the Romanian roots of Brăncuşi and it was extraordinary that he was such a prominent modernist. Brăncuşi had been born in 1876, in a small village in the foothills of the Carpathians, not far from Tărgu-Jiu. He showed a talent for woodwork. As a young man, Brăncuşi moved from folk art to the international avant-garde but always managed to retain a sense of his origins. Brăncuşi had made his way first to a school of crafts, then to art school in Bucharest and finally there is the almost mythological story of him walking, on foot from Romania to Paris. Brăncuşi worked as a finisher and carver for the production centre that Rodin's workshop turned into, where numerous versions of the same work by the master could be produced for the buyers across the world in marble or metal, from Rodin's clay or plaster original. Brăncuşi left, with the famous phase, that "Nothing grows in the shadow of great trees" and for a while, earned his living washing up dishes in a Parisian restaurant, rather than suffer artistic exhaustion.

Years later, when Barbara Hepworth was visiting Brăncuşi's studio, she immediately felt the passionate bond between her own artistic work and Brăncuşi, whose studio floor was covered with stone and wood chips from the direct carving that Brăncuşi did himself.

There are many versions of the *Infinite Column*, but only one real instantiation of it that has so deep a meaning, and that is the one in Tărgu-Jiu. It is a pity that the huge *Infinite Column* in Tărgu-Jiu and its sixteen and a half large rhomboid beads has been visited by only a handful of people, and is impossible to photograph as the eye can see it in the flesh: this giant work has to be seen in the flesh otherwise it is just a two-dimensional abstraction in a coffee-table art book.

The *Infinite Column* is the problem: it consists of a mild steel spine, on which are threaded, like giant beads, sixteen elements in cast iron, finished with a thermally sprayed zinc undercoat and finally a brass thermally sprayed finish. The upper bead is half rhomboid to suggest that the work continues for ever, into the atmosphere.

What Sydney Geist in his book on Brâncuşi, published in 1968, has to say about the Infinite Column is as true today as it was fifty years ago. He writes "Marvelous is the fact that the elements of the Column do not diminish in size as they mount. The persistence of size and of shape, the constancy of the repetition, causes the Column to remain near to the mind as it moves off from eye. We have here a poetry of the actual, without illusion or compensation, without tapering or entasis. The tension between the sameness of what is known and the perspectival variety of what is seen is unique in art"

This Column is Brâncuşi's only experience with the concept of a golden reflective finish in the outdoor environment, and the intention of the artist was that the surface would remain shiny, reflective, golden in hue. Instead, the brass began to corrode, the zinc undercoat began to fail in some areas and ugly streaks of ferrous corrosion ran down the surfaces. Graffiti, mostly in chalk, defaced one of the lower modules, and cracked concrete surrounded the base. The broken concrete may have been due to a failed attempt by the communist Romanians to tear the infinite column down in the 1950's, as an example of degenerate abstract art, rather than the socialist realism preferred by their communist masters. Being nearly 100 feet tall, and the same dimensions at the base as at the top, the Romanian engineers did a superlative job in ensuring the structural stability of the massive and unique artwork: it continues for fifteen feet underground in concrete foundations.

Brâncuşi was famous for the superlative finish of his bronze sculptures, such as *Fish*, which is a work displayed indoors, like his superb, thin, *Birds In Space*.

The GCI were approached by art historian Dr. Radu Varia, for help in the conservation of the three artworks. Dr Varia founded the International Brancusi Foundation, whose principal aim was to restore and preserve the *Infinite Column*, the *Table of Silence* and the *Gate of Kisses*. David Hockney and some slinky British actress friend turned up at the Marina del Rey location of the Getty Conservation Institute, as it then was, miles from the Getty Museum, to listen to a very esoteric talk by Radu Varia about Brăncuși, along with the rest of the GCI staff. We were indeed honoured with his presence as he was a friend of Radu Varia, and as Hockney never showed up for anything on offer at the GCI again, apart from the conference we held on Modern Art around 1999, this was a rare sighting. Hockney spoke at the conference, at which I also gave a talk on the *Infinite Column*, and his message was simple: if you love the artwork, then you will strive to keep it. That preservation of art came down to love: love was the only thing that was going to save the art of the present for the future. He is probably right, but it is hard to convince people that love needs money in order to conserve everything we want to keep in the name of love. The other problem being that one group of people might love everything that contemporary art has to offer, and the other group might prefer African folk-art. But you get what he means: the passion to preserve is something that all of us conservators embrace.

Back at the beginning of the project, Dr. Dusan Stulik, then boss of Scientific at the GCI, who had escaped from Czechoslovakia, worked for a while with Dr. Vladimir Kucera at the Swedish Corrosion Institute (SCI), and ended up teaching in America before he joined the GCI in Marina del Rey. He wisely suggested that I team up with the SCI, to form an investigative scientific team to travel to Târgu-Jiu to investigate the environmental, structural and corrosive environment of the Infinite Column. So it was that Dr. Varia arranged to meet us back in Romania to begin the work. Two German photographers had been invited, together with Dr. Kucera and two of his co-workers, and myself. A reception for the assembled guests was held at a small ministry building in Bucharest, not far from where the largest palace in the world had been built for the megalomaniac Ceausescu and his equally appalling wife, who had both been shot in the Romanian revolution only some two years previously. Elena Ceausescu, who had never finished high school or attended university, somehow managed to get a PhD, on the subject of stereospecific isoprene, with a foreword written by Professor Dorothy Crowfoot Hodgkin! It transpired that the PhD on this important chemical had, in fact, been written for her a group of Romanian chemists. Presumably the chemists had not been given much choice in the matter, and Mrs. Ceausescu became Dr. Ceausescu. Our Nobel laureate had no idea that such a fraud was involved. A great pity that more of the world's elite do not hanker after a doctorate in chemistry. The desire for one might do our subject the world of good, and for that we could dish out a few more PhD's to interested politicians.

How typically Romanian that the world's largest palace should be located in Bucharest, rather than America, China or Russia, as being intellectually isolated and partially sidelined their fantasies could assume absurd proportions. The ministry reception that we had been invited to was hurried, as we had a four-hour drive to get to our location near the Infinite Column, and would have been better with a reception on another day, another time, but it was a tribute in a way to how important the work was regarded.

Dr. Varia was married to the famous Romanian soprano, Mariana Nicolesco, and we were later to be whisked around with them in their brand new Volvo, for now we were all on a small mini-bus. On the road from Bucharest to Tărgu-Jiu we passed a huge overturned lorry, lying by the side of the road, deserted and silent, its black underbelly like an enormous beetle struggling in vain to right itself. Much later, we passed a heavily overladen cart on the road, straw in huge bundles protruding from each side of the cart, pulled by an exhausted horse, and managed by a young boy of about twelve years of age. A few ducks waddled across the road, a reminder of the backward agriculture economy of the Romanian region, and the huge gulf between Dr. Varia and this peasant boy. That was 1992, and one forgets just how long ago that is now, a quarter of a century, and I dare say things have changed greatly since then.

At Tărgu-Jiu we were driven to an impressive monastery, surrounded by trees and fields, and had to wait for a while before the gates were heaved open, since it was about 11pm, well past the normal closing time. The monastery was called Mănăstirea Cămărașeasca, and the only thing that had altered since the arrival of Ceausescu and the ghastly communists some 45 years earlier, was that they had lost some of their adjacent farmland: otherwise the Eastern Orthodox Monastery was unchanged over the centuries since its foundation, back in the mists of time, perhaps the 8th century AD.

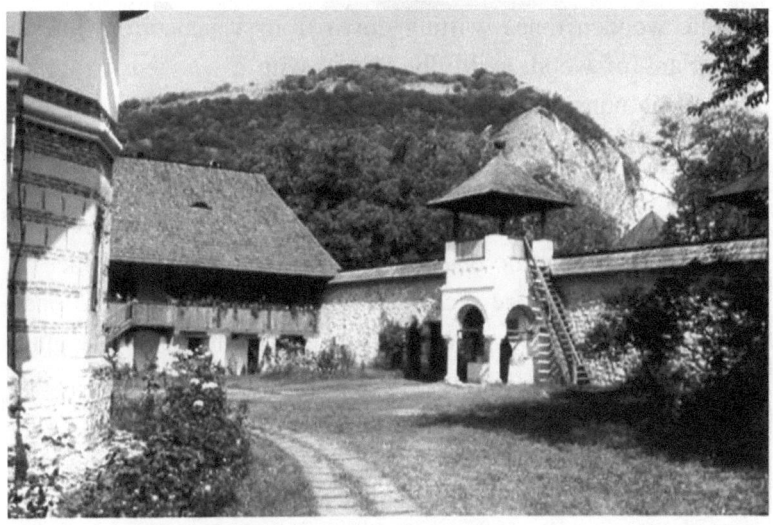

The Eastern Orthodox Monastery of Mănăstirea Cămărașeasca, with the Carpathian Mountains behind where the wolves howled at night and the Romanians discussed poetry, and where we stayed for our work on the Infinite Column. Photograph by the author.

The German photographers arrived a little later and seemed a bit put out by their accommodation and the lack of any hot water. At our late evening meal, a superb-looking beige-coloured cake was brought out and placed in the centre of the table by the Mother Superior. We ate our eggs and potatoes, while the nuns poured out what appeared to be modest glasses of water. One of the Germans took a large gulp and spluttered and coughed: it was very strong plum brandy, made by the monks themselves. The Germans had had enough and decamped to a rather decrepit hotel in the centre of the town of Târgu-Jiu, the monastery being some distance from the centre. This hotel, practically empty, had miles of worn-out carpeted floors and reception area, and did not look inviting at all, but the Germans stuck it out there.

Back at Mănăstirea Cămăraşeasca we were awakened by the rhymic wooden tones wafting down from a semantron, a long thin plank of wood, skillfully played with a wooden mallet by one of the nuns, around 7am. It was quite hypnotic and I was happy to listen to the semantron for ages, but had to rise and wash in cold water, before shivering into clothing, as breakfast was at eight. The same mysteriously beautiful cake was produced again, but no one had the courage to request a slice so it went uneaten for the second time before being removed once more. No Germans at breakfast either, to partake of the plum brandy again, with soup and bread to follow; they would join us later at the Infinite Column. Dr Kucera and I listened in some astonishment as Radu explained that in order to create the tripartite artwork through the town as Brâncuşi had apparently envisaged, a church and railway line would have to be moved out of the way, and that this had already been agreed to by the authorities. We let this unlikely scenario go by, and walked to the *Infinite Column*. If you have not visited this version of the *Infinite Column*, whose dimensions are the same at the base as they are 100 feet into the sky, you cannot appreciate the beauty and majesty of the column and its effect on the viewer, the strange geometry of observing the identical biconical beads as they recede into space above you, and the spare and restrained nature of its surroundings.

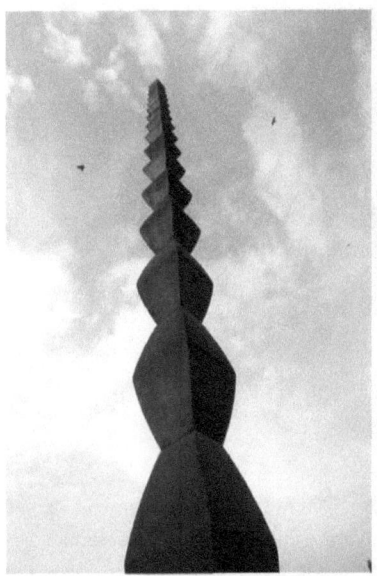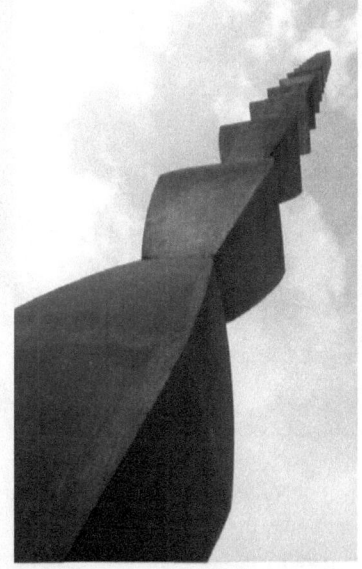

Two views of the Infinite Column. You have to remember that each biconical element is exactly the same size from the top of the column to the bottom which greats extraordinary visual displacements in the mind. Photographs by the author.

Dr. Kucera and I are more concerned with the discolourations and corrosion. Dr. Varia and I take it in turns to inspect the innards of this architectural marvel from an inspection plug a foot or so from the ground. We can inspect the central spine of steel and remove a few handfuls of rust. Dr. Kucera's assistants set up a UN approved environmental testing station on the roof of a nearby textile factory to determine the corrosivity of the area around the infinite column. Data will be collected for three months. Apart from the structural issues, the main problems to be resolved are the degree of penetration of water between the biconical modules, what to do about the corrosion of the cast iron, what to replace the discoloured brass coating with, and what organic coating can be used to protect the new brass or bronze surface. None of these questions could immediately be answered.

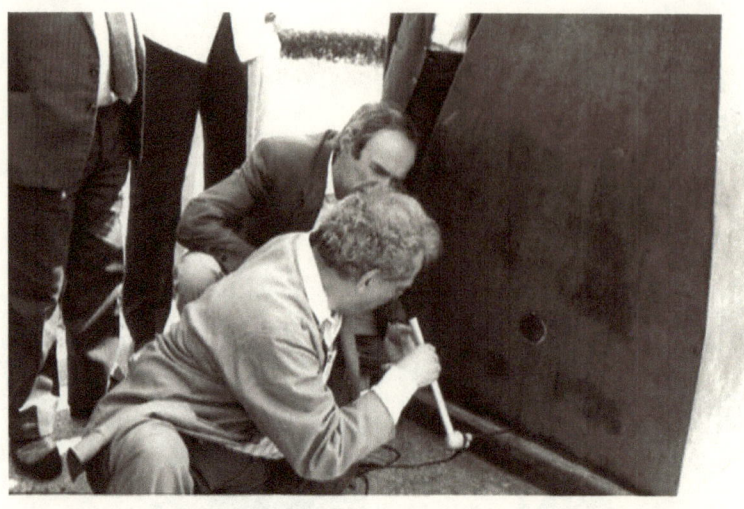

Dr. Radu Varia inspects the innards of the Infinite Column with an endoscope to examine the interior rusting, which proved to be surprisingly non-lethal for the stability of the masterpiece. Photograph by the author.

The engineering problem centered around the need to dismantle the column to carry out a thorough inspection. One of the Romanian engineers working with us had lived in a solid 1930's apartment block not far from the gargantuan palace that Ceausescu, the Romanian president, occupied. One day, Ceausescu was looking out of a window in his massive palace and thought that the apartment block in question was obstructing part of his view down the avenue. The demolition team was ordered to remove the offending block of apartments: everyone was ordered out on the street, with their possessions, and the wrecking ball machine trundled down the avenue and began to demolish the building as the stunned former occupants watched in disbelief. The process of checks and balances in countries like Romania are fractured and broken by the human failures of feudalism, medievalism, religious devotion, despotism, communism and foreign domination. The combination with the inherent poverty of the region demeans the democratic process and leaves the outsider bemused and worrying about the stability of life in Romania. Indeed, in later years, Dr Varia had to deal with an endless succession of Ministers of Culture, about eleven of them, each of them claiming the kudos of having undertaken the restoration of the *Infinite Column.*

That night, back at the Monastery, the engineers and the monks engaged in a long debate on the subject of Romanian poetry, while in the thick dark night outside, the wolves howled over the Carpathian Mountains. How could that memory ever fade? An area of the world made famous by the story of Dracula, thought to have been based on Bran Castle, situated on the border between Transylvania and Wallachia, and we were very close to the Transylvanian region. And how could one forget being an honoured guest at this Eastern Orthodox Monastery in aid of preserving a masterwork by Brăncuşi? And washing in the morning in cold water followed by plum brandy at breakfast? And the sounds of the semantron reverberating in the early morning?

I was intrigued by the fact that the Monastery accommodated both nuns, on one side of the building, and monks on the other. This integration seemed fundamentally more egalitarian than the western models of supposedly strict separation of the sexes. I liked the idea that the monks and nuns could live together in their wonderful accommodation, that they could tend the fields, or sew garments, pray or undertake their devotional duties together.

Back at the Column, the fire brigade had kindly brought over a large lorry with cantilevered hoist and bucket, allowing Dr. Kucera the chance to inspect the column at some height, some ninety feet above the ground. This we did and met again with Radu Varia, who was about to be interviewed, for over an hour, for Romanian television. The programme was duly broadcast and one had to marvel at the fact that no such program stood a chance of being aired for an hour on television in the UK or USA in prime-time.

We assembled for a final meeting and the two Germans went off to Bucharest, as did we, but they had booked into a different hotel to ours. When they went out for an evening stroll, they came across two Romanian policemen holding a gypsy by the scruff of the neck and announced that he had been in their hotel dealing in illegal currency transactions, and the Germans were told to hand over their wallets for inspection. The Romanian police duly inspected them, announced that everything was in order and sent the Germans on their way. Next morning at breakfast, one of the Germans took out his wallet to pay for the meal, only to find that his money had gone. The other reciprocated, and found that all of his money had gone too. What a clever scam by the gang of pick-pocketing Romanian thieves.

Dr. Kucera and I collected data and wrote reports: the main problem was going to be the coating. Dr. Kucera came up with a Finnish coinage alloy that had good corrosion resistance and was a suitable bronze colour. We were conducting a battery of tests on alloys and coatings, but at the same time as this was going on, Dr Radu Varia and his International Foundation were sidelined by the World Bank. The Bank paid one million dollars for the Romanian ministry to undertake the restoration work. The Column was dismantled, the biconical elements housed in small sheds, cleaned and recoated, and the whole assembly skillfully reintegrated, together with a lightning rod at the top sticking out into the sky! Paraloid B72 had been provided by the World Bank as the coating agent, and the work was completed effectively, even if its longevity as a conservation treatment was in doubt. The artistic intention of Brâncuşi was that his column touched the sky in the mind, not that a passing storm would use the column as a lighting conductor! In any case, the entire column was made of metallic components so there was no need for a lighting conductor at all, the entire column was its own conductor! Remarkably, my informants have told me that the *Infinite Column* is still doing well in its restored state, some fifteen years later. The problem is the never-ending passage of time: will the coating hold up for another ten? What maintenance is being carried out on the column? I suppose that I will have to make the pilgrimage to Tărgu-Jiu to discover the current state of the masterpiece.

The research that I needed to carry out has given me a deeper appreciation of the achievements of Brâncuşi as an artist and the refined and, to some extent, restricted nature of his oeuvre. As he remained true to himself and his ideals throughout his life, and absolved the clutter of representation from sculptural art, he was a pioneer, but one who has had few books written about him: the most commonly available is the one by Sidney Geist, called *Brancusi*, from which the quotation above was taken, and the one by Radu Varia, also called *Brancusi*, has just been reissued in 2016, and not before time.

The paucity of books about Brancusi contrasts with the huge number written about his famous contemporaries in the artworld, such as Giacometti, for which there is no real excuse. The artworld has, to some extent, just forgotten about him or has taken him for granted, or does not know what to write about him next.

One of the most famous incidents involving a Brăncuşi work of art was the attempt to import, in 1926, one of his masterworks, *Bird in Space,* into the United States of America. Having no clue about modernist art at that time, the Americans, then somewhat in the dark as to what modern art was all about, tried to describe it as a manufactured product, on which duty would be payable, rather than as a work of art, on which no duty is levied, a story often repeated. In fact, it was the Second World War which saved America from its own parochialism, since the European intellectuals, writers, scientists, sculptors and artists ended up in New York in some numbers and that changed everything: New York was to become the hub of modern art, encouraged to some extent by secret funding from the CIA to help to combat Russian social realist art. Avant-garde New York art was seen as a foil to the Russian mind-set.

The Getty were involved with Romania in other ways: the revolution had resulted in the destruction of the University Library, with over half a million volumes and thousands of rare manuscripts destroyed: all gone up in smoke. Scores of Renaissance paintings were destroyed, damaged or stolen, and four of the best of the Italian baroque works made their way to the Getty Center, along with Romanian conservator Simona Predescu. Simona later gave me a wonderful hand-painted egg, crafted by her grandmother, a traditional Romanian gift and one which demands great skill from the painter, as well as knowledge of ethnic patterns for the design.

The most famous damaged work to just about survive was Orazio Gentileschi's 1609 oil on canvas, *Madonna and Child*, worth about 15 million quid, that had an enormous gash down the centre of the canvas, having sustained gunshot damage, forcing a stretcher bar right through the artwork. The total financial loss to Romania for all of the destroyed works and books is in the hundreds of millions. Elizabeth Mention, formerly of the Getty Paintings Conservation Department did a great deal of work on this Gentileschi, now back on display in Romania. In 1992, the Getty held an exhibition on the restoration called *"Innocent Bystander"* of which not the slightest trace remains. I cannot find it on the Getty website, but perhaps others can. The innocent bystander is no longer standing as far as I can see. Just recently, in 2016, the Getty purchased their second Gentileschi, after its display at the Met, for over 30 million dollars, a huge inflationary payout for a Gentileschi which should ensure that they continue their upward spiral in monetary value in the years ahead.

Back on the street, Los Angeles is home to untold numbers of fascinating characters who one might meet in the most mundane of circumstances. One day, sometime in the 1990's, deep now in a past LA life that no longer exists, I ran into Harry over the tie rack at Macy's department store. Harry was an old UK car mechanic who told me that for many years he had worked for this chap who had gone to Antarctica with Scott of the Antarctic. That would have been between 1910-1913. I gawped in disbelief: how could that be possible? I invited Harry up to the Getty Villa for lunch later on, and he recounted his amazing tale. While he was working as a mechanic in the UK he had done some work for Charles Wright, who had indeed gone with Scott to Antarctica. That was Sir Charles Seymour Wright, KCB, OBE, MC (1887-1975)! Sir Charles was a very dedicated worker and Harry served as a sort of fixer and odd-job man for whatever it was that the important scientist needed, such as arranging a suitable tent for one of the scientists who happened to be 6 foot 7 inches tall.  On one occasion, Harry interrupted Sir Charles while he was busy with some of his mathematical physics lab work.  He seemed to pursue his work with utter dedication and determined sense of purpose.

"Sir Charles, Sir Charles"

"What is it Harry?"

"The men are complaining that they haven't been paid yet"

"Good God Harry is that all"

Sir Charles took out his cheque book and wrote out the monthly salaries for each of his staff and returned to his task.

"Now can I get on with my work Harry?"

On another occasion, by which time Sir Charles was in Canada, working for the Defense Research Board of Canada's Pacific Naval Laboratory, Harry had to bother Sir Charles again.

"Sir Charles, Sir Charles" He looked up from his work.

"Yes Harry what is it?"

"Customs have impounded that special magnetometer that was ordered from England.  It's arrived safely but Customs won't release it"

"What? What? Pass me the telephone"

Harry passed the telephone and Sir Charles dialed a number.

"Get me John on the line" He demanded.  It was then that Harry realised he was asking to speak to the then Prime Minister of Canada, John Diefenbaker.

After the conversation, the very sophisticated magnetometer was released from customs the following day.  Presumably this was all secret Canadian defense work in the north to track or detect Russian submarine activity off the Canadian waters.

George Roberts was the man who invented the deep blue liquid we all know from flushing of our bodily ablutions in aeroplane toilets or portable loos.  He was consequently rather rich. George Roberts first love was astrophysics, but his passion was for capsicums from South America, with a deep interest in ancient Peruvian colourants and dyes.  At one stage, somewhere in the distant past, LA had a botanist who was the expert on capsicums for the entire state. He was retired with perhaps not too long left, and no one had replaced him, needless to say.

George tracked him down and they had a wonderful exchange of information and knowledge.

George and I met because the Getty Conservation Institute, for some forgotten reason, had come up with the idea of hosting a series of lectures on Ancient South American art to be given at the Fowler Museum auditorium at UCLA, to be paid for by the Getty. This had been agreed to around 1992 with the then director of the Fowler Museum, Professor Christopher Donnan, aka Mr. Moche, and Dr. Miguel Angel Corzo, Director of the GCI . Who at the Getty to get to organize such a thing? Well, which GCI project would be inconvenienced the least? Obviously, the Museum lab was not in desperate need of anything, so get David Scott to do it all! That was the obvious choice of lead person. So we began to plan a series of Saturday afternoon lectures at UCLA on this topic over about eight weeks, one each week. Deborah Gribbon used to show up regularly and a few GCI folk, but not that many, in fact, very few. The audience was predominantly the UCLA crowd, not the Getty crowd. At one of the Peruvian talks, on ancient Inca stone building techniques, George Roberts and his wife showed up and we got into conversation, eventually being invited over to his house in a desirable LA canyon location. At that time, work on Peruvian dyes was going on in my lab at the Getty Villa, where I was hosting Ran Boytner UCLA graduate student, to enable him to finish up his PhD. Another non-Getty project which was going on under the radar.

Roberts was keen to get us hooked up with all the Peruvian labs and sources he knew of to really turn this work into a mega-project. We had neither the time nor the resources to do that, but George was nothing if not determined, and I had to prevaricate on that topic. As part of his astrophysics work, he knew of an astronomical centre in Chile which was in dire need of suitable books. George collected many together that were then going to be shipped off to the observatory in Chile. He had a large crate made which he filled with rocks, which was dispatched at vast expense to the Chilean observatory from LA. The crate never arrived, which I guess he was half-expecting. George then arranged for the Chilean navy to take the actual crate of books to Chile when their frigate docked off of Santa Barbara. This time the astronomical books did make it to a happy observatory. When we visited his house he took us around the garden where the capsicums were grown in raised beds, each protected from possible predators by being totally enclosed in netting some eight feet in height. There were several of these, forming an exotic pepper zoo, and at the end of the garden, a thirty foot high octagonal wooden structure. I asked George what that was for. "Oh yes" He replied "That's a prototype for the structure we built for Paolo Alto"

I am not sure how many gardens sport such an impressive prototype, but I would guess just one in the world. Visiting that evening was a prominent Peruvian archaeologist, Kauffman-Doig, who had written books about the sexual proclivities of pre-Columbian Peru and much else besides. In fact, Professor Dr. Federico Kauffman-Doig had been the Peruvian ambassador to Germany. He was the first Latin American to be awarded the Neuberg Medal from Sweden (I learn on Google) and a number of other prestigious awards from all over the place. Apart from that, he was General Manager of the Monumental and Cultural Patrimony of Peru and Director of the Museo Nacional de Antropologia y Arqueologia and History of Peru. I have to admit that I had no inkling of how elevated this slight figure of an elderly man was at the time we met. He was very reserved and retiring and just offered me a couple of books to give to the Getty library as he thought they might not have them, which was indeed the case.

There was a curious link between the remarkable George Roberts, myself, and Charles Craig. Charles Craig was an eccentric, who lived only for art. Hus house in Santa Barbara, where he had worked for the Crocker Bank, was essentially a totally disorganized and over-stuffed art storehouse to which no-one was ever admitted. Charles had collected drawings, paintings, prints, Dali or Warhol signed shopping bags, pre-Columbian art from across the continent, the work of the Cornish group of UK artists in St. Ives, modern art, Mexican retablos, Russian icons, the list went on and on. He had a tendency to swap one artwork for another, so that when he would visit an artists studio, he took one of the Dali signed blank sheets of paper with him, or perhaps a Russian icon, and then swapped that with a painting by the artist he was more interested in at that time. He had a small portrait of the artist's mother, painted by one of the St Ives group of artists, so one day Charles decided to visit him. He flew with the portrait from Los Angeles to London and then took the train down to St. Ives where he found the house of the artist and knocked on the door. The artist rarely answered the door as he disliked visitors, but Charles persisted and eventually the irascible artist appeared demanding to know what Charles Craig wanted. "I thought you might like back this portrait of your mother that you painted in 1973" Replied Charles. The artist was, of course, astonished, invited Charles in and promised that when Charles was next in London, he would travel up to paint Charles's portrait. That was typical Charles Craig: another artistic exchange in which no money was necessary. Charles had a deep admiration for the goldwork of Costa Rican and Panama, and had built up quite a collection, some of which I had looked at for him. At one stage the five hundred dollars I had accumulated from this paid work enabled us to buy a new gas cooker, so it must have been around 1992, when we were really hard up and had about a thousand dollars in the bank in total, if that. Somehow, Craig had also got hold of

Peruvian goldwork from the Sipan treasures, whose excavation had been undertaken by Walter Alva with great help from Professor Christopher Donnan. When Donnan learnt about the parlous state of the finances for the excavation of this very important site, he simply gave his two Nikon cameras and hundreds of rolls of film that he had brought with him from Los Angeles to Lima to Walter Alva, and retuned to Los Angeles in search of additional funding for the excavation. The famous site had already been partially looted and these finds were scattered across the globe, some hidden behind a false wall in Charles Craig's kitchen, which were found when the place was raided by US Customs.

It was George Roberts who hired and paid for the attorneys to prosecute the dealers who had brought in this priceless goldwork to the USA. The case was eventually dismissed for lack of evidence, but it was a generous act of George Roberts, and Charles Craig simply gave the pieces back and moved on to his next obsession: it did not matter to him that much, he just loved art, regardless of where it had come from. He died a few years ago now, leaving the legacy of a house crammed with thousands of artworks, and a headache for the relatives and art dealers to decide what to do with it all.

I remember being with Dr. Fawzi Zayadine and the goat-herd perched on a high rocky ledge in Petra as we sipped tea together with Lesley from tin mugs in the late afternoon. The goat-herd had made the tea for us on an open fire, high up, away from tourists, off the beaten track of any regular visitors. Fawzi's family came from an area not far from Petra and they knew every trail through these mountains. How had we ended up here on this deserted rock, miles from anywhere, at one of the world's most extraordinary archaeological sites?

It was a remarkable time, Amman was awash with Kuwaiti and Saudi businessmen, the Iraqi army was about to invade Kuwait and Jordan was tense and expectant, on edge, with very few visitors from the West that year. American Express cards could not be accepted at the hotel we stayed at in Amman, but luckily we had Bank of America credit cards too, and they were acceptable.

We were in Jordan for the Dead Sea Scrolls, the Copper Dead Sea Scroll which had been found in a cave in Qumran in Jordan in 1952. That is the reason why we are here: for their conservation and investigation. The aim of the project is to see what we can do with the Copper Dead Sea Scrolls. Why is that? The copper scroll, covered with early Hebrew script detailed the supposed location of over sixty treasures of gold and silver, was in dire need of conservation and an updated display context for this unique artefact. The scroll was found rolled up like a Swiss roll, and unusually has been totally corroded during its nearly 2000 years of sitting in the Qumran cave. This meant that the scroll could never be unrolled to read all of the text. The scroll was sent to Professor H. Baker Wright, at Manchester University, who devised a unique machine to cut the scroll into segments, followed by careful cleaning of the surfaces. Having handled the cut segments myself, I have a great deal of admiration for Professor Wright and his accomplishments, largely unsung in our profession, have drifted off into the unknown past. During the early part of the sixties Professor Baker was chief UNESCO advisor for the Central Mechanical Engineering Institute, Durgapur, India, which sounds like a really wonderful thing to do in the early sixties.

We are the guests of the Jordanian Ministry of Culture, Professor Bill Fulco, from the Department of Religion at USC, Lesley and myself.

The first set of introductions involved endless cups of teas in antechambers before being ushered in to see the Minister in person. There seemed to be about three separate ministers, and tea and meetings consumed the entire day, so that nothing was actually done at all. On the second day in the morning it was the same, and only in the afternoon did I get to see and handle the famous Copper Scrolls. Despite being totally corroded and having the strength of a piece of hard biscuit, they were in remarkably good condition, but the curators had placed them on black polystyrene foam, which must have seemed like a good idea back in the 1960's. Today we know better: we would never have used black polystyrene foam under any conditions, because it slowly degrades. It either turns to a sticky mass or a decayed brownish-black powder. Unfortunately the sticky version of the black goo had adhered to the underside of the copper scroll segments, so that now they had polystyrene goo stuck to them! No-one will have even noticed this, because the curators just look at the copper scroll through the display case, unaware that the acidic emanations inside the case have slowly increased to unhealthy levels. They know nothing of the finer points of conservation. The Jordanian curators are not alone: in the massive collections of the Belgian African Museum, the curators had placed all of the wonderful African iron artefacts, swords, blades, and ceremonial objects on sheets of black polystyrene foam. Now one side of these iron objects are covered with sticky degraded foam! The problem is widespread, due to ignorance, neglect, and lack of resources. Communication is a world-wide necessity but some forms of knowledge become stuck in the past, pun intended.

In the 1970's the conservator in Amman had gone to the British Museum to learn the rudiments of metallic conservation. But the techniques they were taught were the chemical treatment methods of the 1960's, with coins fizzing away in dilute nitric acid or sodium hydroxide or alkaline glycerol, or Rochelle salt. Not that there is anything wrong with these forms of treatment on a prime facie basis, but they need to be carefully monitored and preferably the coin examined under a binocular microscope as gentle swabs of reagents or the tip of a scalpel is prodded into the corrosion covering the coin. That way, taking twenty times as long, we can get the best results in surface preservation of each coin. You can't criticize these curators: they were only trying their best, it is just that they have no idea, sympathy and smiles, keeping quiet is the diplomatic option here. If it were in my power, another offer of advanced training at the British Museum would be on the cards, but none seems to come. The conservation problem of the sticky black mess can be dealt with later. My time with the scrolls seems to be rather limited and there did not seem to be a definitive meeting with the curators to hammer out the details of shipment of the scroll sections to the Getty for treatment.

The next day we meet Dr. Fawzi Zayadine, a Jordanian archaeologist of international repute. We are going across country to visit some archaeological sites. We stop at Jarash, where Getty himself once stood, between the colonnaded way of still-impressive parallel columns. There is an old black and white photograph of Getty standing at Jerash between the columns.

Two young boys approached me and tried to sell me small coins they had found at the site, but they do not know that Fawzi is a prominent archaeologist and he deals with them quite severely, taking their coins and telling them to never again touch the site. I felt sorry for the boys, but Fawzi has no such feelings. Jerash is a magnificent wreck, a site which goes back to the Bronze Age. Some of the ruins, include an Arch from the time of Hadrian and Corinthian columns of the Temple of Artemis. Small shops were located along the central avenue in Roman times. It is an impressive site whose complex history is hard to deal with.

Somehow Professor Bill Fulco of the Department of Religion, University of Southern California is with us too. Professor Fulco was also a Jesuit priest with a residence at Loyola Marymount University, at Los Angeles, not far from where we lived in Mar Vista, and I lectured for them occasionally. Professor Fulco was dark-skinned with looks which could be from anywhere in the Middle East. When he was in Israel they looked on him suspiciously as an Arab, and when he was in Palestine, they thought he was a Jew. One day on the bridge between Israel and Palestine, he rescued a young Palestinian girl who was about to be trampled on by mounted Israeli police. This infuriated the Israeli police and they pursued him. He dashed into the Post Office and the counter staff, who were quite aware of what was happening, lifted the wooden serving hatch and thrust him into the back and out through a side door away from the bridge and the Israeli police lost him.

We travelled together to Petra and each of us took donkeys to get to the site through the mystic pass where the rocks narrow together before opening out into the wide vista of the temples carved in the solid rock, the soft pink sandstone. The Nabateans were the inhabitants od this important trading post which is how the money accrued to make this extraordinary and unique site, now visited each year by well over half a million people, but when we were there, we were the only visitors to be seen! The first time I ever saw pictures of Petra was when Lutfi Khalil gave us a lecture back at the Institute of Archaeology in 1980. I never thought then that we would be esteemed visitors to Petra itself, eleven years later. Fawzi explained how the Romans had tried to take the site of Petra, but the Nabateans retreated to the high stone platforms and pelted the Roman soldiers below with rocks, so that in the end the Romans gave up and went back to base. Defeating the Romans however was never easy, so what the Roman authorities did instead was to re-direct the trading routes to bypass Petra altogether. That marked the beginning of the end of the Nabatean kingdom's power.

Fawzi would stop the jeep in the middle of nowhere and point out the significance of a worn stone tablet, from the time of the foundation of the Eastern Empire All of this travelling around was totally fascinating, but I began to get a bit worried as to what progress I was making with the Copper Scroll. What I did not know was that Noor Al-Hussein, the Queen of Jordan at the time was involved with the decision as to what to do with the Copper Scroll and it may be that there was an anti-American sentiment in the decision to get the French to conserve the scroll rather than allow the Americans the kudos of undertaking this work. From 1994 to 1996 extensive conservation efforts by Electricité de France (EDF) included evaluation of corrosion, photography, x-rays, cleaning, making a facsimile and a drawing of the letters. The facsimile was the obvious thing to do, and at the Getty we had planned to taken silicon rubber molds from the curved sections, lay the silicon rubber flat, join them together and then cast a copy from the silicon molds. The scientists at Electricité de France clearly thought the same way, as perhaps an electrotype in copper might be the way to go. I can't imagine the

UK Central Electricity Generating Board taking any interest in ancient Hebrew copper scrolls as Electricité de France did, and even less the ghastly privatized entities which have replaced it since the 1990's rolled by into privatization and the capitalistic heaven that the UK has become. The customer in these cases is even less likely to be an ancient copper scroll, which has been sitting around for 2000 years. Its ability to pay an electricity bill is very much in doubt.

One day at Windsor Castle in the late 1990's, a new curator opened an obscure cupboard to find to his surprise an unknown bronze satyr by Benvenuto Cellini, long forgotten. Only at a place like Windsor Castle might one find a world-class bronze by Cellini just lying about in a cupboard for perhaps a hundred years, with the Royal family in total ignorance of what they had! None of this, of course, is mentioned on the Royal Collection website.

Now this bronze satyr is actually one of a pair, the twin being in the collections of the Getty Museum, designed by Cellini for the transformation of the Porte Doree at Fontainbleau flanking a bronze lunette, which is an enormous bronze casting and one of the treasures of the Louvre. The rest never got cast and the small bronze satyrs was all that was completed, apart from two large plaster model satyrs which have disappeared now completely.

The Getty have had theirs for over twenty years, and before that it was in a collection in Vienna and before that it too was in the Royal Collection at Windsor Castle, because there is a 19th century photograph of it in an inventory at Windsor Castle! So, my theory is that Queen Victoria gave the bronze as a Royal gift to a visiting dignitary from Austria, and that they then disposed of it or had it stolen during the First World War. The true historiography of the displaced Cellini satyr is actually much more interesting. To start with Cellini was commissioned to make a huge bronze version by King Francois I of France but had to flee the country in 1545 as he had been accused of theft. One theory is that he completed the wax models for the two satyrs but never had time to complete the castings, so later hands took the waxes, and had them cast. In the chaos of the First World War, the Getty version was sold by the Drey Gallery in 1918 to an August Lederer, who died in 1936 and left the bronze to his widow Serena Lederer.

During the Second World War, the bronze was confiscated by the Gestapo at the direction of the Zentralstelle für Denkmalscuhtz, on the orders of the Wiener Magistrat. While in Nazi hands, the satyr was valued at 200 Reichsmarks and, by autumn 1939, it was stored at Zentraldepot at Neue Burg, Vienna, before being moved to Wollzeile, then in 1944, to Thürntal Palace, Fels am Wagram, which was taken by the Allied Russian troops in May 1945, at which time it was released to the Republic of Austria. The Austrian government restituted the satyr to the son of Serena Lederer, Erich Lederer in 1948, who then passed it on to his widow, Mrs. Elisabeth Lederer of Geneva in 1985. She sold the satyr to the J. Paul Getty Museum that year, which is how the bronze went from pillar to post across our troubled 20th century, ending up at the Getty, and how its companion stayed unnoticed in a cupboard in Buckingham Palace, tranquil and forgotten. The tale can be seen as an archetype or paradigm: any trail of European art stretching across the terrains of desirability and possession, collection and disposal, theft and restitution, encompasses the kind of detail recorded here, often with depressing regularity. We should be grateful, I suppose, to the incomparable efficiency of the German bureaucracy, whose meticulous records make this kind of history possible to unravel.

Having analysed the Getty *satyr*, the Royal Collection *satyr* was sent over to the Getty for a closer comparison. Remarkably similar in facture, they are very alike apart from one salient detail: the Royal Collection version is coated in platinum! This remarkable fact went unnoticed by curators, or art critics, and the report by James Fenton in the *Guardian* in October 2003 makes no mention of this extraordinary and rare patination. The Getty *satyr* simply possesses a standard bronze patina with nothing unusual about it: it is a typical Renaissance bronze in appearance. The French were the masters of electrodeposition of platinum patinas, which suggests that the Royal Collection *satyr* was given a coat of platinum in the 19th century, replacing a previous patina made sometime after 1545. For some commentators, the subject of patina has either become too scientific a concept for them to be bothered with, or they simply have no idea what they are talking about. The old connoisseurship of Ernst Gombrich is referred to, by scientists and art historians alike, but has seldom been emulated or taken further in new studies.

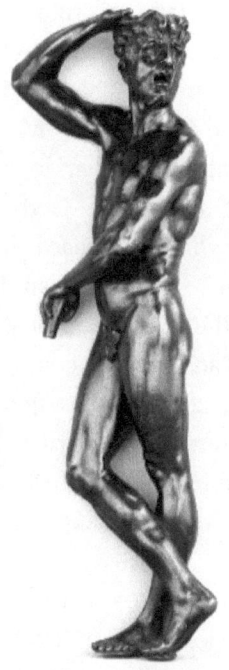

Bronze Satyr, Benvenuto Cellini, Italian 1500-1571, Artist unknown, 1543-1545, 85.SB.69  56.8 cm x 8.9 cm x8.4 cm.  Photograph by courtesy of the J. Paul Getty Trust.

Around the period from 1992-1997, I used to regularly travel to LACMA to learn from, assist, and discuss Chinese, Cambodian,

Near-Eastern, Egyptian, Iranian and Iraqi metalwork with Dr. Pieter Meyers and John Hirx. It was the time when Mr. Horuruchi was travelling the world, buying art for the Shinji Shumaki Religious Foundation who were having a new building, designed by I.M. Pey, built for them on a hilltop site outside of Kyoto, costing untold millions. With limitless wealth and buying power, some of the great artworks of the civilizations mentioned above, that had found their way onto the market at Sotheby's or Christie's were purchased by the Foundation, and shipped over to Los Angeles for Dr. Meyers to authenticate.

There were some superb artworks among them: large bronze Egyptian statues of Sekhmet and Osiris with the most desirable and aesthetically pleasing cuprite-red patina I had ever seen, not matched by anything in the British Museum. There were extraordinary Sasanian gold masterworks, ancient Iranian or Samartian silverwork of exquisite quality, Chinese gold belt-buckles with animal designs, a magnificent ancient Iranian bull weight cast in lead. It was art from areas of the world that the Getty did not collect, or art from sources that the Getty would have been unable to collect from, as the obvious question was: where was all of this astonishing artwork coming from?

If Sotheby's or Christies had taken it in and it had been sold to the Japanese religious foundation, it was too late for any archaeological provenance to exist. Is it possible to buy such works of art? There does not seem to be an answer to this question, especially in the 21st century while Isis and the Taliban continue to destroy our world heritage. The gulf between the archaeologists and the still-acquiring museums has widened over the past thirty years as the looting and destruction of archaeological sites has become so prevalent and the prices paid for works of art at auction has risen way above the rate of inflation. There are essentially two camps here with conservators caught in the middle. The archaeological purists maintain that no works of art without proper excavation data can be acquired by museums. The universal museums with world coverage such as the Metropolitan, the Louvre, the British Museum, the Boston Museum of Fine Arts, etc., etc., have a philosophy which has allowed huge numbers of works of art to be acquired without any provenance information whatever.

Is there a dialectical argument, like a Hegelian spiral, which can take us out of this impasse and create a new synthesis? Should works of Renaissance art, such as a Predella from an Italian church, be returned to the church concerned today? What can be done with practically all of the pre-Columbian goldwork in the Metropolitan Museum of Art? Should it all be returned to Colombia because it was purchased from dealers and has no known archaeological site?

Some of these problems are very hard to deal with. For example, when a farmer in Colombia found that his tractor had partially fallen into what was obviously a pre-Columbian tomb, he dug down and found so much goldwork, that he simply abandoned the tractor. Word spread and armed police came to protect the site together with some archaeologists. They were confronted by hundreds of local villagers advancing towards them, armed with picks, mattocks, shovels, buckets and spades, and they were not going to stop. So what were the police going to do? Shoot one or two of them? Clearly not an option, so they abandoned the site to the looters and in three months of frenzied looting the new cultural area, the Malagana culture, was practically destroyed in terms of its archaeological context. Now there are hundreds of Malagana goldworks floating around the international art market, they have no exact site description, and no exact date, and all of these disastrous series of events took place in 1992. Such goldwork then becomes lost in a limbo of a quagmire of looted art, much of it in private collections, which will be unavailable for study for decades.

One of the most salient cases I can recall is that of the ceramic depiction of an ancient Peruvian smelting operation, with a number of men with long blowpipes, heating up a metal smelting furnace. This ceramic masterpiece is the only depiction that we have of this kind of ancient Moche metalworking technology, and it has been published and illustrated in many books over the past twenty years or so, because it so important and significant. Professor Christopher Donnan, one of my eventual colleagues at the UCLA Cotsen Institute has spent many years of his working life hunting down and cataloguing Moche ceramics. The depiction of ceremonies, rituals, and events concerning Moche society on these ceramics has revolutionized ancient Peruvian studies, and made the Moche culture world-famous. On one of his many trips to Peru, where he also excavated Moche sites, Professor Donnan had heard of a local guy with a small collection of Moche ceramics in his house. He tracked him down and was shown into the modest home. There, on top of the television set, covered in household dust, sat the priceless Moche ceramic in question. Professor Donnan was able to purchase it on the spot and to publish it in an academic paper devoted entirely to this one ceramic vessel. Now, there are various ethical problems with this event from the perspective of the politically correct, first of all, the purchase from a private individual of a looted archaeological ceramic, and secondly, the publication of an important archaeological artefact without any site specific information in a prestigious archaeological journal. Therefore, under the philosophical position that such works cannot be published at all, especially in the *Journal of Archaeological Science*, the premier journal in the field today, this ceramic, of outstanding importance, would not be able to be seen by scholars in print. Clearly, something is wrong with this picture: for purposes of archaeological research it is important that we have knowledge of this one ceramic vessel. Yet because of the looting of archaeological sites we would not be allowed to publish it, so we would have no knowledge of it. And in the middle sits the conservator, who might be wondering which set of dictates to follow, should the vessel in question need to be conserved or treated to assure its stabilization. Should we refuse to treat it, because it might increase its monetary value and we would be considered to be an accessory to the encouragement of looting in virtue of the action that had been taken? It is all a matter of seeming to be on an ethical platform, when we know that some parts of the platform have no real foundations. I wrote a review article for *Latin American Antiquity* in 2011 on ancient Ecuadorian metallurgy, which was published, but since most of the artefacts discussed in the article were from looted contexts, should the entire article have been prohibited and sent back to the author for destruction? The artefacts the article is based on were smuggled out of Ecuador in empty toothpaste tubes to Denmark in the 1930's, which formed two seminal publications on the topic by Paul Bergsøe. Without these works by Bergsøe, we would have little knowledge of the La Tolita metalwork and its superb technological accomplishments, such as the use of platinum for coating gold, the fabrication of gold-platinum alloys of a whole host of colours. This culture, the La Tolita-Tumaco area, was the only one in the ancient world to make use of platinum. For readers who cannot believe that such cultures could use platinum even though it could not be molten, should look at Bergsøe's work. Professor Bray and myself continued this work much later with a stream of further publications, the finishing touches being made by Susan LaNiece and Nigel Meeks at the British Museum, and that is why I wrote the review for the Journal of *Latin American Antiquity.*

When the looting problem is being discussed in the press, it is usually Greek, Roman, Egyptian, African and Chinese artefacts being held up for scrutiny: by comparison, debate concerning preHispanic goldwork from Colombia makes only occasional mention.

As you can see pragmatism may be a course of action here, because a blanket prohibition cannot work. Is there a difference between the publication of looted material from societies where the culture has long since died, or from societies where the culture is still extant? The human stain is a deep one and could permeate both kinds of situation, but it is the living descendants who are the most troublesome for museums. Maori ritual artefacts kept in the British Museum became a subject of controversy when the British Museum, stupidly, hesitated in returning them to the Maori descendants. The curators at the British Museum were less than keen, although ethically they hardly had a choice, and consequently they were eventually sent back. In an article I wrote in the *International Journal of Cultural Heritage,* I postulated that one of the ways out of the impasse is to create perfect copies of the objects to be returned, especially when these objects are fundamentally appreciated for their aesthetic properties. Take the *Elgin marbles*: if they were replaced one night with perfect copies, would any member of the public actually notice? The answer is no: the only people who could readily distinguish between the different instantiations would be conservation scientists and conservators. Many Chinese museums display copies all the time, and the public appreciation of them is not limited in terms of the 'aura' of the work if the person viewing the art object believes that what they are viewing is actually the authentic object itself. For more on this topic you can read my book, *Art: Authenticity, Restoration, Forgery*.

There were a series of acquisitions going on constantly in the Getty Museum, although on a far lesser scale than the Met, these were usually weeded out by the conservation departments concerned, some of these did pass through the Villa lab when the occasion demanded. When I had been originally interviewed for the job at the Getty by Frank Preusser and Luis Monreal, Luis remarked to me that later on, long after I had left the museum, I would be able to write my memoirs concerning my experiences in dealing with the art and its authenticity at the Getty. Well, I am following Luis's word, although to recount everything here would begin to get indigestible for the reader, so a few choice items have being highlighted here.

The problems in the acquisition of antiquities began to get more and more fraught as the 1990's headed north. Some had to be sent back, as they were proved to be fakes, such as the Scopas Head, which came from some French connection and proved to be a student copy of a marble head held in the collections of the National Museum in Athens. There was an absolute stunner of a masterpiece of Lydian metalwork which has had to be kept in storage out of the public gaze for its own safety ever since. This bed, which eventually Jeffery Maish and myself were able to publish, in *Studies in Conservation*, is made of copper, bronze and iron, with cast bronze rails, beautifully finished with simulated mortise and tenon joints to each other, as if made in wood, delicately worked with a floral design, cast over an integral iron rail for internal strength and a cut copper lattice for the bed frame itself, overlaid with layers of fine linen, some of which are still in situ! It is unique in the world, an absolute masterpiece, a bed only fit for a Princess, and which deserves to be on display in Turkey in a small room dedicated to it: that is how special it is. The issue which prevents its display to the public is that the bed was looted from a tomb in Turkey, we know where the tomb is, and the bed should never have been able to make its way to the Getty in the first place: it is looted art of international significance.

The Turkish antiquities authorities know that the Getty have this unique object in storage, and are simply awaiting the day when it might be possible to take it back to Turkey and give it the very careful conservatorial and curatorial care that it needs to ensure its survival into the future. If the Lydian bed were so admired as it should, then perhaps a replica could be put on display in Turkey so that the local inhabitants could learn what their ancestors were capable of producing long before the Islamic world took over, as it could be even more years languishing in storage and being viewed by nobody.

Kathy Tubb, our former laboratory supervisor for practical work at UCL, became so passionate in her detestation of anyone involved in examining and publishing unprovenanced artwork that she became an international expert on the problems of looting of archaeological material. She has since deprecated the work of Jeffery Maish and myself in print, castigating us for the publication of such looted art that no one should forebear to dissociate him or her from such an endeavor. This is understandable but does not help the bed in its current predicament of being a prisoner in a museum crate, which cannot be seen. Lord Renfrew has a fancy phrase for the semi-legitimated publication of such works, something like "post-excavation recontextualization" Even the archaeologists have been forced to come to terms with the publication of the Lydian bed, which was the subject of a PhD thesis and impressive article by Elizabeth P. Baughan of the University of Richmond, entitled

*A Bronze Kline from Lydia,* an article which ended with another ethical statement that the bed provoked, but being unique in the world, its very existence is a paradigm of itself.

The *Getty Bronze Youth* is another masterwork, this time on display, which was originally fished out of the Adriatic Sea off the coast of Fano. There is some argument recently that the Adriatic find was not in Italian territorial waters, but who knows? A recent review of the case by Luis Li in the *Chapman Law Review* (you can read it online) makes much of the fact that it was a Greek bronze found in the sea not an Italian one, and that this alone makes the case for restitution to Italy doubtful. Personally I do not buy that legal argument, cross-cultural artefacts between Greece and Italy happen all the time, so one simply can't make an argument based on cultural origins in the simplistic way the article in the *Chapman Law Review* tries to over-emphasize, which does their legal case no good at all.

The bronze masterwork would have been on display in some Greek villa, and was ripped off of its stone base, breaking its feet, as cast in a leaden support, to bring away on a boat bound for Italy and a new owner, who would lovingly restore the feet and have the bronze on display in his own Villa, but unfortunately the boat sank in the Adriatic on its way, lost in a storm.

The tangled tale of how it ended up at the Getty is quite extraordinary. When the fisherman unloaded their remarkable catch, covered in barnacles and stuffed with sea creatures inside the hollow bronze form of the body, some local guy bought it from them: they got 400 lire each, and this chap took it to his cement factory to keep it out of view as far as possible.

The police as well as art dealers got wind of the catch and it was then hidden in a bath, stinking of fish, before making its way to a local priest's house where it was hidden under the stairs. Somehow, it was shipped out of Italy, as being too hot to hide from the authorities forever, and was secreted away in a Brazilian monastery, probably through clerical or monastic connections of the priesthood. What an amazing itinerary the work had suffered, and we are still not finished.

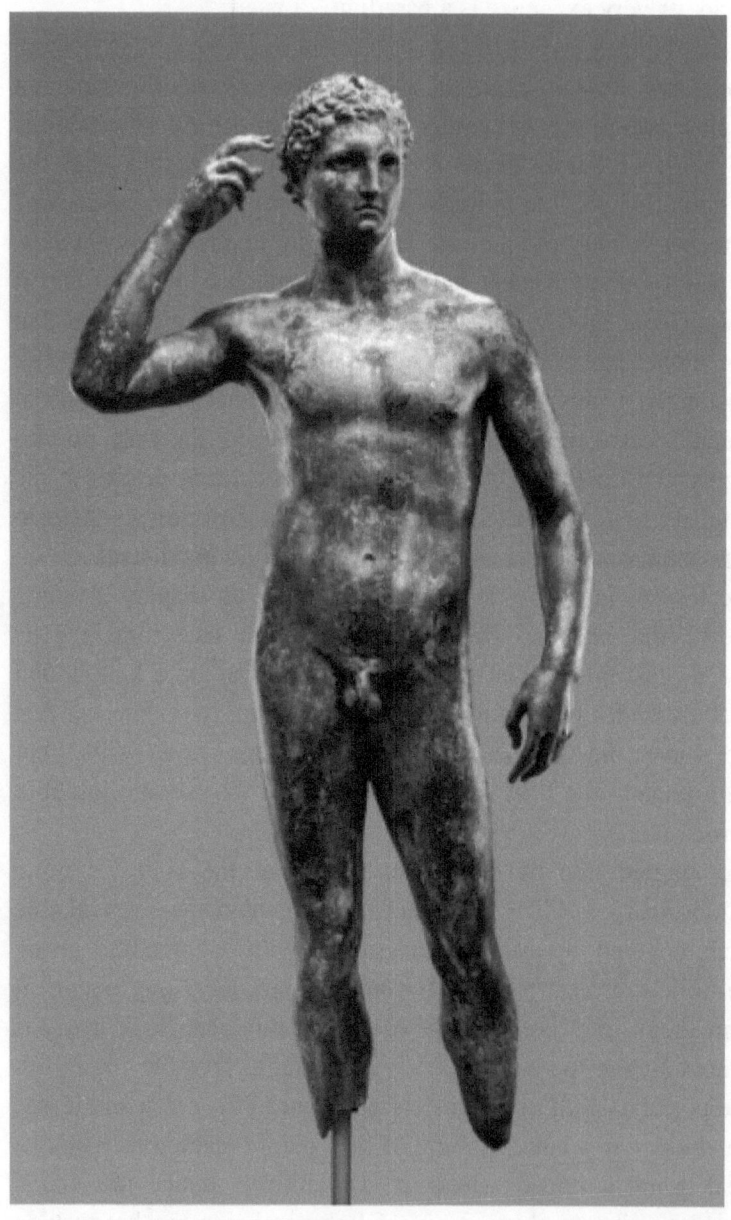

Statue of a Victorious Youth. Greek, 300-100 BC, Bronze with inlaid copper, 77.AB.30. 151.5 cm x 70 cm x 27.9 cm. Weight 64.4108 Kg. In theory, reclaimed by the citizens of Fano. By Courtesy of the Getty Trust.

The fugitive bronze then made its way to London, where the dealers began to drool over it, and it was then shipped off to Munich for a couple of highly skilled restorers to scrape away the barnacles, attach a broken arm and carefully clean the surface to some kind of patina. They did quite a good job, although the conservators at the Getty would have done it better, and the bronze made its way back to London, where buyers began to wonder if they might buy the unique work. Getty was approached, of course, but he would not buy it because he was not satisfied that the provenance papers were in good enough order for his careful mind to conclude that the purchase was not without risk, it was also rather expensive. How very astute of J. Paul: he was quite right. It had to wait for Getty's death and then the freewheeling Jiri Frel, who was the Antiquities Curator at the Getty at the time, purchased it for a few million dollars. Jiri Frel was a charismatic guy, who hosted what were virtually Roman orgies for the staff at the Getty Villa in the 1970's. The very thought of it is unimaginable in the Getty of today: perhaps a virtual re-enactment of a lengthy Roman senate meeting where the strategic management of the roads are discussed at length or whether or not to tax the urine collectors who stand at the intersection of major streets in Rome, used for the leather trade, that would be appropriate I think today rather than a Getty sexual orgy.

Jiri Frel eventually had to flee the United States, having been found to issue inflated art appraisals for tax write-offs for rich donors, and various odd scams for money, as well as collecting a lot of dubious material, some of which has had to be quietly repatriated to the countries from whence they came, especially Greece and Italy. So that is how the *Getty Bronze Youth* got to Malibu: Jiri Frel bought it with the blessing of the Trustees, but then Frel used to manipulate them as a bunch of civilized uninformed men, mostly art ignoramus's.

Jerry Podany and his staff did an excellent job on the technical examination, conservation and display of this rare Greek masterpiece, which is on display at the Getty Villa to this day.

When a negotiated settlement of the dispute between the Italian authorities and the Getty was reached, which helped to keep Marion True out of even more trouble, the Getty Bronze Youth was excluded from the special deal that enabled the return of the forty other artworks to Italy.

Poor Marion True, who followed Jiri Frel as the Curator of Antiquities at the Getty Villa, was effectively hung out to dry by the Getty Trustees, who ensured that she was the one who took the entire blame for the purchase of unprovenanced artworks, some of which were, in fact, unprovenanced and therefore looted. In a quote in the Los Angeles Times, Marion True complained that her Getty colleagues had not stood up for her, and that no one had spoken out on her behalf. That may be true of the Getty senior management, but it was not true of the sentiments on the museum floor that I came across at that time, I can tell you. I have made sure, in particular, to mention Marion True in the lectures I give on Art and Looting or The Bronzes of the Getty to graduate students and on the occasions I am invited to give a guest lecture at other Universities. Marion True was also an important voice in encouraging the formation of the new Archaeological and Ethnographic Conservation Training Program, which I was later to head up, and is another tribute to her now forgotten presence at the Getty.

Americans know that they have to be very careful to keep all criticisms to themselves, as that is part of the psychological mind-set of savvy or experienced Museum workers: it is not in one's interests to appear too critical of anything: it is essentially un-American. Our friend Doug, in Los Angeles, refers to it as having drunk the cool-aid. After imbibing the cool-aid, one becomes completely uncritical of an institution's treatment of you as an employee or the behavior of the institution itself, with regard to other employees, even if these employees are partially disabled grounds staff who are laid off with no word of protest from anyone else. A happy state of affairs which means lessening the existential angst of one's working life: definitely to be preferred to being a critic of a powerful institution.

I can hardly believe that someone who knows the life, body and entrails of the Getty Museum better than me has not written an expose or personal account which would be both more entertaining and revealing than what I am able to write, for I was at the periphery of so much of what went on and was but a humble scientist and not at all at the centre of the gossip routes that permeated the various entities and their associated departments.

The percipient chief curator of the Getty Villa, John Walsh, as we have seen, had already gone for early retirement and he was off, and rarely seen again. Deborah Gribbon, the assistant director, she went too over something else, as did Marion's deputy, Karol Wight, to the Corning Museum of Glass, the Villa Librarian, Barbara Furbush, was judged to be superfluous to requirements, and even Jerry Podany himself retired in 2016, at a younger age than me, although he still does contract work for the Getty, and most of the administrative staff at the Getty just come and go anyway in the natural course of museum life. All in all, not much is left of the old Getty that formed such an exciting group of people back in the 1990's, except for the highly dedicated Antiquities conservation staff of Jeffery Maish, Susan Maish, Eduardo Sanchez, Lisbet Thoresen, and Erik Risser, and one or two of the Antiquities Curatorial staff, such as Claire Lyons, and I understand that Eduardo Sanchez has himself retired now in 2017, Lisbet going around 2004.

Well, the citizens of Fano were very unhappy that their bronze was still in captivity at the Getty: they took the Italian culture ministry to court and the court of appeal ruled in favour of the citizens of Fano, who therefore have the legal right to seize or demand back the famous Bronze Youth. I guess that the Getty Bronze Youth will not be travelling to Italy for a loan exhibition anytime soon. Presumably the Italian Ministry has not actually demanded that the Getty return the bronze statue, because of international sensitivities and political agreements which have sidelined the inhabitants of Fano again, despite their court victory, they are smaller players on a world stage in which they barely have a walk-on part.

All of this has just changed in late 2019, when the Italian Supreme Court ruled in favour of the return, so we will have to see how that scenario plays out in the American courts over the next few years, creating more happy lawyers on nice commissions. As we say in the conservation world, art is a dirty business, but someone has to do it. Usually it is us who get to handling the art, and that keeps us happy, as well as the lawyers working in the field of art restitution, authenticity and contentious ownership.

One of the questions to be asked is: does the Bronze Youth perform a more important function at the Getty Villa than it would do in Fano? I think that the answer is probably in favour of the Getty if we follow that question to its logical conclusion. As J. Paul would say, to hold back the uneducated and to think that barbarians might not be moved by the presence of a Greek masterpiece of bronze is no idle boast or thought. The large numbers of visitors who stop to photograph or admire the Getty Bronze Youth are a testament to its function as an ambassador for Greek and Roman art. I am sorry, but the citizens of Fano can travel to view many other fine life-size bronzes in Italy and, if they wish, Greece, while Los Angeles, with its teeming millions, has only one. Let it remain a captive for it possesses more goodwill in itself than many ambassadors are able to show. The idea of a perfect copy comes to mind again, and with today's technological achievements in this respect, a superb copy could be made that would fulfill the aesthetic function of the bronze for the citizens of Fano.

I have my suspicions that one of the small bronzes currently on display at the Getty Villa, an Etruscan striding figure, is actually a forgery. Funnily enough it is a small Etruscan bronze kouros, which the curator Claire Lyons tells me will actually be taken off display in the newly revamped Getty Villa display in 2019. It has been on display for decades, which again raises the question as to whether a work of art so much appreciated by the public, even if a forgery, has distorted the public understanding of small Etruscan cast bronzes.

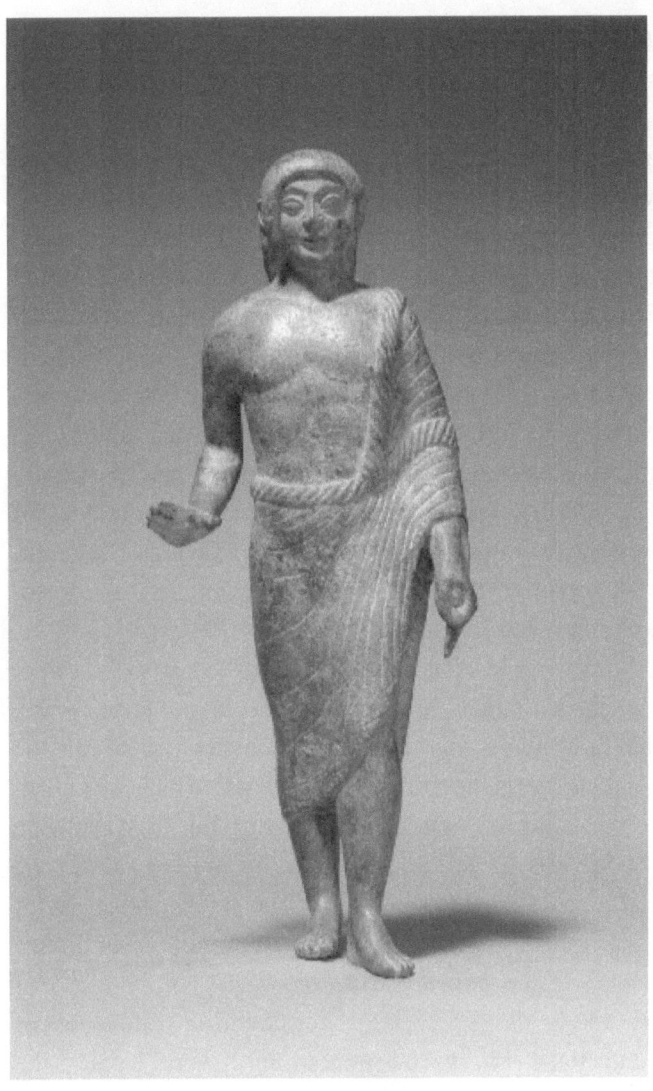

Etruscan bronze figurine. The patina of this bronze is questionable and David Ortiz thought it an outright forgery. This Etruscan bronze has been on display at the Getty Villa for decades, but may now be removed from display. Further investigation is needed but it is not clear yet that the Getty intends any.

If viewing of works long regarded as authentic, which are now judged to be inauthentic, does that sway art appreciation of a culture or does it matter? Does anyone else notice except us cognoscenti? Can it create an aura of interest in Etruscan bronzes even if we think that it is not authentically old? One of my favourite artists of the Renaissance who lived in modern times was Giovanni Bastianini, creator for example of the marble bust of *Lucrezia Donati,* carved in1865 and purporting to be a representation of the mistress of Lorenzo the Magnificent, carved in the style of the 15th century Florentine sculptor, Mino da Fiesole. Even knowing that the work was a 19th century forgery, it was purchased by the Victoria and Albert Museum as if it had been a genuine Renaissance sculpture, for the same amount of money that a genuine Renaissance work would have fetched! That is how admired Bastianini came to be in the late Victorian-early Edwardian period, and there are those who admire his works still, this author among them. My book, *Art: Authenticity, Restoration, Forgery,* is much concerned with the subtleties of cases of forgery that highly skilled craftsmen such as Bastianini have created, and how these have come to be restored, or copied, exhibited, or consigned to storage.

All of the work that Marion True accomplished is to be swept away in a chronological arrangement of art objects which became the fashion du jour after the Tate decided to do the chronological categorization thing a while back, which was much lauded by the critics. Not that the Getty has a worldwide coverage of the arts of antiquity in order to present that to the public, but I expect it will do its best. The reinstalled galleries opened in April 2019 after I had left LA and the Etruscan bronze kouros statuette that is believed to be a forgery will be included among the likely forgeries in a forthcoming catalogue of Etruscan and Italic art, to be written by Claire Lyons, the erstwhile senior curator. It might be a good idea however, to augment the doubts with a proper scientific examination in depth. All of the senior management of the Getty Conservation Institute, such as Jane Slate Siena, Dr. Miguel Angel Corzo, Mahasti Asfar, Rona Sebastian, Kris Kelly, and Dr. Stefan Simon, Dr. Alberto de Tagle, Dr. Giacomo Chiari, Christopher Grey, Dr. Nicholas Stanley-Price, Marta de la Torre, and of course the late Dr. Frank Preusser, went onto other things when they retired, or resigned, or were sacked from the Getty. Despite their supposed passion for art conservation, most have probably not touched an issue of the *Conservator*, or *Studies in Conservation* since their departure from the Getty, and have certainly not written anything for them recently. Being a Fellow of IIC, the publisher of *Studies in Conservation*, I can see that none of their names are present as subscribers or fellows.

# Chapter Twelve: The Getty Conservation Institute and Conservation Training

When the Getty Villa site was being rebuilt, renovated and restored, there was a fair amount of space that no one had any idea what to do with. One of the obvious additional activities was to create an Archaeological and Ethnographic Conservation Training Program. The GCI, Jerry Podany and myself had already been involved in several exploratory ventures regarding such a training program. Our first exploration was at the University of Arizona, with Marta de la Torre, Frank Preusser, Nicholas Stanley Price, Jerry Podany, and myself. There was a strong conservation program at the museum associated with the University, headed by Nancy Odegaard, and this would have formed a substantial backdrop to a new conservation-training program at Arizona. However, the typical academic understanding of the field of archaeological and ethnographic conservation is so limited, that one of the principal Arizona academics thought that the new program would have to be a PhD program in conservation, not the MA program that we were seeking to establish.

The meeting was getting nowhere: they simply failed to understand that a conservation graduate program had to be an MA degree. This is because the students would already have a BA or BSc degree, and taking an MA degree for another three years is usually quite enough time already, rather than the five-eight years of an American PhD degree, and that was not the aim in any case; the whole purpose of the new degree as the evangelists of the GCI saw it, was to train foreign students who would go back to their third-world countries and spread the message of conservation to the uninitiated. A worthy if totally unattainable concept. So Arizona was out: our next stop was the University of Washington, Seattle, as they had an impressive ethnographic collection, ideal for the students to work with.

Jerry Podany and I were, for some reason, charged with drawing up in a hurry suitable course content to help with the dialogue with our new potential partners, when we had already arrived in Seattle. This we did, and we reconvened with Marta de la Torre, Nicholas Stanley Price and the Washington State academics. It all seemed most promising, even if rather a long way from LA, and things seemed to be chugging along until it became obvious that one of the Washington folk wanted to be the Director himself, even though he had no training in conservation. Disagreements began to surface, and it meant that Washington was off the slate too. So what was wrong with UCLA our academic powerhouse just down the road in LA? The problem of UCLA is that the subject of Archaeology does not reside in a department, it is the Department of Anthropology one would have to deal with, and between anthropology and archaeological conservation there is an intellectual chasm that is virtually unbridgeable. So why no Department of Archaeology? Dirt archaeologists have not been that welcome in the rarefied atmosphere of US anthropology departments, something that Professor Merrick Posnansky, the first director of the UCLA Institute of Archaeology, does not address much in his autobiography *Africa and Archaeology*. Archaeological Departments are much better represented in the UK than they are in the USA. According to Dr. Shott, writing in *World Archaeology*, the Americans lost their chance for independent archaeology departments in the 1960's, when there was an opportunity for innovations previously beyond reach. If the Americans had, there would probably be many more archaeologists in the USA than there are today. Only an archaeological department can contemplate an interaction with a conservation department, since their interests in the preservation of archaeological artefacts, called objects in the USA, can meld together without an intellectual gulf being apparent, while the physical interaction with objects to conserve them or alter their appearance by restoration or cleaning is of no interest to an anthropologist at all.

At the time when Professor Posnansky was charged with the task of getting those interested in archaeology across campus to come together instead of existing in offices spread over seven separate UCLA buildings, there was no obvious building they could occupy. Anthropology had no interest, but around 1984, the Fowler Museum building was coming along, and the archaeologists fought for the basement space in the large building being planned.

Since there could not be a Department of Archaeology as such (why one wonders?), the Institute was configured as an Organized Research Unit (ORU) and as an IDP (inter-departmental program). Back in the UK, Archaeology Departments often had substantial numbers of undergraduate students, but the ORU/IDP itself, at UCLA, was predicated on being a graduate program, which seemed a pity to me, as back at the Institute of Archaeology in London, there were many undergraduates, helping to spread the message of archaeology and even archaeological conservation to a wider audience. It always seemed amazing to me that the Cotsen Institute of Archaeology at UCLA could fawn over five or possibly six students that they took in and funded each year. If competition was intense for one or two of them, the numbers coming to UCLA that year might be three! Three! That must be like a dream to some UK academics, stuck with teaching scores of undergraduates every year. In their home departments, since the Cotsen Institute could not be a home per se, the academics might indeed teach 200 undergraduates Ancient Rome every couple of years, complete with teaching assistants to do a fair amount of donkey work for them. No such luck at the Institute of Archaeology in London! Archaeologists were to some extent a colonial lot, in the sense that American or British archaeologists could get funding or could chose to work in Peru or Syria, but Peruvian or Syrian archaeologists could not get to work in Sussex or Washington State. The world is still our oyster. True, there are now areas of the world which are too dangerous for UK or USA archaeologists to work in: even Egypt might be tricky now in 2019 following the terrible fate of an Italian student, found dead in a gutter somewhere in Cairo. Too dangerous to take errant students to.

OK, back at Los Angeles, Marta de la Torre and Nicholas Stanley Price had approached UCLA some time in 1985 and been told by the then director of the Institute of Archaeology, that UCLA had no interest in hosting this new program at all. This might have been Professor Timothy Earle, an expert on the development of early societies, who moved his expertise from South America to Scandinavia for the kind of safety reasons alluded to above, whom I think was the director at that time, and whose home department was indeed Anthropology. Eventually, Professor Earle was succeeded by Associate Professor Richard Leventhal, who had worked with conservation to some extent at the site he had excavated at Xunantunich, an ancient Mayan site in western Belize, where Shin Maekawa, one of our late lamented colleagues had once undertaken the environmental survey work, and Professor Leventhal was much more receptive to the idea. Professor Leventhal even undertook several trips to discuss conservation with the few other academic conservation-training programs in North America, at NYU, Delaware, and Buffalo. This was looking promising now, and we interviewed several candidates for the position of Director of the new program. It transpired that the candidate, who was the obvious choice, could not be appointed at a level of a full professorship, and then the office charged with helping the candidate find an area to live in LA showed them around the Pacific Palisades! For those of you who do not know LA, the Palisades are a somewhat exclusive enclave and far from cheap. It simply was not going to work, the associate professorship status was also not that great, and she declined the directorship. We were back to almost square one again, especially as Richard Leventhal's publication record was judged by the UCLA committee of academics and principals (CAP) to be insufficient to merit advancement to a full professorship. He subsequently left UCLA and the helm at the Cotsen Institute was taken up by Professor Chip Stanish, although he too eventually left the Cotsen in 2016, much to my surprise, but then Professor Stanish had high ambitions and was ready for new pastures when his directorship of the Cotsen Institute came to an end.

However, Professor Stanish was less than keen on the idea of taking in the new conservation program too, but the late Lloyd Cotsen, our principal benefactor, told Chip that yes, the Cotsen Institute should take in the new conservation training program, which Professor Stanish subsequently agreed to do. Not that he was convinced, I think, by the intellectual content of the aegius of conservation, which might just as well be done by carefully trained janitors.

The strange thing about Lloyd Cotsen, is that I remember, a long time ago, it was in fact 1979, being in England and listening on the news to the remarkable story of a Californian businessman, whose wife and kids were being held at gunpoint by a crazed individual, wearing a ski mask in their Beverly Hills home. The wife and child were the family of Lloyd Cotsen, and they were shot dead along with a thirteen-year old friend. Lloyd heard about the deaths of his family on the radio as he was travelling out of town. The police eventually deduced that the person responsible was a forty-six year old Belgian businessman, Erich Arnold Tali, who was taking revenge on Lloyd for some business deal gone sour. Tali committed suicide in Brussels, the day he was to be questioned by the LA police, who had travelled to Belgium to arrest him.

I also remember the translucent bar of amber-coloured soap, Neutrogena, that was so brilliantly marketed by Lloyd that by 1994 he was able to sell the business and pocket 350 million dollars. One of his passions was archaeology and the collecting of art, and that is how Lloyd Cotsen became involved with the UCLA Institute of Archaeology. Following several donations to UCLA, the entire institute was re-named the Cotsen Institute of Archaeology, to honour their principal benefactor. I got to meet Lloyd several times, or work on some of his collection, examining the authenticity of his Chinese bronze mirrors, vetting a purchase for him, or acting at the Oxford agent for the thermoluminescence dating (TL) of a Chinese pottery figure. We only really trust the TL results produced by Oxford

Authentication Ltd., which at one point had to be hived off from the Research Laboratory for Art and Archaeology, due to the ethical problems of dating African ceramics. Lloyds collection of ancient Chinese bronze mirrors was housed in a penthouse suit in Beverly Hills, where I used to travel to, on several occasions, in my old battered Ford Windstar passenger van. The valet parking folk, all Hispanic, did not bat an eyelid as my old wreck was taken away to the garage to be parked next to Bentleys, Lexus's, BMW's, and other desirable automobiles. Lloyd's apartment, with a magnificent view over central and western Los Angeles, was completely given over to an art storage area on the 15th Floor of this Beverly Hills apartment block. Lloyd's immediate neighbour on the other side of the hall was an apartment owned by Cher, although the only person who seemed to be coming or going down the immaculately clean and spotless white carpet of the communal lobby seemed to be me.

Over a period of several months part-time work I gradually developed an "eye" for ancient Chinese bronze mirrors and the assorted problems of their authenticity, which are intriguing and complex. I wrote a long entry for the two superlative volumes on these Chinese mirrors for the books published by the Cotsen Institute Press, and was amused that the small square mirror, selected for the cover of one of the volumes, was actually a mirror I had shown to be a forgery! That aspect of the authenticity of art or its apparent indistinguishability from forgeries could consume many pages here, so for readers who are interested in the topic, I would recommend the two excellent volumes that the Cotsen Press Produced. Shortly before Lloyd gave away the entire collection of mirrors to the Shanghai museum, there was a series of lectures devoted to these mirrors at the Huntington Library in San Marino (effectively Los Angeles as far as us locals were concerned). I gave one, on something like a Tuesday night in November 2011, in the large auditorium at the Huntington, which must seat upwards of 300 people to an audience of about....eight. Yes, ancient Chinese bronze mirrors are something of a specialty topic.

If we go back to the period just before I left the GCI, around 2002, Nicholas Stanley Price had resigned from the GCI, just when Marta de la Torre had announced she was going on sabbatical leave. Whether this was a co-incidence I leave as an open question for the reader to decide. Shortly after that, Marta de la Torre herself resigned, as her family was moving to Florida, so she was off after many years of sterling work for the GCI, although we never really got on with each other.

I was beginning to think that I should now apply for the post, as a move from the Getty seemed a good idea, the only problem being that it was hardly dissociated from the Getty as the new program would be called the UCLA/Getty MA Program in Archaeological and Ethnographic Conservation and it was based in LA. Before I had even thought of applying for the position, a couple of years previously, I was involved in several planning meetings for the new program at the GCI, where Erica Avrami, Kathleen Dardes, Jerry Podany, Marta de la Torre and others were involved. The evangelists thought the new program should accept twelve students, mostly from foreign countries, and that no air-conditioning would be provided in the storage areas because the neophytes would need to learn how to conserve their ethnographic and archaeological artefacts without the aid of first-world country contraptions. I kept my mouth shut, since I was not about to contradict the entire group of GCI worthies, but remember thinking that the whole idea was unworkable, especially the straightforward problem of the lack of air-condition, which seemed to me to be an unjustifiable omission, and a false-consciousness as Sartre might have said, because one knew that if metallic objects were going to be loaned to the program for treatment by the students, then one of the prerequisites of the lenders would be that they are taken care of properly in terms of relative humidity. Normally, for metallic works of art we do not want the relative humidity to rise higher that 45%, and the only way to do that would be to install a special cabinet. This is exactly what Vanessa Muros, our lab supremo, had to eventually arrange to have installed.

I was charged with coming up with a list of equipment and expenditures for the putative new lab at the Getty Villa, which I did. Had I known at that time that I would eventually end up as the Director of the new program, I might have made the budget even more generous! It was about half a million for large items of equipment and a quarter of a million for small tools and equipment. This was needed in order to place the amount in next year's GCI budget.

So, the next round in the saga began and I applied for the position. Now I should explain a slightly arcane matter here to do with UCLA, which is a very complex behemoth of an institution. It was not thought that a new Department could be created for the new program: it would have to be an Inter-Departmental Program (IDP) operating in concert with the Cotsen Institute of Archaeology at UCLA which was also an Organized Research Unit (ORU), which has already been explained above. Even experienced UCLA professors run into trouble into thinking that the chairs of the IDP have to answer to the Director of the Cotsen Institute, but such is not the case. Well, in our case, the small number of faculty which would have to be hired for the new program were considered too small in number by UCLA to form a viable department per se. This had the consequence that any faculty hired by UCLA for the new program would have to be taken in by existing academic departments and have a joint appointment in the IDP, so that they each had a departmental faculty home. This is a logical conundrum since by definition skilled conservators are not art historians, anthropologists, culture specialists, information specialists, classicists, chemists or materials scientists. Once I had applied and the wheels had revolved round, I was selected as the new Director, and I accepted the new position. But which department was I going to be acceptable to? The obvious choice was chemistry, as my first degree had been in chemistry and I had many chemical-related publications in my armoire. The chair of the chemistry department was incredulous as soon as we met up at UCLA: the atmosphere of the interview was as if I was somewhat delusional. I was slightly baffled by this, as I thought that chemistry would be a good home for my range of skills. Another great boon is that a new faculty member in the department of chemistry and biochemistry (to give it a full moniker), was awarded about 800,000 dollars for new equipment to help him or her get off the ground. This was amazing to me: now it was my turn to be incredulous as well as excited at all the new equipment I could get to help the new conservation program run. However, the chemistry department, suffering from a kind of purist tunnel vision were not even aware that any scientific equipment was to be found in….a museum! How could that be?? And what use would a David Scott be anyway?

I invited them up to see the very impressive GCI laboratories, which I think did make an impression, but clearly not enough of one. They seemed to regard the new program as a scary venture, one not about to bring in millions of dollars of NSF or industrial funding, or to result in a Nobel Prize, so what good was it to anyone? Service to art in the name of conservation meant nothing to them. Chemistry was going to be a non-starter. So, it was back to the unknown, and as Professor Cecilia Klein was just passing our Dean's office, the Dean, Professor Scott Waugh asked her if Art History was in need of someone who could teach museum studies. She said yes, and the rest is history, even if I was not an art history graduate in any shape or form! So it was that I joined the Department of Art History at UCLA, and a wonderful and impressive bunch they are too. Unfortunately, art historians do not merit start-up funds of 800,000 dollars, so there was a certain mis-match between my new departmental home, and the laboratory side of art conservation. I began at UCLA in 2003 as the founding director of the UCLA/Getty conservation program, and as a full professor in the Department of Art History.

Consequently, I had to devise a couple of courses for the art history undergraduate students in order to consecrate my presence in the department. The first of these was most successful, *Art and Preservation*, which regularly drew between 30-55 undergraduates from a host of different departments across campus, and a few graduate students as well. I am especially proud of the fact that two of these undergraduates, on hearing about the message of art conservation during this course, went on to qualify for the MA in Conservation degree and to become trained conservators themselves.

In 2003, the putative program consisted of myself, and one graduate intern, Chris de Brer, paid for by the Getty for one year, to help get things started up. This was a complex time, and having advertised for two assistant professors to join me in forming the core faculty of the program, I set about trying to find a department who might be interested in taking the first one in. Scott Waugh was our Dean of Social Sciences and he was much involved with the budget and hiring of the new faculty. For our first applicant, I tried the Department of World Arts and Culture, then Anthropology, Art History, and then the Department of Architecture, without getting anywhere. The chair of the World Arts and Culture department that year happened to be a dance instructor, to whom the concept of art conservation was entirely alien. The Departments of Architecture and of Anthropology, predictably, could see no benefit to them in taking in an assistant professor in conservation. The applicant was savvy to these issues and withdrew their application, probably wondering about the willingness of UCLA to put its mouth were its money was. The next applicant was Ellen Pearlstein, a skilled and talented conservator of the ethnographic arts who hailed from Brooklyn Museum, New York, and whose work I knew of. Ellen Pearlstein did not have a PhD, which in the eyes of many UCLA departments meant that she was effectively classed as sub-human. This was going to be a problem, as Art History were not willing to take her in either. Scott Waugh and I thought it over: clearly she was the best candidate so something had to be devised to get her on board. Scott came up with an adjunct professorship at the Cotsen Institute and a lecturing role. It is to Ellen's credit that she took the position under these terms and we began to plan out a possible sequence of courses.

The next applicant was Dr. Ioanna Kakoulli, who despite some opposition from the GCI, I considered to be the next obvious choice. Ioanna had a PhD so surely it would not be too difficult to find her a Departmental home. I tried the Department of Classics, since Ioanna could have taught some Greek, but they were particularly surly, as if they had been press-ganged into a meeting that no-one except Scott Waugh and the unknown David Scott had wanted and requested, so that was hopeless. Next, the Department of Anthropology: that was totally out of the question. They were a department that could never be swayed by issues of a wider import. Next, the Department of Art History: the answer from the then chair, the late and gracious Irene Bierman-McKinny, was a very quick no, probably in realization that this fellow Scott from Conservation had already been accepted, and seemed rather useless, so the thought of taking on another one was too much to stomach.

Obviously the Department of World Arts and Culture was still out of the running, as it was still in the hands of dance experts. I returned to discuss the matter with Scott Waugh, who was a very experienced hand  "I don't know what to suggest" said Scott, raising his hands to heaven. "How about the Department of Materials Science?" I suggested. "You can give it a go" Said Scott.  Now Materials Science comes under a completely different Dean, as it is not in the Social Sciences at all, and Scott would therefore have to come up with the salary for the post, giving the Materials Science Department an extra bod for free, in a manner of speaking. I despondently trooped over to Materials Science to meet with the then chair, whom luckily for me had done his PhD at the Massachusetts Institute of Technology (MIT). MIT, is one of the few American universities which has a relationship between the Department of Anthropology and the Department of Materials Science. At UCLA this is more or less impossible due to the high-falluting nature of the Department of Anthropology and the mental distance to the Department of Materials Science. It just so happened that Cyril Stanley Smith, metallurgist, and Heather Lechtman, anthropologist, important names in the study of metals and ancient metallurgy had been based at MIT and the two departments had collaborated with each other, or at least seen their mutual admiration in a mirror of possibilities, including student training, even if jointly authored papers was not one of them.

The Chair of Materials Science therefore saw the potential for collaboration, and there was another reason: at that stage the Materials Science Department had no women faculty members, and therefore Ioanna would be a first, and add to the diversity of the department. He was quite open to the idea, which almost made my eyes bulge forward, but I acted cool and, scarcely able to believe my luck, I reported back to Scott Waugh and the wheels were set in motion, and an impressive amount of work for the Materials Science Department has been done by Professor Kakoulli since she was hired, as well as her teaching for the Conservation Programme.

We also needed a skilled conservator as the laboratory supervisor for the Getty-located lab for the MA students at the sublime Getty Villa. I met with the GCI folk to discuss the issue and Kris Kelly objected, saying that the lab did not need that kind of person, but just a technician. I argued with them and prevailed, and so Vanessa Muros was taken on as the Villa lab supervisor. At this stage the revamped Villa, at a cost of 250 million, had not yet been finished so all of us, including our very able secretary, Amber Cords-Cole, were based at UCLA. We began the process of interviewing potential students for the September 2005 date for the first entry for our new course. Now, this is where the reality of life shows a serious departure from the visions foisted on the program by the GCI. There were no foreign applicants, and we had rapidly determined that we could only afford to support six students in any case, not twelve! And so it has remained ever since. One year we took on seven or eight to gain brownie points with the Social Sciences budget figures, which was just a waste of time: no kudos accrued to our program in the 2008 period when the budget was in need of being trimmed due to the fiscal crises of that time, so we reverted to six after that. The program was designed to accept six students every second year, since we would not have been able to teach the large variety of courses that the MA program demanded, just the three of us, and in their third year, the students went on paid or financially supported (by us) internships all over the world. Both Ellen Pearlstein and Ioanna Kakoulli were much more adept at raising funds for the program than I was. My principal success was in transforming three graduate funding positions from the Social Sciences, which is what we had been set with, into a budget for the six students overall. We had an endowment of one million dollars provided by the Getty and in the end Ioanna was successful in getting the matching one million dollars, giving us the interest income from two million, which really helped to sustain the entire program.

At the same time Ellen and I (principally Ellen) had been in many conversations with Angelica Zander Rudenstein, at the Andrew W. Mellon Foundation in New York. The Mellon Foundation is our fairy godmother in the field of art conservation, as it is one of the five core areas it is prepared to fund. Their endowment is a staggering 6.1 billion, founded in 1969, a perfect time for art conservation, as the field was just finding its new feet about then. In 1993, Angelica Rudenstein took over the Museum and Art Conservation section, and I have to pay her a considerable and sincere tribute here, as otherwise her contributions may be lost to history. Angelica wore a pair of large, round red glasses that matched the large spirit and drive she brought to the subject of art and conservation. Combined with her intelligent understanding of the needs of the field of conservation, her indefatigability, her wide geographical knowledge of the needs of conservation across North America, and her gracious presence at meetings, Angelica really did become the incarnation of a fairy godmother. Perhaps because she also had the mind of a scholar I felt an affinity to her, which was unusual for me, as no highly placed Getty employees had the same attraction for me. After she had waived her magic wand, new conservation positions sprung up in numerous museums across North America, new positions for those who already had conservation departments, new scientists for departments who had none, the deepening of the academic engagement of college and university art museums; the identification of needs in the area of photographic conservation and the creation of programs to meet those needs; the development of science within art conservation, bringing to bear the highest level of scientific expertise; the strengthening of advanced conservation training programs, and the creation and support of positions for conservators in a wide range of institutions.

Much more could be said about her ability to bring together professionals at the highest level to pursue issues in which conservation, science, and art historical scholarship intersect powerfully. Each of us could add still more from our personal work with her and would be able to let her know how very much we value what she has accomplished.

Angelica retired from the Foundation in March 2010. However, thanks to the art historical community having discovered the issues revolving around the issues of materiality, the coinage of art conservation has been much revalued, as we were the ones dealing with materiality over the past 100 years, during some of that time the art historians had forsaken materials as rather old hat, until it gradually dawned on them that a great number of different kinds of hat could be placed on materials, with all kinds of interesting results and discussions. True, this has not greatly helped advance the causes of ethnographic conservation or natural history conservation, some of our largest collectives in terms of object numbers. For example the Natural History Museum of Los Angeles County houses 33.5 million objects or specimens alone and has one or possibly two conservation staff!

So, with our complement of academic and administrative staff complete, and the Getty Villa labs well on their way to completion, we could now get on with the business of teaching. Space was still a problem. Admittedly we had our offices at the new Getty/UCLA labs over at Malibu, but the spaces allotted to the program at UCLA were fundamentally inadequate. Yes, I get your lack of enthusiasm for this gripe. However, the archaeologists all had "labs" which were essentially huge rooms with books, desks and computers in them. We had a "lab" which, in the end result, I was not allowed to actually mount in resin or etch with chemicals any of my metallographic samples, due to the usual draconian health and safety regulations. The four of us ended up with one large lab space and tiny offices for the three of us, or the four of us, depending on how we are counted, as our administrative officer occupied a desk in the "lab" space. We had an x-ray diffractometer in that room, complete with computer, desk, chiller, pump, and water pipes, polishing equipment for preparing samples, two microscopes, a hand grinding machine, books and accessories, a diamond cut-off machine and associated chemical supplies. A lot of kit. It made for a messy and aesthetically unsatisfying assemblage of personnel, offices, equipment and chairs. In order to create something that would have worked properly at UCLA for the students as well as the staff, two separate large "labs" would really have been required, but as faculty are prepared to battle over the smallest square inch of space across campus, one might as well have asked for the moon. Our wonderful lab space at the Getty Villa and associated offices were very gratefully received, but the physical separation between the proper laboratory spaces for the conservation students at the Villa, and the necessity to undertake teaching based at UCLA, meant a split existence and a military approach to time and location.

Only once did I leave home in the car to attempt to get to UCLA on a Monday morning when I should have been travelling to the Getty Villa! Parking was free at the Getty Villa, and there was good, subsidized food at the staff refectory. No ordinary visitors were allowed in our area of the Villa, and the library, then run by Barbara Furbush (until her position was deemed redundant) was for the use of our conservation students, staff and visiting faculty only. Any book that the students wanted on conservation was either already at the Getty Villa library, or it was sent over from the main library at the Getty Center. The reading room was a joy to behold, being part of the old Ranch House, Getty's first building on the site all those decades ago. On a wet Wednesday in November, the central area of our zone was like a mysterious painting by De Chirico, all sharp angles, staircases, courtyards, the clean lines of buildings totally bereft of any human beings, illuminated by a diagonal slice of sunlight.

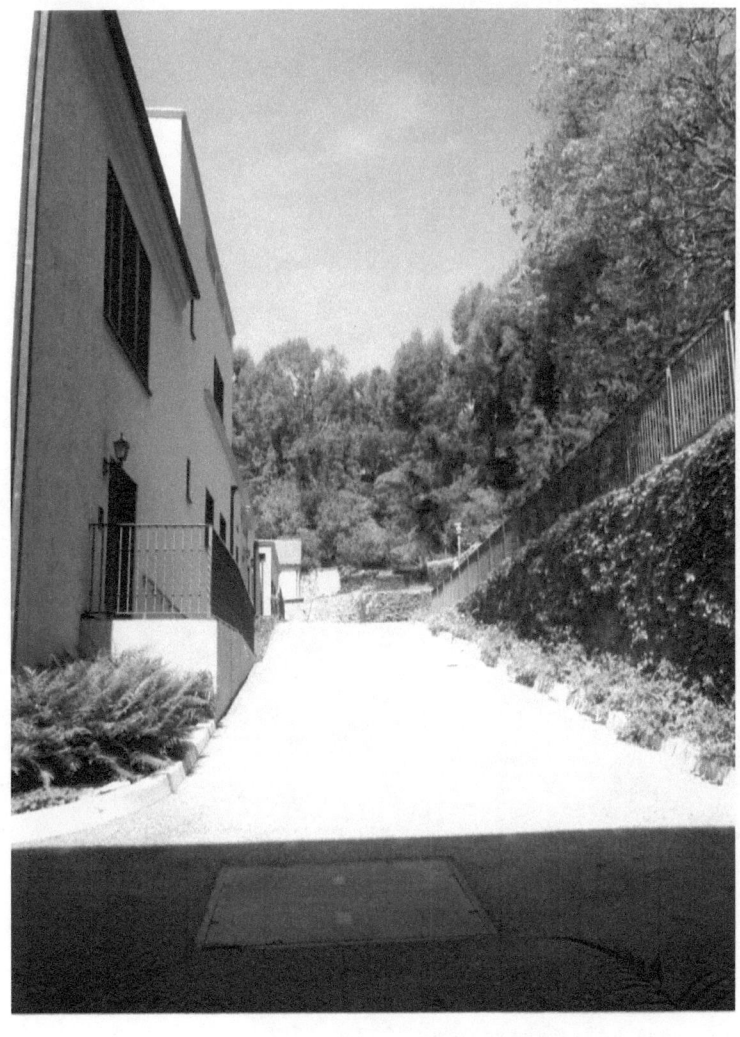

The view of the side of the back of the Getty Villa from my office window. The architects had not thought that a desk looking out at this tranquil view was of any benefit, and I made my own desk which did afford a view. Photograph by the author, March 12thr 2016.

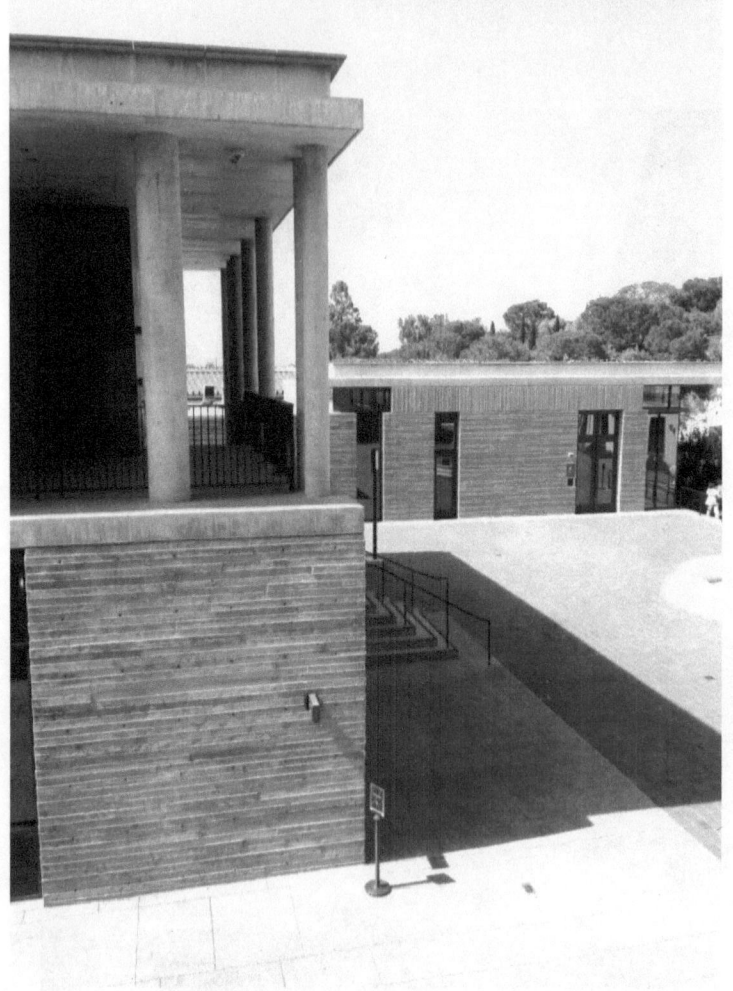

The Ranch House rebuilt. Rectilinear forms with a De Chirico ambience. Cast concrete with wooden batten impression finish from the casting battens. Photograph by the author 2017. This area of the Villa is for staff and faculty only, but often looks stark and empty. 12th June 2017.

This ambience could give the paradise of our part of the Getty villa an unreal, surreal, presence. Our library facilities here were augmented by the massive holdings of the University of California system, and of course, the increasing number of papers and books available on-line at the touch of a button. The University system, like most other standard libraries, had no idea what archaeological and art conservation was all about, but had every scientific and mainstream humanities publication going. This meant that the combination of the Getty Villa library and the UCLA library produced between them a world-class resource for art and archaeological conservation unequalled anywhere else in the world. This was of great benefit to me in writing two of my books in particular, the volume on *Copper and Bronze: Corrosion, Colourants, Conservation*, already referred to above, and my 2016 volume, *Art: Authenticity, Restoration, Forgery*. The latter volume really tested my skills of library use. The Getty and UCLA were an inspiration for such a wide-ranging volume as the literature reviewed or read for my book went from the Palaeolithic to the Contemporary art scene, from Plato to Derrida and Deleuze, and from Pliny to Arthur C. Danto and Paul Craddock, and practically all of it one never had to order from outside. Exceptions were rare, such as some of the work of H.H. Coghlan, a retired railway engineer, who wrote a number of papers published in the *Transactions of the Newbury Archaeological Society* or equivalent obscure British journal, which had to be ordered inter-library loan from Boston Spa in the UK!

My book was a natural outcome of one of the new courses I had prepared for the Art History Department, called *Art and Authenticity*, which proved both popular and intellectually rewarding for myself as well as, hopefully, a few of the students. The first general course I had devised for them was *Art and Preservation*, which was also a success, already mentioned above. In an effort to generate some awareness of the desirability of preservation and conservation to the archaeology students, they were invited to attend the course as well, as all the other art history, classics, near eastern students etc., but they did not seem to like the message, and all six of them backed out of the course after three or four lectures. This act of volition was quite within their rights, but was somehow symptomatic of the lack of integration of archaeological conservation within the Cotsen Institute as a whole.

UCLA had introduced a series of lectures called the Fiat Lux series. As a cornerstone of an innovative undergraduate curriculum, UCLA offered up to 200 seminars annually through the *Fiat Lux* Freshman Seminar Program. These seminars provided students and faculty with small group settings to engage in meaningful discussions on a range of topics. Students received one-unit of academic credit and faculty members from across campus had the opportunity to share with undergraduates their areas of intellectual passion and expertise. True to the University of California's motto, *"Fiat Lux* – Let There Be Light," these seminars illuminated the many pathways of discovery! We, who taught the Fiat Lux seminars, also received $1500 for our efforts, although teaching the Luxes did not result in a credit for another teaching course as such. I taught a Fiat Lux every year, once I had understood how they worked, about 12 years of such courses. They were given under the rubric of Chemistry and Biochemistry Section 19, and most of the students were from the sciences across campus. They were not an easy target to entertain, those students, so I enjoyed the challenge. Most of my colleagues never taught a Fiat Lux course, neither Ioanna or Ellen were tempted to teach one every year, which I thought a shame. The same was true with Art History: there were one or two who did, but that was the extent of it. As the Fiat Lux with the science students evolved over the years from more or less teaching, more or less discussion, it gradually became clear that most of these students had never worked with their hands at all: no woodwork, no pottery, no plaster, no metalwork, and little painting. I introduced them to mold-making and casting in plaster, to pigments and colour, and revolved any discussion around that. Mostly they were intrigued, and it was then that I realised what huge gaps there were in most of their educational training: being rather clever, they had neglected the practical side of their lives to such an extent that their balance of activities was completely skewed. A few of these students were very grateful for the chance to talk about and work with making casts of their own hands. As there was no budget for supplies, I cobbled together some casting supplies from our labs at the Getty, and the rest I had to fork out of my own pocket. I managed to give them a behind-the-scenes tour of the Fowler Museum, and of course, they had no idea what went on in a typical museum. The storerooms, packing, crating, receiving, accessioning, mounting, exhibition, labelling, photographing, conservation, compact storage was all new to them. Chris de Brer who had graduated from our course by then had been lucky: the previous conservator Jo Hill had gone back to the biological sciences in a hospital and Chris de Brer had become the conservator at the Fowler Museum, a post he relished. One or two of the undergraduate students who we had shown round later volunteered to work at the Fowler, another success for our process of indoctrination of the general public into our world of museums and conservation.

As our MA students undertook three years of work for their degree, two years of taught work and one, a year-long internship, they had to be visited by a faculty member while they were on their internship, usually in some far-flung location. We should note in passing here, that a three-year MA degree program is not the European norm. MA degrees are usually regarded as money-generating courses lasting somewhat less than a year. Ours was a money-giving course spread over three years! One of my memorable visits was to assess our Belgian student, Siska Genbrugge, who had ended up working at the British Museum for her internship. I remember interviewing this student, as since she was finishing her studies in Amsterdam at the time she applied, we conducted a telephone interview with her, and were most impressed with her background, degrees, and preparation for the conservation graduate course. She was one of the six students we accepted that year, and we had to provide financial support for all of them, a situation almost incredible for the poor UK universities to imagine.

So it was that I flew over to the UK in February 2010, economy class, as usual, to stay for a couple of nights with my mum and Val in Chandos Crescent, Edgware, both of whom are no longer with us. I wrote up my trip for this visit as it seemed both memorable and nostalgic. I took a minicab with a voluble Kenyan Asian Brit lady who derided all the lazy dole-takers hooked on benefits. We were going to the British Museum outbuilding in Hoxton, down Orsman Road. I had been to this dump many years previously in a different life, when I was still a lecturer at UCL, following up on my PhD research on ancient Colombian metallurgy: that was around 1984, at a time when Hoxton really was the back of beyond. I had parked the Austin 1300 nervously, outside a scruffy block of council flats, I remember that as there was not a soul to be seen anywhere, which seemed even more sinister. Like many areas of London, this previously working-class area of the dispossessed was now becoming even trendy, or at least livable in. Well, the minicab driver had no idea where 48-56 Orsman Road was, so used her SATNAV to plot out her route. Not the best option, as the plotted path went down Holloway Road, which Val had strenuously advised against, giving me detailed written directions on a post-it which the Kenyan lady ignored completely, relying instead on her abstract electronics rather than the street-cred of the locals. Needless to say, we came to a complete halt down Holloway Road.

48-56 Orsman Road on the N1 side of the divide, E8 is the assignation of the other side, forms a shabby factory-like frontage running some distance along the anonymous warehouse and storage buildings making up this dead stretch of Orsman Road, once bustling factories perhaps one hundred years ago. The Stag Head pub and council housing on the other side, in fearful E8, had a forbidding ambience.

Indeed, staff from this British Museum outpost have to be transported by shuttle bus to Liverpool Street Station at night for their own safety, when both N1 and E8 come out down Orsman Road, with young women having a cat-fight outside the pub, or a careless block of ice might be tossed at the unwary female conservator hurrying home. Over the decades enough unsavory incidents had occurred that the British Museum had kept the shuttle bus going, even when the shuttle between BM HQ and the BM of Orsman Road was terminated a few years ago. Now it takes staff an hour to get to the BM by public transport and another hour or so to get back if they attend meetings at Russell Square, not exactly an efficient use of a conservator's time.

A portly Irish BM security officer with rather pale skin, baldhead and twinkly eyes signed me in. He knows that I must be a special visitor, as David Saunders, Head of Conservation at the BM, has already made the trip to Orsman Road on my behalf. Siska Genbrugge, Belgian, with her bright blonde hair and light amber skin looks like the visitor, the foreign graduate intern from our programme in LA that she is.

Quite undeterred by her dowdy surroundings, we enter a series of strangely malformed corridors and out across a rainy porch covering to another segment of the old factory where the textile conservation resides. En passant, we encounter Maori masks, Inuit canoes, Congolese drums, broken down furniture and historic paintwork a strange and sickly shade of yellow. Siska's supervisor is the somewhat fey, ethereal Pippa Cruickshank, a survivor, perhaps institutionalized, underrated textile expert, one of the few to have lasted over twenty years at the British Museum. She quietly darts her fingers over a keyboard that needs attention, of a network of strings, each holding a textile in the new position ordained for it as aesthetically desirable or necessary for its survival.

Siska and I examine a sown gut parka with decorated polychrome borders from the Aleutian Islands, brought back to Cornwall by some intrepid Cornish sailor and donated to a local Museum a hundred years ago. The Cornish museum, seeing that the gut had no connection to Cornwall, ordered its deaccession, and so, shorn of its local history, the parka ends up dirty and damaged in this prison-like outbuilding where it has been mouldering away for the past fifty years or so. And now Siska is lovingly restoring the tears and losses with specially designed and flattened sausage casing, cleanly bordered with thinner stock, so that the repaired edge adheres to the remaining gut and doesn't look too opaque when the translucent gut is held to the light. Siska uses non-woven spun-bound polyester for patching holes, as it is very light and strong. She also tested Japanese papers and goldbeaters skin, but they were too weak for this job. For adhesion Siska used Klucel G and Vinamul. Vinamul is stronger, so she used it for the structural repairs to try to hold the precious parka together, with Klucel G for the edges. Siska was lucky – the previous intern had spent several weeks just clearing dirt and grime from the parka. A gut decorated hat would have completed the outfit: a ceremonial ensemble that the Aleutian Eskimos used for what especial purpose or ritual? "If the repairs are successful this gut cloak might make it to display in the refurnished North American gallery" said Pippa. "How will you support it?" I asked. She makes a face. It obviously would be a task in itself as the cape is very full and wide by the time the bottom hem is stretched out.

We go off to another corridor which opens to an enormous square room with old industrial metal alloy framed windows along two entire outside walls. On a series of tables, a few conservators are busy at work on various textile fragments from the Andean region. Most ethnographic cultures of the world are represented in this unlikely building, whose principal claim to security is that no-one knows what goes on inside its fusty walls.

From the mist of the grey exterior, a view of the asbestos-fibre board roof of the warehouse kiosk next door and on the other – a stunning view of a three-story disused factory building across the canal that runs along the back of Orsman Road. The decrepit factory is glass-paned all the way along its 400 feet length with angled glass skyfacing along the top. God knows what kind of factory life took place there in the distant past, but the entire edifice was now deserted and had been so for decades.

"A storm whipped up debris from next door and it shattered some of the glass" said a Canadian conservator sitting at one of the workbenches, looking lost in the huge volume of space surrounding her table.

"Have they fixed any?" I said

"No, no-one's doing anything about it"

Next door to this elephant of a building, a more modest factory had a couple of super-trendy lofts now perched incongruously on top of it, the vanguard of the Middle Class reoccupation of Hoxton.

"Hoxton? You don't want to go there mate" advised my late Father-in-law a few years ago "that's where they find bodies stuffed down drains"

It was certainly an ambience of Hoxton's past which made it the kind of place no-one would ever visit, not in those days.

"You can see milk bottles hanging up in one of the flats over there " said the Senior Textile Conservator "and it's obvious there's no furniture"

That was the E8 side of Orsman Road, not over the canal where the lofts sat, expectantly, of the gentrification to come. The days of the sinister glass-enveloped monster were clearly drawing to a close. The canal looked too cold and too wet. Suddenly a narrow barge drifted into sight and chugged past the BM outpost. Two mad joggers in the freezing February rain stamped along the towpath and disappeared in the mist.

It was a strange vista. A landscape in transition, with the canal like a life-blood, now pumping, now reviving the squalid and neglected with its presence, and the possibility of a new life, both for itself and for those who surrounded it. These buildings were so old they were almost in need of conservation themselves as historic sites of the late Victorian side of the Industrial Revolution. Another twenty years or so and they would all be gone, replaced by expensive canal-access gardened detached houses or edgy lofts for a couple of million each. It was a property developers dream. Across the water, a scary and precarious-looking hole was being chomped at by one small and one large JVC, while sturdy labourers worked without any shoring, fifteen feet below ground level. No health and safety experts in sight. These were the first signs of new beginnings underfoot in 2010.

We chatted with the head of textile conservation. An experienced hand, but somewhat typically, had only been at the BM for three years. It is a feature of the place, as David Saunders himself has now, in 2015, taken early retirement and is off enjoying various courses and consultancies, rather than serve out his time for the mantelpiece clock. Complex beings, Museums, especially hallowed institutions such as the British Museum.

"Yes" she said, when I had remarked on the paucity of staff, "it looks a bit deserted here, but we do have more staff – they all work part-time"

"How is that possible?" I said, with genuine amazement. I had obviously been in America too long to understand how practically all of her staff worked four or three or even two days a week.

"It means a heavier burden if you're full time" She said. "When they want consultation about design or exhibitions or whatever, then that might fall to me to do, as the others aren't here"

I nodded sagely, marvelling at this humane approach to permanent part-time employment. I don't think it applied to conservators at the Getty Museum. There was one married couple who split their work down the middle, but that arrangement was a historical relic of a bygone age of a gentleness and consideration to its ordinary staff that the Getty had forsaken sometime around 1997. No new hires at the Getty could split their working lives for their own purposes: all allegiance was now to Getty only.

It was time for lunch. As quietly as David Saunders had disappeared when we first shook hands that morning before Siska had whisked me off upstairs, he reappeared and the four of us, David, the Senior Textile Conservator, Siska and me left for lunch. Poor Pippa was, of course, not invited for this, tacitly, was going to be a BM lunch paid for out of what John LeCarre would have called the reptile fund – the meagre BM hospitality fund set aside for this purpose.

Having last visited Orsman Road in 1984 to rummage around in the old drawers of Peruvian maceheads, badly conserved and forgotten, I feared what kind of food either this end of N1 or E8 might be able to dredge up: on my last visit there was not a restaurant or even a chippie in sight. But this was 2010 and we were on the canal side now, with a brand new sustainable food-serving Hoxton trendy-hangout only fifty yards down Orsman Road.

"You can't get orange juice here "explained the Senior Textile Conservator "but you can get apple juice, because apple juice is sustainable"

I mulled this over without really solving the problem. Coming from

LA where the entire San Fernando Valley used to be devoted to orange groves, it seemed a bit hard to grasp. Indeed, in 2008, Tropicana, one of the largest orange juice creators in the world, was using landfill gas for a portion of its operations. In 2007, approximately 30% of the facility's thermal energy demands were derived from this renewable resource. I read "Tropicana's production process aims to utilize the full life-cycle of the orange. For example, Tropicana recycles peel and seeds to make 150,000 tons of beneficial cattle feed, avoiding more than 700,000 tons of raw peel becoming landfill waste annually". So maybe that is what it was all about.

The restaurant side windows looked out over the canal as we gazed at the hazy view through the translucence induced by the rain. Another barge with a group of young BAME schoolchildren on board, undeterred by the weather, churned up the still grey water, and behind them, the pastel shades of freshly painted wall came into view, divided into large coloured squares – the communal work of some Japanese artist which had already attracted artwork of the local graffiti artists along the lower level of the squares, adding an authentic touch of the indigenous population.

We chatted about old times, old colleagues, the latest twist and turns of the politburo which organizes and controls the political life of museums, the pre-emptive cuts David had introduced and the next round of depressing budgets ahead. I had a sustainable fish dish – pan seared mullet in a tasty gravy of boiled mussels with herbs and minute squares of potatoes. So minute that I finished the main course and was still hungry, a not uncommon experience in posh or trendy restaurants these days.

The colour of the mullet looked as if it could have locally caught in the canal - the Regents Canal as it happens – but I trusted that such fishing would not yet be a sustainable enterprise and was probably banned by the Regent, so pulling back the little flap of grey skin, I ate it up. The chocolate fondant dessert was also very good. The whole restaurant had been established for re-employment of freshly trained young folk, taken from the unemployment register, a laudatory venture to create new job possibilities by some enlightened millionaire.

The eco-credentials of this restaurant were way ahead of anything in Los Angeles. The restaurant used the ambient water temperature from the canal (under license from British Waterways) and the latest in heat pump technology to produce energy- efficient cooling for ice cream, roof-mounted solar panels to provide hot water, photovoltaic cells to produce renewable electricity, hydrocarbon fridges to reduce energy consumption, a waste management system using a wormery to digest raw food for composting, a localized waste management technology, and even made its own premium-filtered and chilled bottled water on site with some new-fangled filtration system. Back in the US of A, our then beloved Californian governor, Arnold Schwarzenegger, had the gall to attend the global meeting on climate control as if energy-sucking LA was in the lead of reducing its huge carbon footprint in 2010 or its car-driven polluted air. As usual, when it comes to saving anything, the Americans were way behind the curve in 2010.

Way, way behind this restaurant, that was certain.

The Regents Canal – part of the great watery tributaries of the Grand Union Canal, are preserved thanks, amazingly, to the efforts of one man – Ted Rolt, who saw their value and charm in the 1930's when this stretch of the canal was an overgrown, polluted, dangerous and inaccessible place, just about to be infilled with concrete. Now, its waters are clean, navigable and safe, a desirable relief from the ill-tempered streets clogged with a grumpy assortment of cars, vans, lorries, articulated vehicles, the odd moped, brave cyclist and scores of buses. No wonder that today, the followers of Ted Rolt are so grateful for all that he had done: he had preserved something precious that could never be replaced at a time when few could see any benefit from the canal at all.

There was certainly no hope of seeing any change to the area in 1984, the last time I was here, in the dark days of Thatcherism with her vacuous work schemes which just created cheap labour for fat-cat companies and took numbers off the unemployment statistics: Hoxton continued as it always had, with dreadful unemployment and rife with crime. We walked back in the rain to the other end of Orsman Road where the affable white-headed security chap let me ring for a mini-cab. This had been done so many times before that the cab number was glued to the front of his telephone. Yes, 2010 was just before the days of the iPhone for many of us. David Saunders had left already, en route to St. Albans and hence to Lisbon with the family for a short break. We bade farewell. As the Nigerian taxi driver looked up Val's Chandos Crescent address, we began the crawl up Holloway Road with the SATNAV on again, as we had made our way down, jostling through the grimy traffic as best we may and coming to a standstill yet again. God knows if I'll ever be down Orsman Road again, but one thing is certain: the view through the misty haze floating over the Regents Canal in winter will not remain the same. Through the haze a new life will be born out of what remains of Hoxton and the canal will flourish once more. Hoxton may even become a place to live.

The Regents Canal remained special to me, having been such a long-term residence of the Regents Park Council Estate and so often the wonderful Canal was a backdrop for me, or nowadays for thousands of Londoners and visitors to Camden Lock and Camden market.

That was my world: the schizophrenic duality of London Museums and LA Museums, LA and London, the USA and the UK, we were always backwards and forwards, forwards and backwards over the years until eventually we escaped back to the UK in 2017. The world of Museums is an international world, linked together by objects, events, exhibitions, loans, conferences, interns, travel and research. It is a world that greatly involves both conservators and curators, because when objects travel across borders, they have to be accompanied by a human for their own safety, usually a skilled conservator, especially when they are de-installed or re-installed in Vienna, San Francisco, San Paulo, St. Petersburg, Paris, Turin, New York, Copenhagen, London, Beijing, or any one of another score of locations across the globe. The spoilt darlings usually have to be provided with the perfect temperature and constant relative humidity that they are accustomed to, otherwise no-end of trouble may occur: they may warp, corrode, become contaminated, weep, desiccate, swell, shrink, discolour, or even fall to pieces.

These complaints the human being must try to prevent at all costs. The cosseted ones arrive or leave carefully cushioned in relative humidity controlled crates, made specially for them, taken across country in the best lorries with air-cushioned suspension to avoid any jolts or bumps. Meanwhile we sit in economy class, trying to find something to eat in the increasingly disgusting offerings of food. On arrival or departure from the museum the darlings have to be logged in, inspected, a condition report perhaps prepared for them, and installation or de-installation arranged with the preparation department who are responsible for the safe mounting or hanging of the artworks. Since some of them weigh tons, this is an important function. Special display cases may have to be ordered or built to house them, the total cost often exceeding 100,000 dollars, and these may be used only once, for the special exhibition being put up or being taken down. One of the problems of present-day museum display in Europe and North America is that they are all supposed to change over every three months. Even working at the Getty Museum might mean that an exhibition you fancied seeing had come and gone before you realised it. One special exhibition at the Getty, called *Devices of Wonder*, was indeed a wonderful exhibition, except that it had taken almost twelve years to plan and has ended up being on display for eleven weeks, with temporary cases costing over 150,000 dollars alone! Clearly, the museum world was one in which these kinds of ridiculous costs would always be happening, even if the insane amount of time that went into putting this particular exhibition together might not work out too well as a role model! The punters have to be given something new every three months otherwise they might not continue to flood through the doors.

Some of these exhibitions are simply brilliant, but without a detailed record of them, they come to reside only in the memory and gradually fade until they are lost in time, or some faint spark of remembrance takes you back there. Some of these exhibitions do not have exhibition catalogues, which guarantees their consignment to the oblivion of fading memory. A properly detailed video of the entire exhibition would be one way to assist with the fond memory of their existence, but there is a major problem with the idea: some lenders would refuse any permission to film their artwork as they want to keep the aura of the work entirely for themselves and their own museum, rather than making it available for posterity as part of a holistic vision.

One of the exhibitions I am recalling is that of the bronzes of Adrien de Vries, held at the Getty Museum in 1995. Everything about this exhibition was quite outstanding and unique: it will never be repeated in our lifetime. The de Vries bronzes were mounted on cool grey pedestals or stands, the lighting was perfect, the space for each bronze was carefully balanced to complement the show, and the overall impact of the exhibition stunning. H.M. Queen Elizabeth II of England and H.M. King Carl XVI Gustaf of Sweden loaned sculptures. Insurance indemnities was provided by respective government ministries in the Netherlands, Sweden and the United States of America, which essentially made the exhibition possible, otherwise insurance costs would have been prohibitive. There is an excellent catalogue for this exhibition, but it is just a book: it says nothing about the exhibition itself or its inspiring ambience. The exhibition spurred the book, but the book cannot represent the exhibition, it is only an abstraction of it. And so by comparison, the exhibition had a life of its own, and the book not even a pale reflection of it, just a collection of scholarly articles on De Vries.

Lenders would never have agreed to have a permanent film made of the exhibition, as it would compromise the sense of possession that each King, Queen, Museum, or organization, feels for their artwork, so matter how feeble that sentiment seems.

Another brilliant exhibition was the display devoted to the classical marble sculpture of Antinous, which the Russians had looted from Dresden at the end of the 2nd world war. The life-size sculpture had been stuffed into a wooden crate, thrown on the back of a lorry, and transported with a host of other art spoils to Leningrad. When the curators at the Hermitage opened the crate, the looted sculpture had been broken into scores of pieces. They shut the crate up again and consigned it to storage in the Hermitage basement. There it lay for sixty-odd years until the Russians decided that the useless fragments were better repatriated to the Germans. So the crate of broken bits went back to the Skulpturen Sammlung, Staatliche Kunstsammlungen, Dresden, who percipiently had noticed that the best conservators in the world to approach for any potential restoration, were the stone conservators at the Antiquities Conservation Department at the Getty Villa in Malibu. In this they were perfectly correct: no real time pressure, excellent materials, superb facilities, no money worries, and highly skilled conservators to work on your broken sculpture. And, after a six-month exhibition of the restored Antinous at the Getty, Dresden gets the sculpture back again, all costs covered, and the work beautifully restored. What could be better?

The American group, Friends of Heritage Preservation, run by an ex-Getty conservator, Suzanne Deal Booth, even put up funds to assist with the restoration! The reason why the 200-odd fragments were so significant is a matter of the problem of identity of the work of art. When found in Italy in the 1600s, the sculpture was missing its head, right arm, and parts of the feet and drapery. Over the next two centuries, the identity of the statue was reinterpreted, restored parts were removed and replaced, and the figure assumed a variety of titles, from Alexander the Great to Antinous in the guise of Bacchus, to Bacchus or Antinous himself, each with different marble heads but the same body with different arms or attributes.

The exhibition of the headless sculpture, surrounded by photographs of the work in the guise of its three different identities was simply brilliant. As Cesare Brandi writes "For restoration to be a legitimate operation it cannot presume that time is reversible or that history can be abolished." Brandi captures our ambivalent attitude to the removal of time's effects on works of art and whether that constitutes a denial of their historicity or not. Time can be attempted to be reversed in a number of ways: a work can be stripped of all later additions, it can be disassembled, if various components are not thought to be original to it, it can become a collection of fragments, or a pastiche reconstruction as an ersatz masterwork. Time is the handmaiden or the tyrant of restoration, but some survive through time to be admired, as Keats writes, of the Elgin Marbles, having seen them for the first time:

My spirit is too weak; mortality
Weighs heavily on me like unwilling sleep,
And each imagined pinnacle and steep
Of godlike hardship tells me I must die
Like a sick eagle looking at the sky.
Yet 'tis a gentle luxury to weep,
That I have not the cloudy winds to keep
Fresh for the opening of the morning's eye.

Such dim-conceived glories of the brain
Bring round the heart an indescribable feud;
So do these wonders a most dizzy pain,
That mingles Grecian grandeur with the rude
Wasting of old Time -with a billowy main,
A sun, a shadow of a magnitude.


The actions of rude time on artefacts is what we try to mitigate, to lessen the wasting away of the past. David Bowie writes in one of his songs, that time is waiting in the wings to play with us. If we had thought, for example, that Alexander the Great had not been Antinous but someone else all along, and maybe now we think that Augustus's favourite was shown in the guise of a god, a timeless one, while the identity of the sculpture changed constantly over the past three centuries. The artifice of time is that the sculpture is Roman, from 1st-2nd century AD, and may itself have been inspired by examples from ancient Greece, now lost to us, and probably covered in coloured pigment that so upset the sculptural purists like John Pope-Hennessey.

So where had it been for one thousand four hundred years until dug up in Rome? It was time that buried its presence as an irrelevancy. Our poets capture something of the sense in which Michel Foucault, in his *The Order of Things*, sees museums as embodying a heterotopia of time. The museum can be seen as a space that encloses objects from all times and styles: they exist in time but also exist outside of time because they are built and preserved to be physically unsusceptible to time's ravages. Foucault's views are of interest to us, because conservators deal with time, and preventing the ravages of time is part of the job description: heterotopia is conservation's raison d'etre or a Platonic desire, that our artefacts would last forever.

Time cannot be reversed, its arrow points only forward, but we can imagine what once might have been, and the Getty exhibition captured that thought by leaving the restored sculpture headless. The different disembodied heads were isolated in sealed glass vitrines around the small gallery space that Antinous's body dominated, together with a truncated arm held as if at rest, in space, timeless, as immolated in a permanent limbo devoid of a body. Time brought still or one could imagine it being reversed to create again an Alexander the Great.

I doubt that the Skulpturen Sammlung, Staatliche Kunstsammlungen, Dresden, could ever have conceived of the exhibition or been able to continue to display the assemblage over time. No one else could possibly have created the exhibition that the Getty did, but once again, although the Getty did make an effort to preserve a vestige of the work, as a pdf on the Getty website, the modesty of this presence is the only remnant of something which no longer exists. If we cannot reconstruct identity, can we show it to the public as the problem that it is? This wonderful exhibition, on the construction of identities, took on the challenge of that problem and exemplified it, to the general indifference of the wider world of art. I do not remember seeing a review of this show, which was up for a full six months rather than three, from December 2008 – June 2009, and have not been able to find one on Google, searching in 2019. The reason why the Getty is so pre-eminent here, has nothing to do with the curatorial staff, but rests entirely on the availability of a group of skilled conservators, the excellent facilities for conservation, mount-making and manipulation of heavy stone sculpture, which is one of the major strengths of the Antiquities Conservation Department. At no cost to the Dresden museum, over 200 shattered marble fragments have been resuscitated into something viewable, something with historical and material significance.....what could be better? Many museums still do not posses a conservator, let alone a skilled and experienced conservation department, and the tendency over the last fifty years has been for museums to jettison or not employ their own conservators, but to rely on those in private practice to hire out their services to museums for whatever job needs to be done. That modus operandi would not have worked for something like Antinous: there is no way he could have been hired out commercially for reconstruction. Time is money and he would have been declared financially unviable.

The last exhibition I will mention here was a major assemblage of bronzes from the Hellenic world that I managed to see at two of its locations: in Florence at the Palazzo Strozzi and at the Getty Center in 2015 which cost a small fortune to mount. This was a superb exhibition of major Greek and Roman bronzes from: Athens, Boston,

Brindisi, Chiati, the Vatican, Copenhagen, Corinth, Florence, Fort Worth, Heraklion, Houston, London, Madrid, Malibu, Mantua, Naples, New York, Paris, Pompeii, Pothia, Rome, Salerno, Sofia, Tbilisi, Thessaloniki, Tunis, Vienna, Washington, and Zagreb. What a list! This event will never happen again in our lifetime and is a testimony to the brilliant work of Jens Daehner and Kenneth Lapatin of the Antiquities Curatorial Department at the Getty Villa. Both are true scholars whose achievements have been outstanding, although one sometimes wonders if the Getty fully realizes what they have got. The bronze boxer, from the Museo Nazionale Romano di Palazzo, was found in 1885 on the Quirinal Hill in Rome. Intriguingly, the fabulous bronze boxer seemed to have been carefully buried in the foundations of a house sometime before 200 AD. I like to think that it was a fellow lover of ancient bronzes, who could not bear to see the work destroyed by invaders or later Christians. Copper inlays were used to outline the cuts of his skin and to represent the blood dripping from his wounds. The swollen right cheekbone was cast in an alloy with less tin to imitate the colour of a haematoma. The skin cuts are actually cast into the bronze. The body was cast in a bronze of 12% tin, 12% lead, 76% copper, while the cheekbone was cast in 3% tin, 31% lead, 66% copper. He is shown with his foreskin tied, a hygienic practice of Greek athletes. The technical skills required to cast this bronze and the subtlety of the different alloys used are a testament to the bronze casting and alloying skills of the late Bronze Age.

Viewing this masterpiece at the Getty Center was overwhelming. The thought that it could even safely travel from Rome to Los Angeles is staggering. Our major bronze at the Getty was the Bronze Athlete, which compared with the Bronze Boxer, is a fairly middle-of-the-road achievement for the Greek metalworkers and there was something even incongruous in being able to see such masterpieces in a modern museum space in Los Angeles in a building that had only been open for ten years. I suppose the thought occurred to me that really, the entire exhibition should have taken place at the Getty Villa. That would have been truly magical as providing the perfect backdrop to such a magnificent exhibition, but I suppose the logistics of freeing up this amount of space in the Getty Roman Villa was just too hard to do. One of old favourites which I have studied the metallurgy of is the

Herm in the Getty collections shown below.

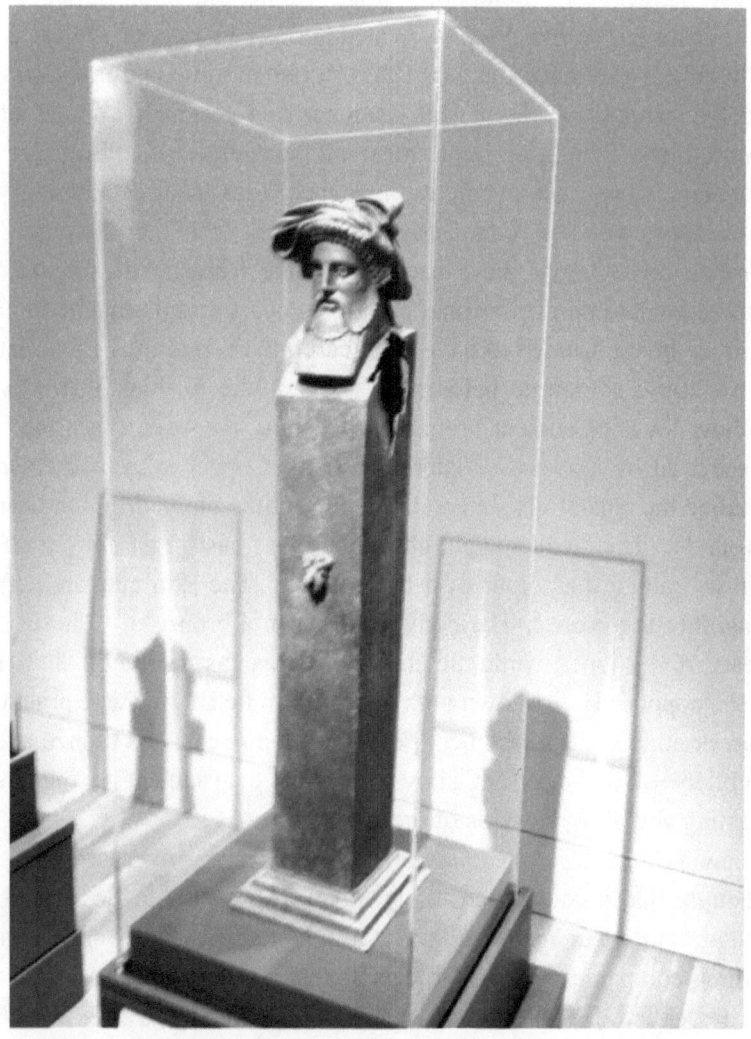

The Getty Herm, long on display at the Getty Villa, and here transported to the Getty Center for the exhibition. 200 – 100 BC. A most interesting bronze, with bronze rods passing up the center of each side of the internal sides of the base. Attributed to Boethos of Kalchedon as Herm of Dionysus. 103.5 cm x 23.5 cm x 19.5 cm. Collection of the J. Paul Getty Museum. Small casting flaws nicely filled by small rectangular bronze patches. Related to the superior Madia shipwreck Herm shown below. Photograph by the author.

Once again there would have been an once-in-a-lifetime opportunity to make a comprehensive film or documentary of these superb bronze sculptures, but that is not to be. There is no film of them together, as that would countermand the wishes of the lenders, who often enforce a strict policy of NO PHOTOGRAPY at loan exhibitions because the lenders want to retain their exclusive rights to the small remnants of the ancient world they possess.

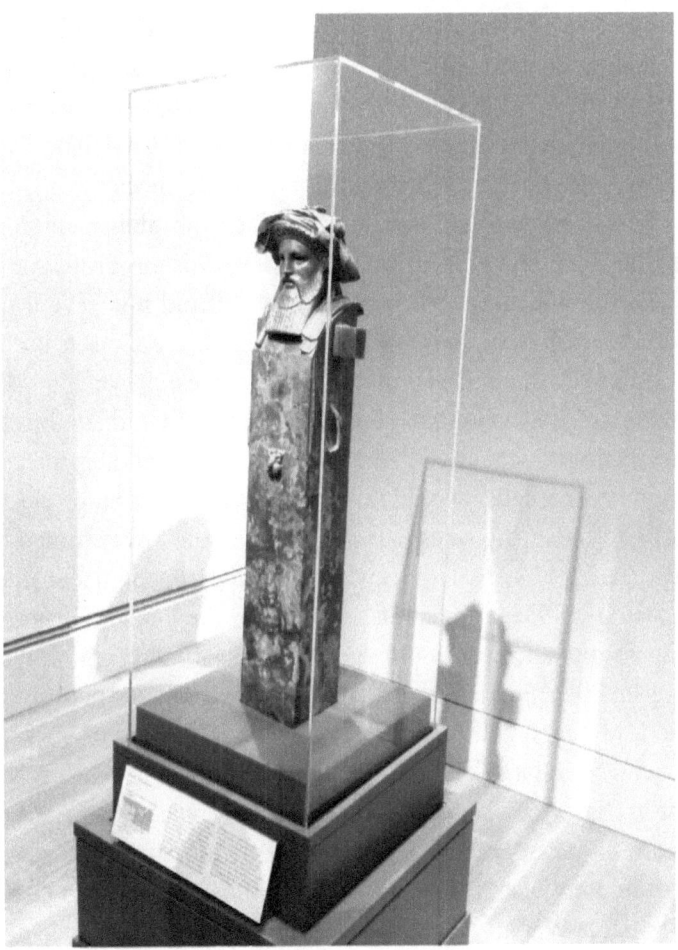

Madia Herm of Dionysus 200 – 100 BC. Bronze on display at the Power and Pathos exhibition. Dimensions 130 cm x 24.8 cm x 19.5 cm. L'institut National du Patrimoine de la Republique Tunisienne, Tunis. From the Madia shipwreck off the coast of Tunisia. The two herms come from the same workshop and were cast at a very similar time using the same batch of bronze.

The exhibition at the National Gallery, Washington, managed a small audio tour for a few pieces and that was it. I did manage to snap the Madia herm because it was so perfectly displayed to match its offspring in the Getty collection.

Being at the Getty Villa part-time after we had left to become a UCLA professor, we retained a close relationship with the Department of Antiquities Conservation and some with Antiquities Curatorial, a department I much admired. Even at the Getty Center, our students had a presence and were welcome in many ways. The same was true across many departments at UCLA, from Materials Science, Engineering, Art History, Near-Eastern Languages and Culture, Anthropology, Chemistry and Biochemistry, World Arts and Culture, and Information Sciences. Why Information Sciences? Well, that is where Ellen Pearlstein had ended up! When the higher-ups realised that the title Ellen had been given, that of an Assistant Professor in the Cotsen IDP, would not work because she still did not have a proper departmental affiliation, and such a title held at the Cotsen itself was not possible, the then Dean of Social Sciences, Reynaldo Macias, suggested that I try to approach the Department of Graduate Education and Information Sciences (GEIS). This was a remarkably perceptive suggestion and certainly would never have occurred to me. So it was then that I resumed my salesman pitch and ambled over to one of the buildings that this very large and active department occupied. Of course, this GEIS Department was also not in the Social Sciences! But I was pleasantly surprised by the generally positive reception the idea of taking in Ellen Pearlstein received, having had so much trouble in the past few years with Departmental homes for faculty, including myself, who was hardly an art historian. Professor Reynaldo Macias was not to last too long as Dean, being replaced with Professor Alessandro Duranti. Duranti lasted longer than Professor Macias, but even he could not last as long as Professor Scott Waugh had managed. Professor Scott Waugh went on to become executive vice-chancellor, dealing with a host of complex issues, but he too has now returned to being a common-or-garden history professor after several years at the top of the administrative tree.

One of the last general memories I have of Professor Duranti is a meeting with the entire Cotsen Institute faculty around 2013. We had been summoned to this meeting at Duranti's request, and then he kept us all waiting for 35 minutes before showing up. As none of us had advance knowledge of what the meeting was for, we all began to get a bit twitchy. Duranti appeared, and launched into an account of how we all might raise money for the Division and what were our ideas for suitable projects or ventures that could benefit both the Cotsen Institute and the Division as well. I did think of suggesting the odd bake-sale, but did not think this might go down very well. There was general bafflement, and one or two faculty suggested that conservation was the possible contributor to patents and moneymaking ventures, since they could not really think of anything else, and we were in the best position to do that. I was also about to suggest the idea of paid authentication work on antiquities that could bring in masses of moolah, except that such work is totally beneath the professoriate and now morally banned as non PC. There was a memory here too: many years ago, the then Vice-Principal of University College London had called a general meeting of the archaeological and conservation faculty together around 1985 it would have been, at the Institute of Archaeology. The message from the professional administration then had been exactly the same: how were the archaeologists going to help themselves and the Institute by raising funds? Outside of bake-sales and authentication work on artifacts, there was little to say. I hardly need to add that as a result of Professor Duranti's prompting and the rather bullying tone adopted by the UCL Vice-Principal, that absolutely nothing happened in either case! There had always been the odd commercial contract for paid work or collaboration with the local archaeology units in the UK, so that did not mean anything happened at all which would not have been in the general run of events. When UCL did began to undertake paid conservation or authenticity work, sometime around 1991, the workers were soon given their marching orders by the Institute, as the conservation work was deemed incompatible with the archaeological nexus of excavation and the increasing importance of known provenance. On one of my teaching weeks, to the Institute of Archaeology, London, while I was still working at the Getty, I was amazed to see one of the priceless silver ewers from the Sevso treasure just being removed from a cleaning vat of ethanol. It is a scene stuck in my mind: first of all, it is not everyday that one sees an object from the Sevso treasure, especially in the Institute of Archaeology around 1991, and not everyday that we conservators dunk such an object in a complete chemical bath, rather than carefully proffering a cotton swab to it. Why was this event so amazing? Well, the Sevso treasure, probably looted from Hungary, worth over 200 million dollars, is the most pre-eminent silver ever found from the Roman Empire, and the Romans knew a thing or two about silver. No-one can actually see this treasure today, this unique collection of silver, a work of genius, even though we know where it is, in London in a dingy basement vault of Bonham's. Why? The answer to that question was well explored by a Time Team TV show, called the *Mystery of the Roman Treasure* which aired in 2008. Once again the trail involves the Getty, and the thread connects the Getty to the Institute of Archaeology, London and to the treasure itself, because Lord Northampton, the owner, obviously thought that the right place to unload the Sevso treasure, for untold millions, was the Getty Museum. The then curator of Antiquities, Arthur Houghton III, could read Arabic in both hand-written and typed manuscript, a rare talent, and he could see that the export papers and signatures, ostensibly from the Lebanon had been forged. That was the end of the story as far as the Getty was concerned: they were unable to touch it. The tangled tale of disputed ownership has continued ever since, with millions being spent on lawyer's fees in New York and London. The claim by Hungary to have the treasure returned to it has been stalled, because of the sheer stupidity of the American legal system, and even the Time Team TV folk were denied any sight of the treasure in London or any questioning of Lord Northampton or his lawyer in 2008. This is the safe legal option: the longer the treasure remains hidden away in a vault, the better for everyone concerned in the process of obfuscation, except the public, the archaeologists, the Hungarians, the rightful re-examination of the legal case, and so the orphaned status of the masterworks will continue, long into the future. That such a fate should befall the world's best collection of Roman silver ever found is essentially a tragedy. Found in a large copper cauldron, as a complete collection worthy of a king, although we have no idea who Sevso was, his name is on one of the silver vessels, at the time it represented immense wealth in itself because the sheer quantity and craftsmanship is so extraordinary.

Anything to do with dealers was, or is totally verboten, UCL Vice-Principal or no: better to do without funds rather than have they tainted. Shortly after the 1991 period, the archaeologists at the Institute of Archaeology saw the writing on the wall, and the private venture that involved looking at antiquities for the trade and others had to decamp to Birkbeck College, and finally to decamp to Belgium. A similar problem beset Oxford University, regarding the dating lab, which has already been mentioned a while ago here: it was hived off as a private venture.

Things were financially tight at UCLA, and there were budget stresses, but no professors were laid off! A tribute to UCLA and its regard for education. Our little inter-departmental program was too small to be noticed, thankfully, so we survived unscathed. Both Ioanna Kakoulli and Ellen Pearlstein proved to be exceptionally hard workers, and Ellen carried on, undeterred by being found a home in the Department of Graduate Education and Information Studies, such a strange department for us conservators, and seemingly a long way from archaeological and ethnographic conservation, but her tenure case went by without a hitch, and was ratified by CAP a couple of years back, around 2016, for which I had written strong letters of support.

So what is tenure? In the bittersweet play, *Educating Rita*, by Willy Russell, which premiered in 1980, Frank, the professor tests just how far tenure can be taken when he trashes the Vice-Chancellors place and gets blind drunk. His reward then was to be sent off to Australia on a year's paid sabbatical leave.

Now, in 2019, there would be no reward, as tenure in the UK was effectively abolished, decades ago by the ghastly Margaret Thatcher and the Conservative Party. Today, there exists in the UK a theory and a practice regarding "permanent" positions at universities. This is a typically British solution to the problem that theoretically means that you will not be sacked if keeping up your publication, research, teaching, and fund-raising work. In practice, the Brits still have ways of getting rid of you that would create a storm of academic protest in the USofA in elite institutions. One senior colleague, close to retirement age, at the University of Edinburgh was called in to meet with the Departmental Chair and told, "Either you resign or we will have to get rid of two junior faculty members, what would you like to do?" His retirement was still a couple of years away, but he did the decent thing and quit. At the University of Cambridge, since an official retirement age was abolished a while ago, they have a gentleman's agreement, that all things being equal, you will retire at the age of 70. Over in Europe, these retirement ages are fixed at different levels. One of my colleagues at the Rijksmuseum had to retire at the age of 65, when he would have been very happy to continue working. Over at UCLA, many professors continue into their 70's, some into their 80's or even their 90's. It depends on how arduous your academic life is: for those working in philosophy for example, if your brain is still going and you enjoy the stimulation of good graduate students, then why retire at all? Over in our conservation field, it is most unusual to continue past the age of 65, because there is simply so much to organize: teaching, equipment, chemical orders, scientific grants to be applied for, software updates, student project supplies, student internships, object loans, object returns, artefact security, student interviews, matching funding, essentially no technicians to help you, as in larger scientific departments, and in our case dealing with essentially two departments at the same time. All hard work and no play compared with carrying on in a philosophy department until the age of 88. That old Hollywood actor, and great pal of Margaret Thatcher, Ronald Reagan, never undid the tenure system: probably the States of the US would not have bought it, the academic status of professors in the United States in elite establishments is so much higher than in the UK being one reason for this. Tenure still has meaning and substance in the best American universities as it used to have in the UK, but the UK system is so mean, so austere, that it has become a scenario with sinister undertones. One retiring colleague at the University of Durham told me that the teaching would be divided into those who just taught and those who actually did research. Conservation was not a department much suited for research, so he was off, heading into the calm waters of early retirement. I did not quite understand this dichotomy, but perhaps I should, as the schism between "lecturers" at universities such as UCLA and "teaching staff" at universities such as UCL, is quite analogous. Perhaps the idea had even been imported from America, because when I last taught at UCL in 1987 there was no such distinction between those feted brains conducting "research" and those primary activity was "teaching" According to the Guardian newspaper for August 2019, around a quarter of academic staff in the Russell Group of research-intensive universities, such as UCL where I used to teach, are categorized as teaching-only – fewer than across the sector as a whole, but the number is growing. This is partly as a result of the government's new teaching excellence framework (Tef), which aims to help redress the balance between research and teaching. Having published over 140 peer-reviewed papers while carrying a fair teaching load over the past thirty years, I find the need to redress the balance between research and teaching very strange. Presumably, the balance needs to be reset because government has been placing so much emphasis on research that no-one really cared who was doing the teaching anyway. All this is doubly odd, since universities in the UK are supposed to greatly value teaching, while keeping an increasing number of lecturers on short-term contracts. I am not sure how you get a mortgage if your contract expires in two years time and you have no certainty that it will be renewed. One study found that many research-intensive universities offloaded heavy teaching allocations to teaching-only staff to give researchers more time to publish. Some even threatened researchers who failed to publish with extra teaching, and rewarded those who published particularly significant research work with less teaching.

These gripes about the UCLA professoriate will find little sympathy then with young colleagues in the UK today, those who hold a PhD but are stuck on temporary contracts rather than "permanent" positions. The main barrier for obtaining a permanent position does not seem to be the lack of qualified academics but rather a lack of positions established and offered by the universities. It is cheaper for universities to keep staff on temporary fixed-term contracts than to promote them to permanent lecturer appointments. Another barrier is the fact that young scholars are supposed to focus both on teaching and research and it is only the latter that matters in the research excellence framework. This whole exercise, as far as archaeological and ethnographic conservation is concerned, is one fraught with difficulties.

Young researches are hit with a double whammy: undertake masses of teaching or what use are you? At the same time undertake great research that will pull in mountains of funding. Where to find the time to do both on a salary of about 30,000 pounds a year? You may recall that my final salary as a distinguished professor at UCLA was $220,000 a year. They are not compatible amounts as you can see. The whole system, one could argue, is a reflection of what has happened to society as a whole. Instead of cohesion and collectivism there is division and difference. These differences, like the rest of UK society, have drifted apart like two planets whose orbits are becoming increasing distant from each other. They still communicate, but the system cannot be put into reverse to bring them closer together. One feels like saying, please, give us the old liberal democratic philosophy as espoused by people like Paddy Ashdown. Not the liberal philosophy of Nick Clegg, which resulted in tuition fees trebling in costs, something that the Liberal Party will never live down, as their manifesto gave an undertaking not to raise UK tuition fees at all. I could never vote for them now as a result of that broken promise, and neither could many of the British electorate, although with Brexit boosting the Liberal appeal, some of the electorate appear to have short memories. Nick Clegg had travelled from the centre of power to having no power at all, as he had lost his seat in Parliament, and the experiment in giving one's support to the Conservatives shown to be a failure.

While Los Angeles teachers were at one time, around 2010, being laid off from the Los Angeles Unified Public School District (LAUPSD), us university professors were still getting pay rises and any financial problems at UCLA were simply dealt with by not hiring too many replacements for those that had left, resigned, died or otherwise vanished. There is no holistic concept applied to education across boundaries. It is each entity for itself with no regard for the other. If the UCLA professoriate were told that in order to help the State of California with its educational responsibilities, that they were not going to get any pay rise at all for the next three-four years, in fact a small pay-cut might be necessary, many of them would simply have left UCLA altogether to find another university prepared to give them a raise. The chosen few did that in any case.

One researcher in Earth and Planetary Science had a whole research group modeling the Chinese economy using fractal mathematic modeling, on multiple funding from Chinese agencies. Things got a bit tight at UCLA about that time, and that was enough! He relocated to the University of Geneva and took his entire PhD cohort with him. The rest of us have to carry on: keep calm and carry on is our motto in archaeological conservation, because we are the Time-Lords of artefacts whose existence will stretch out into the future long after we are gone.

Back at the IDP in Conservation, Ioanna and Ellen were going great guns. Ioanna becoming accomplished at managing both Materials Science students and their needs as well as the IDP and Ellen building up strong relations with local Indian and Indigenous Museums, which were of great benefit for internships and paid work for our conservation students, as well as upping her game regarding publications, which she had not concentrated on in her working life at the Brooklyn Museum of Art in her prior existence as a museum conservator. With Vanessa Muros as our highly skilled laboratory supervisor, and Amber Cordts-Cole as administrative officer, we were set and ready to go. Since 2005 we have now finished the training of fifty-six conservators, many of whom have even gone on to find paid employment in conservation! Still so much easier than finding paid employment in anthropology! One might have imagined that our relationship with the Getty Conservation Institute was an intimate and deeply collaborative one, but such is not the case. The Getty Conservation Institute even has an education department, which the unitiated might imagine to be our very close buddies. The education department of the GCI encompasses a broad array of resources including those developed for workshops, courses, retreats, and training, as well as programs for scholars, fellows, and interns. Quite so, but where was the interactive relationship with our conservation training programme? It seemed to me to be rather minimal. How about developing workshops for our students, or bringing in guest scholars who could also teach our students too and work on GCI related educational goals? This is perhaps too much to hope for, because the two entities, UCLA and the Getty are fundamentally different, while the Getty has become much more corporate over the last twenty years or so and its interest in joint ventures with the likes of us, rather muted. There is hope however: nothing remains static and future collaborations may yet prove fruitful and useful for both the students and for the GCI. Even within UCLA there are mind-silos, in which interpenetration of intellectual activity is practically non-existent. The Cotsen Institute is housed in the Fowler Museum building, and one would imagine that joint exhibitions or lectures or other things might be very prominent connecting threads between the two rich neighbours. Such, however, is not the case, and the Fowler Museum might as well be in a separate universe, let alone a separate building. But there are useful links between the objects in the Fowler Museum and our conservation IDP, because object loans are an essential ethnographic component for our students to work with, and Professor John Papadopoulos used to take students to see some of the pottery at the Fowler. The avenue between us which creates this stream of objects and reports appears to have no impact on exhibitions per se at the Fowler Museum and therefore, to external eyes, there is no useful contact, but that would be an oversimplification and would neglect how important it is for us in so many ways.

Every five years there is an external report carried out on different departments by an assembled group of civic-minded professors who then prepare a report for the Vice-Chancellor. A recent external report on the Cotsen Institute highlighted the communication problem between the Fowler Museum and our archaeological colleagues, but since our own collaboration does not really constitute "research" it seems like small beer to the experts, so it was not even mentioned. In a never-ending saga, the external review continued to point out that the Director of the Cotsen Institute needs help to improve the collaboration with the Getty in the area of conservation. These suggestions begin to seem like old chestnuts, dragged out without any really constructive possibility beyond repeating these trite comments every three-five years. Without the participation of all parties involved and a Getty-style endless series of conversations, little is likely to change in that regard, but you never know – hope springs eternal.

The external review went on to state the need to: "Recognize the inherent challenge of the inability of the inter-departmental unit to make faculty hires. This can result in a circular logic where departments argue that archaeology is already provided for by the Institute so that other areas should be favored in hiring priorities" This topic reared its awkward head again as a result of my retirement and the familiar problem of finding departmental homes for conservators, such as my replacement, whose who do not fit in easily in the elevated UCLA department silos: trying to scale the wall of these is not an easy task. I had gone by April 2017 and as at October 2019 the poor IDP is struggling to keep going with help from......LACMA. Los Angeles County Museum of Art I here you say? What about the bountiful resources of the Getty? Is it not supposed to be the UCLA/Getty Conservation Programme? Well, yes, but the Getty Conservators are only helping us out under the radar, so to speak, the idea that a couple of them would be able to give two forty-hour classes a term and deal with marking, papers, evaluations, timetables, etc, is of course quite out of the question. This would be a major radar-observable event and would clearly never be sanctioned. It is now September 2019 and at last, Professor Glenn Wharton has been appointed to my old position, even in the Department of Art History, vacant now for two and a half years, and he is very likely to be an improvement on the old incumbent, as one not laden with the baggage from another era replete with hypercritical evaluations of the surrounding institutions, but one with renewed energy in which there is plenty of scope for new initiatives. It is a good time for this in 2019 as Los Angeles is awash with money at the moment and is full of new possibilities of benefit to the conservation programme and its excellent students.

UCLA, vis a vis the department silo issues, is not very good at sorting out Catch 22-type problems, due to the lumbering behemoth of the administration: small problems like ours are hardly going to be solved in a trice, given the protocols designed by prominent scholars over the generations, and either a series of exceptions or fudges would be involved or the whole point of the external review committee will just be buried in the electronic filing cabinet.

As regards the Getty Conservation Institute, we have to rely for some of our analyses on the kindness of strangers in the shape of Michael Schilling, Herant Khanjian and Joy Keeney who accounted for most of our reliance on the GCI and the guest teaching for our program has been performed out of the goodwill of Maya Elston, Eduardo Sanchez, Jerry Podany, Marie Svoboda, Jeffery Maish, Susan Maish and Erik Risser, all present or former members of the Getty Antiquities Conservation Department, who obligingly have carried out many functions for us. I used to carry out some work for them too which was also under the radar. Erik Risser brought samples of the Antinous sculpture for me to examine for him to UCLA, and one or two Egyptian pigment issues were undertaken to help Marie Svoboda.

Jeffery Maish is one of the unsung heroes who regularly used the Getty Villa x-ray facility for our students conservation work on baskets, pottery and metals. For the innocent, I should explain that this is not the feeble kind of x-ray used by dentists, it is military-industrial grade x-ray work, because very high accelerating voltages have to be used to penetrate through heavy cast bronzes or thick stone sculpture. The room has to be lead-lined, has huge lead-lined doors operating in concert with remote opening and closing locks and safety warning lights and sound systems. All manipulation of the machine in terms of powering it up is done remotely from outside the room. Exposure to 240 KV 35 mA x-rays for even a few seconds might even kill you! I used to operate the same kind of massive machine at the Getty Center, when I was in charge of the Museum Lab after it had moved to the Center, so it was always a responsibility to help others, in my case usually the Department of Decorative Arts and Sculpture. But it was not the responsibility of Jeffery Maish to always help us with our x-ray work, and we all owe him a deep debt of gratitude for the unfailing generosity with which he undertook this chore, because that is essentially what it was as far as his own work was concerned, it was nothing whatever to do with his own work. Would any of this actually be recognised by the powers that be in HR or other administrative functionaries at the Getty? No, the life and spirit devoted to helping the students from our program by Jeffery Maish was invisible to them. If they had realised the extent of the additional work, they might actually have issued a directive to stop it! Occasionally Jerry Podany, the former head of Antiquities Conservation, would get tetchy with the requests for x-ray radiography from us or our students, because they, the Department of Antiquities Conservation, were stretched that month with the work expected of them, were not getting any additional resources or Brownie points from the Getty Trust, and what they were doing for us was as invisible as an over-developed x-ray radiograph would be to them. Jeffery was busy helping us rather than conforming to the work expectations foisted on him. During one of those periods of withdrawal of the x-ray services, we would have to wait a few weeks before Jeffery Maish was allowed to help us again, which had its own irritations as we were so dependent on the kindness of strangers, or rather the generosity of our colleagues. As I mentioned already, I was a trained x-ray operative, as I had installed and used the x-ray radiography facilities at the Getty Center when I was still an employee of the Getty, but of course it would have been out of the question that I be allowed to operate the equipment for the students at the Getty Villa. We used to have to attend x-ray safety training every year at the Getty Center, which became increasingly boring. The equivalent of this, for a member of the general public, those who drive cars capable of running into folk, or employing explosive and carcinogenic substances (petrol, electric or diesel engines), or who carry passengers, would be the need to attend a car safety driving course every year, before they were allowed behind the wheel again. I think you will agree that such a measure might prove unpopular.

Real advances in understanding works of art had been made using invisible means of study, made manifest in the real world, such as UV radiation, IR reflections, X-ray penetration, False-colour photography, Photoluminescence excitation, Multi-Spectral Imaging, MRI, etc. Skill has to be developed in interpretation of the results of these studies of artworks, but the overall impact is tremendous. Ioanna Kakoulli possessed especial skills in this area, which has served the students well as part of their graduate training.

The next stage in the development of our program was to begin to offer a PhD in conservation. This was potentially important because of the ridiculous inflexibility of the American academic system. While being resident in the US, Alice Paterakis took her PhD abroad, at UCL, as did Glenn Wharton. Nancy Odegaard took hers from the University of Melbourne in Australia and Arlen Heginbotham from the University of Amsterdam. So what links these outstanding practitioners in the USA and the fact that they had to go abroad to get a PhD, part-time? None of them were acceptable to American universities to undertake the kind of research they wanted to do, and the names mentioned above were, or are, highly significant in terms of contributions to our teaching at UCLA, not to mention their achievements in the conservation profession at large. Yes, truly incommoded, but saved by European universities for the most part.

lamentable reflection on the American academic system and its complete inability to understand or appreciate what conservation research might entail and to be able to engage with conservation research in a meaningful way, as several European countries manage to do well.

When one of the gifted conservators at LACMA thought of trying to get into UCLA to undertake his PhD, he even bothered to take a couple of classes with me, received an A grade for them, applied twice and was rejected, out of hand, twice. Not by me, I hasten to add, who simply could not understand what the problem was. He eventually found a sympathetic ear from the University of Ohio, and ended up part-time, being taken on there. The University of Ohio is not considered to be in the same academic league as UCLA or UCL, and therefore there is an additional leeway towards applicants working on bizarre topics. This is one reason why a PhD in Conservation would be a good idea at UCLA once it has been established. It has taken us fifteen years, in a manner of speaking to get there, but I think we will do it. So how is it that American students can be taken on part-time in the European context? We are just more adaptable than the Americans, with no absurdly restrictive pre-conditions that are prevalent in America. We can look at the work history, the level of individual attainment within the conservation sphere, the international standing of the applicant in the conservation profession, the publications which have already been produced, the nature of the intended research project, and the dedication and ability of the researcher to finish the work.

Few, if any, of these criteria mean much to PhD programs at UCLA, what might be more important is if you have three languages as a backdrop to your work on Greek ceramics, rather than a deep knowledge of ceramic fabrics in general and how that fits into the world picture of the development of ceramic pastes, way beyond the confines of Greece, or the conservation of Greek ceramics per se, for which knowledge of ancient Greek might be mostly irrelevant.

I found the dissonance between the art historical world and the scientific interesting, especially as I was surrounded by world-class art historians at UCLA. Ultimately it lead to a deeper appreciation of the problems of authenticity in art, and hence to my 2016 book on the subject of art and authenticity. I enjoyed the twin threads, three really of ancient metals and their structure and microstructure, the world of authenticity, and the general conservation and preservation that I taught for the Art History Department. In 2019 I retired to Hastings, aged 70 to begin a new chapter of events. I am still teaching the ancient metals and metallography course in Hastings, and got talked into writing yet another book on Metallography of Ancient Metals, to be published by Springer in 2019. To keep me on the straight and narrow, I inveigled Dr. Roland Schwab to help me write the book and this has strengthened the book considerably, so much so, that I began to enjoy writing on the topic with Dr. Schwab spurring me on. The book is called *Metallography in Art and*

*Archaeology* and is in full colour throughout, something of a rarity these days.

I hope to get back to the subject of art restoration in the near future, which will form another opportunity for gathering together an interesting group of artworks and sites to write something new, something that will encompass a grand narrative of art restoration, except that the days of grand narratives are over and we have to be content with what we can accomplish rather than what we wished we were able to do. There are those who work to live and those who live to work, as long as the work concerned is congenial and mentally stimulating, otherwise it would be back to working in order to live, a phrase that Professor Emeritus Clifford Price used in an email to me when he retired from UCL.

I have led a fortunate life in which the work I wanted to do became part of my life, which in one sense, it always was. I shall carry on teaching my Summer Course on *The Metallography and Microstructure of Ancient Metals* until infirmity or death intervene, and in the meantime amuse myself with the philosophy of authenticity, aesthetics, fakes and forgeries, join a U3A group and continue to prepare and photograph interesting microstructures for my Instagram site, *Davidscottmetals,* which has over four hundred followers. In fact, I have just joined the Hastings and Rother U3A Science group and started up a group on Technical Art History. In 2020 I intend to plan to hold an international conference on Philosophy and Conservation to be held at East Sussex Coast College if I can pull it off.

My wish is that others like me could have been so rewarded, with a family to boot and one grandson already and another just born in Chicago this week in August 2019. I wish you to also enjoy a comfortable retirement, something that many folk of the next generation will not find so easy to attain, especially those from a working-class background.

One thing the past teaches us is that any of those kinds of predictions is a foolish enterprise, based as it is on mere supposition, so I am secretly hoping that it will be proved wrong and that the future for us working-class Brits over the next one hundred years, is as bright and satisfying as mine has proved to be, largely due to the old-fashioned liberal values of both Conservative and Labour governments. It is quite possible that the entire concept of the working-class Brit will disappear in the decades that lie ahead, just as those old Liberal values have been frittered away in the name of an increasingly capitalistic society.

## Appendix 1

(Apropos of the account of my Mother). Despite Dr Inglis's already notable achievements it was her efforts during the First World War that brought her fame. She was instrumental in setting up the Scottish Women's Hospitals for Foreign Service Committee, an organisation funded by the women's suffrage movement with the express aim of providing all female staffed relief hospitals for the Allied war effort. The organisation was active in sending teams to Belgium, France, Serbia and Russia.

When Elsie Inglis approached the Royal Army Medical Corps to offer them a ready-made Medical Unit staffed by qualified women, the War Office told her "My good lady, go home and sit still". It was, instead, the French government that took up her offer and established her unit in Serbia.

Elsie Inglis, herself, went with the teams sent to Serbia where her presence and work in improving hygiene reduced typhus and other epidemics that had been raging there. In 1915 she was captured and repatriated but upon reaching home she began organising funds for a Scottish Women's Hospital team in Russia. She headed the team when it left for Odessa, Russia in 1916 but lasted only a year before she was forced to return to the United Kingdom, suffering from cancer.

In April 1916, Elsie Inglis became the first woman to be awarded the Order of the White Eagle (V class) by the Crown Prince Alexander of Serbia at a ceremony in London. She had previously been awarded the Order of Saint Sava (III class). Another forgotten heroine of our past.

## Appendix II

(Apropos of the account of my Mother). The Dean Bank Institution was established in 1832 by a small band of women and worked from buildings in the Silvermills/Stockbridge area of Edinburgh from 1832 - 1912.

Prior to the establishment of the Institution a number of women inspired by the work in England of Elizabeth Fry "began systematically to visit the female wards of the Edinburgh Prison". They recognized however that many of the female prisoners quickly returned to prison as they found it difficult to find employment. Their solution was to establish the Dean Bank Institution, a place where girls could be taken out of close association with hardened criminals and trained for domestic service. The Institution's fiftieth anniversary report noted:

"The difficulty of finding employment suggested the idea of a "Home", where those really anxious to do well might be taught and fitted for the service of employers, willing to give them an opportunity of recovering their position in life. A house at Dean Bank was taken, and in 1832, the Institution was opened. Entrance was entirely voluntary, and the expenses were met by the contributions of those interested, and the proceeds of washing and sewing done by the inmates"

It is important to recognise that the establishment of this Institution marked a significant step forward in social reform as it was the first such refuge in Scotland.

["

Department of Antiquities Conservation, 264, 275
Derrida, 22, 245
Dewey system, 134
Dickson, 7, 8
Diwana, 103
Doerner Institute, 139, 140, 179, 181
Donald Maclean, 140
Dorset, 56
Douglas-Home, 28
Dr. Bruce Kaiser, 112
Dr. Dusan Stulik, 159, 191
Dr. Fawzi Zayadine, 205, 208
Dr. Ioanna Kakoulli, 237
Dr. James Mellaart, 104
Dr. Mellaart, 104
Dr. Radu Varia, 190, 196
Dresden, 257, 260
Drey Gallery, 211
East Coast, 131, 133, 175
East German, 92
Eastern Orthodox, 193, 197
Eddy Grant, 56, 60, 61
Edgware, 8, 247
Edinburgh, 7, 9, 11, 37, 267, 280
Eduardo Sanchez, 172, 174, 223, 274
Egyptian, 5, 7, 34, 36, 110, 134, 158, 213, 216, 274
El Alamein, 9, 11
Elena Ceausescu, 191
Elephant and Castle, 24
Elgin Marbles, 258
Eli Broad, 138, 149
Elizabeth Mention, 200
England, 8, 27, 31, 46, 62, 63, 64, 66, 68, 89, 94, 111, 116, 126, 145, 153, 176, 201, 232, 257, 280
Enigma Code, 12
Eric Hebborn, 140, 144
Erica Avrami, 234
Etruscan, 175, 224, 225, 226
Europe, 14, 19, 74, 90, 108, 112, 117, 149, 167, 256, 268
Euston, 27, 30, 41, 42, 58, 59, 60, 68, 102
existential, 17, 222
Faringdon Road, 47
federal, 136, 187

First World War, 6, 8, 10, 27, 61, 64, 66, 97, 175, 188, 210, 279
Fontainbleau, 210
Foucault, 22, 259
Fowler Museum, 202, 230, 246, 272
France, 8, 32, 52, 63, 176, 209, 210, 279
Frank Dobson, 36
Frank Lambert, 140
Frank Preusser, 100, 117, 139, 141, 158, 170, 174, 183, 217, 226, 228
Friese-Green, 15
Fritz Haber, 61
Garry Kasparov, 40, 146, 147, 148
Gas Board, 12, 42
Gay people, 46
George G. Heye, 106
George Goldner, 145
George Roberts, 201, 202, 204, 205
Georgian, 24, 26
Germany, 52, 61, 89, 107, 111, 140, 169, 176, 203
Getty, 4, 100, 110, 112, 117, 120, 121, 123, 126, 127, 128, 129, 130, 131, 133, 134, 135, 136, 137, 138, 139, 140, 141, 142, 143, 144, 145, 146, 147, 148, 149, 150, 151, 152, 153, 154, 155, 156, 157, 158, 161, 162, 164, 165, 166, 167, 169, 170, 171, 172, 173, 174, 175, 177, 178, 181, 182, 183, 184, 185, 186, 191, 199, 200, 202, 204, 208, 209, 210, 211, 212, 213, 217, 218, 219, 220, 221, 223, 224, 225, 226, 228, 234, 236, 237, 239, 240, 241, 242, 243, 244, 246, 252, 256, 257, 259, 260, 261, 262, 264, 265, 271, 272, 273, 274, 275
Getty Center, 4, 131, 133, 135, 146, 147, 149, 155, 156, 164, 199, 242, 262, 264, 274
Getty Museum, 128, 130, 136, 137, 153, 154, 171, 175, 182, 191, 262, 266
Getty Villa, 128, 131, 135, 149, 156, 182, 183, 202, 221, 222,